PSYCHOLOGY'S GRAND THEORISTS

How Personal Experiences Shaped
Professional Ideas

PSYCHOLOGY'S GRAND THEORISTS

How Personal Experiences Shaped Professional Ideas

Amy Demorest
Amherst College

LEA

LAWRENCE ERLBAUM ASSOCIATES, PUBLISHERS

2005   Mahwah, New Jersey   London

Senior Editor:	Debra Riegert
Editorial Assistant:	Kerry Breen
Cover Design:	Kathryn Houghtaling Lacey
Textbook Production Manager:	Paul Smolenski
Full-Service Compositor:	TechBooks
Text and Cover Printer:	Sheridan Books, Inc.

Cover art by Robert T. Sweeney, depicting Sigmund Freud, B. F. Skinner, and Carl Rogers.

This book was typeset in 10/12 pt. Times, Italic, Bold, and Bold Italic.
The heads were typeset in Americana, Americana Italic, and Americana Bold.

Lawrence Erlbaum Associates, Inc., Publishers
10 Industrial Avenue
Mahwah, New Jersey 07430
www.erlbaum.com

Library of Congress Cataloging-in-Publication Data
Demorest, Amy.
    Psychology's grand theorists: how personal experiences shaped professional
ideas / Amy Demorest.
        p.   cm.
    Includes bibliographical references and index.
    ISBN 0-8058-5107-0 (alk. paper)—ISBN 0-8058-5108-9 (pbk.: alk. paper)
    1. Psychologists—Biography.   2. Psychologists—Psychology.   3. Psychology—
History.   4. Freud, Sigmund, 1856–1939.   5. Skinner, B. F. (Burrhus Frederic),
1904–1990   6. Rogers, Carl R. (Carl Ransom), 1902–1987   I. Title.

BF109.A1D45   2004
150.19—dc22   2004007577

To My Father

Contents

Preface

I first had the idea of writing this book when I was in my senior year as an undergraduate at Williams College. I had just read Robert Heilbroner's book, *The Worldly Philosophers* (1972), for a class on the history of economic thought. In his book, Heilbroner brings the field of economics to life by showing how the theories of the major economists emerged from the particular social contexts in which they lived. As a psychology major, I thought that the field of psychology could use a book like this. But whereas economic theory makes claims about social systems, and so an analysis of the theorists' social contexts is in order, psychological theory makes claims about individual people, and so here an analysis of the theorists' personal lives is called for.

This idea was elaborated in the following years as I pursued further studies in psychology. The most significant influence was my graduate work with Irving Alexander. Irving himself explored relationships between the works and the lives of psychological theorists in a class he taught. The class was not taught to my cohort, but I heard others talk of it when he returned to it the following year. Most importantly, in another class and in my thesis work with him, I learned from Irving a method for extracting themes from narrative material, whether that material was autobiographical writing explicitly about the author's life story, or professional writing ostensibly irrelevant to the author's private life. I was also able to see how Irving employed this method in an analysis of the theorist Carl Jung, when he read aloud to a number of his graduate students a talk he was to give at an upcoming American Psychological Association meeting. He would later publish this paper and others on Sigmund Freud and Harry Stack Sullivan, along with a paper on his method, in his book *Personology* (1990). Anyone who has read that book will immediately see that my debt to Irving is great. I had the idea for writing this book before I met him, but he gave me the means to do it.

It has also been important to this project that I found a job in the psychology department at Amherst College. If you talk to psychologists who focus on the study of lives, you will find that many have felt a lack of professional support for this rather maverick type of endeavor. I was lucky to find in my senior colleagues at Amherst, and in the college itself, a wholly supportive attitude. I was also lucky to find students who could share in the excitement of this work with me. I am especially grateful to Paul Siegel, my first honors student at Amherst, whose intellectual spirit has nurtured my work over the years. For his honors project Paul wrote a psychobiography of B. F. Skinner, which was published afterwards in modified form in *Psychoanalytic Psychology*. I have benefited in particular from Paul's thinking about Skinner and about the methodology of the study of lives.

As I finalized my plan for this project in recent years, other books played a role in shaping my thought, most notably Alan Elms' *Uncovering Lives* (1994), William McKinley Runyan's *Life Histories and Psychobiography* (1982), and Robert Stolorow and George Atwood's *Faces in a Cloud* (1979). Still, unlike any of these, my goal has stayed focused on doing for psychology what Heilbroner did for economics in providing a broad survey of the major theorists. A survey of the major theorists of psychology would give the reader a sense of the field as a whole, and make the book useful for courses on the history and systems of psychology, personality theory, and clinical theory. Further, a broad survey would provide a good test of whether the claim of work–life relationships is widely applicable.

In the end, I decided to focus my analysis on three thinkers who represent a diverse range of approaches in psychology: Sigmund Freud for the psychodynamic approach, B. F. Skinner for the behavioral approach, and Carl Rogers for the phenomenological approach. There are a number of reasons why I chose these three. On the one hand, there was the decision to write about three theorists rather than about the dozen or so theorists that Heilbroner had surveyed in his book. I chose three, first because I found that a good breadth of theory in psychology could be surveyed with this many people. Second, I believed that my point that relationships exist between a thinker's professional work and his or her personal life would have been made sufficiently after it was illustrated for three people.

Next there was the decision to write about these particular individuals rather than about any others. The first consideration at this point was who the biggest thinkers are. It was immediately clear that these men emerge regularly at the top of all sorts of lists ranking the eminence of psychologists. They are not always literally the top three (although sometimes they are). But then a second consideration came into play: to represent the diversity of approaches in the field. In some surveys, for example, Albert Bandura ranks higher than Carl Rogers; but Bandura's approach falls within the general category of "behavioral" approaches that is already represented by Skinner, who ranks higher of the two in the surveys. As prime representatives of what historically have been the three dominant paradigms in psychology, Freud, Skinner, and Rogers were all obvious choices.

To identify relationships between each man's work and life, I drew on primary sources, studying the individual's theoretical writings to analyze his work and autobiographical writings to analyze his life. If we want to know the inner world of Freud or Skinner or Rogers, we need to look to the man's own imagery. I employed the method taught to me by Irving Alexander to extract salient themes underlying both these professional and personal narratives. At the end of each chapter on each theorist, the reader will find a list of primary sources on the individual's work and life, along with valuable writings by others.

In telling the story of my analysis in this book, I decided to start each chapter with a close reading of the first major case study out of which the man's theory grew. I saw two benefits to beginning this way. The first is for the sake of understanding the theory intimately: A close reading of a specific case would show how the man worked and would bring his ideas to life. A summary of the full theory could then follow. The second is for the sake of better understanding the life: If a theorist's work reflects his personal life, then a close reading of his first case study should reveal the subjective concerns that underlie the work. This would tell us what to be on the lookout for when we then turn to his personal life history. Thus, for each chapter on each theorist, I decided to first examine the work closely to extract salient themes, and then examine the life closely to identify the origins of these themes. It is my hope that after this method is used in the chapter on Freud, the reader will be able in the chapters on Skinner or Rogers to notice clues to salient themes before I identify them, and to anticipate what life sources might be found to account for these themes. In this way, I hope that the book will illustrate not only the claim of work–life relationships but also a method by which such relationships can be discovered.

Once the book was under way, many people helped me during the process of writing. I am very grateful to those who generously gave their time and knowledge in reading what I wrote. Steve Demorest, Helen Dole, Al Goethals, Marcia Johnston, Monica Lee, Steve Ruckman, Bill Taubman, and Tyler Thornton read parts of the book in its various stages of development. Irving Alexander, Dan McAdams, Nancy McWilliams, and Paul Siegel read the complete first draft. The following people served as reviewers of the book proposal and sample chapters: James W. Anderson, Northwestern University; Robert F. Bornstein, Gettysburg College; Christina Frederick-Recascino, Embry-Riddle Aeronautical University; Richard P. Halgin, University of Massachusetts; Wilson McDermut, St. John's University; and John Zelenski, Carleton University. I benefited from the advice that all these people offered me. I thank Isabel Margolin for patiently typing a hand-written manuscript that was sometimes hard to decipher. I also thank my editor, Debra Riegert, and the staff at Lawrence Erlbaum Associates for their support and skill in bringing this book to fruition.

Finally I would like to thank my father. When I went off to college at Williams, the one requirement he made of me was that I take a course in either economics or physics. Without this requirement I never would have taken the course that led to the idea for this book. My father also had gone to Williams, and when he was asked on a form from the college to indicate what Williams needed most, his answer was a department of psychology. I have no delusion that his answer is what led Williams to finally found its psychology department, but I still enjoy the story. I have dedicated this book to him.

REFERENCES

Alexander, I. E. (1990). *Personology: Method and Content in Personality Assessment and Psychobiography*. Durham: Duke University Press.

Elms, A. C. (1994). *Uncovering Lives: The Uneasy Alliance of Biography and Psychology.* New York: Oxford University Press.

Heilbroner, R. L. (1972). *The Worldly Philosophers: The Lives, Times, and Ideas of the Great Economic Thinkers* (4th ed.). New York: Simon and Schuster.

Runyan, W. M. (1982). *Life Histories and Psychobiography.* New York: Oxford University Press.

Siegel, P. F. (1996). The meaning of behaviorism for B. F. Skinner. *Psychoanalytic Psychology, 13,* 343–365.

Stolorow, R. D., & Atwood, G. E. (1979). *Faces in a Cloud: Subjectivity in Personality Theory.* Northvale, N. J.: Aronson.

1

INTRODUCTION

This book is about a few men who have had a profound effect on a great many people. They have done so by changing the ways that people think about their very own lives. It was the ambition of each of these men to develop a theory vast and powerful enough to account for the human experience in its fullest measure. They sought to explain those human phenomena that are so universal and ever present as to be taken for granted: Why do we show emotion? Why do we want freedom? Why do we dream? They sought also to explain those human phenomena that are so odd or paradoxical as to appear to make no sense whatever: What leads a person to develop superstitious beliefs? Or to have a psychotic break? Or to lead a political movement to practice genocide? Fascinated by the complexity of human life, each developed a model for bringing order and meaning to this complexity. For each man, the theory he offered to the world was so bold that it shocked a major part of his prevailing culture. And in each case, what was initially seen as impossible to accept has now come to be so pervasively adopted as to constitute the essential architecture of our contemporary knowledge. These are the originators of the "Grand Theories" of psychology.

The first historically was Sigmund Freud, a Viennese physician whose major treatise introducing his theory was published in 1899. When Freud looked at the human being, what he saw were seething forces arising from different sources within the mind to wage a never-ending war, and all of this going on without the individual's own awareness. The next was Burrhus Frederic Skinner, a Harvard professor whose first major work appeared in 1938. When Skinner looked at the human being he saw a physical body, moved to behave as it does by its environment in the way that a billiard ball is moved by the objects it hits. Finally there was Carl Rogers, an American psychotherapist whose book introducing his approach was published in 1942. Rogers saw yet a third vision when he turned his eye to the human being. What was plain to Rogers was that humanness is defined by one's subjective experience of the world, and that it is this subjective frame of reference that determines an individual's path in life. Each of these men believed that with his theory he had achieved his ambition to discover the means for fully understanding the human condition. And yet what is obvious from these brief summaries of their theories is that their understandings were entirely different.

These three individuals were founders of three distinct paradigms within the field of psychology. Sigmund Freud provided the first comprehensive model with a *psychodynamic* approach to understanding persons. This approach offers us an image of the human psyche that infers powerful forces battling unseen within us, envisioning an intriguing mystery hidden under that which is apparent. In the view of this approach, unconscious forces in the mind seek a way to be expressed in behavior, yet they run into conflict with equally unconscious forces that seek to deny their expression. Human behavior represents the resolution of this dynamic battle as these various forces are modified, channeled, and given compromised satisfaction. In Freud's version of this model, the primary forces motivating behavior are sexual and aggressive impulses and the moral prohibitions with which they conflict. In a successful compromise between these opposing forces, human behavior represents the symbolic expression of sexual and aggressive wishes in a socially acceptable form. Thus, even the most apparently adaptive and rational human behavior rests on a hidden base of passion, conflict, and irrationality. Freud's theory was the first of its kind, but it has been followed by many others, such as those offered by Carl Jung, Alfred Adler, Karen Horney, and Erik Erikson. Together these and other theorists have provided accounts of what it means to be a person that all fit within the psychodynamic paradigm, a perspective that holds a vision of people as at their core driven by dynamic forces in their unconscious minds.

But a wholly distinct view of the human condition is championed by the *behavioral* approach of which B. F. Skinner is a founder. In the vision put forth by this perspective, human behavior is driven not at all by internal forces but by forces in the surrounding environment. In their goal to develop a science of psychology, psychologists from this approach have argued that private mental events simply cannot be measured objectively or reliably. More importantly, such hypothetical events are not needed in order to explain human behavior. Rather, an explanation can be found in public events that are fully visible: in human behavior itself, in the antecedents of that behavior, and in the consequences that follow it. B. F. Skinner was the first to provide a comprehensive application of this approach to understanding persons. According to Skinner, our intuition that we are motivated by wishes, feelings, and thoughts is as misguided as attributing such internal motives to a billiard ball. Behavior that is followed by a positive consequence is more likely to be repeated; behavior that is followed by a negative consequence is less likely to be repeated; and there is no "wish" or "feeling" or "thinking" required to make this so. Although Skinner was the most radical advocate of the behavioral approach, others too have offered theories within this paradigm, such as Albert Bandura and Julian Rotter. Together, these theorists offer a very different account of what it means to be a person from that found in the psychodynamic approach.

Carl Rogers was a pioneer of yet a third paradigm within psychology, the *phenomenological*. In this perspective, humans are not seen as helplessly buffeted about by forces beyond their control, whether these forces be from their unconscious minds or from their environments. An essential fact of humanness in the view of theorists from the phenomenological approach is that individual persons have free will to determine their own course in life, and that this course will be based on their own subjective experiences.

Each individual views the world from a unique frame of reference, and it is this frame of reference that must be understood in order to understand the person. Rogers himself did not deny that outside forces can have a powerful influence on the person, nor that a person might erect defenses against unwanted self-knowledge. But he argued that these influences only move us away from our true selves, and that there is within each of us an inner directive to bring that true self to fruition, just as there is within an acorn the directive to become an oak tree. Other writers have also offered theories from this phenomenological approach, such as Abraham Maslow, George Kelly, and Walter Mischel. What is provided by theorists from this paradigm is a model for understanding humanness that rests squarely on subjective experience, a view of the individual as using his or her own experience to construct the reality by which he or she will live.

From within their respective paradigms of psychology, Freud, Skinner, and Rogers each believed that he had found the means for explaining what it is to be a person. Each felt that he had discovered the truth about human nature. And yet these truths are entirely different. What accounts for this? In this book I argue that differences in these three major paradigms of psychology result in large part from differences in the personal lives of their founders. In developing a model for understanding all human lives, each man drew on his own particular life. In seeking to make objective claims about all people, these theorists were influenced by the subjective experience of themselves as individual persons. Differences among the theories, then, result from differences in the life experiences of their originators and the personal concerns that emerged from those experiences.

It is not my claim that unique personal experiences were the only sources of the theorists' ideas. By all means there were other sources as well. These include, for example, the general cultural climate in which the theorist lived (e.g., for Freud, 19th-century Vienna); the intellectual precedents to which he was exposed (e.g., for Freud, Darwin's theory of evolution); the particular phenomena the man observed (e.g., for Freud, patients with hysteria). My focus in the coming chapters, however, is on elaborating how the unique personal experiences of Freud, Skinner, and Rogers were important sources for their theoretical ideas. In the final chapter, I say a bit more about other sources.

At the outset, I should say a word about what I see to be the implications of my argument. If the major theories of psychology were indeed crucially influenced by the personal experiences of their originators, what does this mean about their scientific status? Surely their basis in subjective sources means that they must forfeit their claims to "scientific truth," does it not? Actually I don't think so. It is my belief that all human ways of knowing are influenced by the subjectivity of the knower. Scholars of the scientific method have pointed out that subjectivity plays an essential role even in scientific enterprises (c.f. Hanson, 1972; Holton, 1973; Pagels, 1982; Reichenbach, 1938; Ziman, 1978). But, in Reichenbach's language, we must distinguish between the *context of discovery* and the *context of justification* in science. In the context of discovery, the scientist first forms a hypothesis by making inherently subjective observations of reality and systematizing these observations in novel ways. It is in the next stage, in the context of justification, that objectivity is paramount, as the scientist seeks to evaluate the truth of his or her hypothesis by submitting it to empirical testing.

A marvelous example of subjectivity in the first stage of science is found in August Kekulé's discovery of the structure of organic molecules. At the time of Kekulé's work in the mid-19th century, chemists knew that there were different compounds composed of elements such as carbon, hydrogen, and oxygen, but they could not understand the rules by which these elements were linked into compound structures. Before becoming a chemist, Kekulé had originally studied architecture and had formed a strong three-dimensional view of the world. As he now began to dwell on the problem of chemical structure, he experienced visual hallucinations of atoms in three-dimensional space. In waking reveries he saw atoms before his eyes in various structural combinations of chains and rings. He recorded these visions in sketches, and developed a theory of the rules by which organic molecules are organized from his sketches of these visions. Kekulé was the first theorist to fully consider the three-dimensional arrangement of atoms in space, and later empirical work was to confirm the validity of his theory (Hein, 1966).

In my view, the subjective experiences of our psychological theorists played a similar role in leading them to form certain hypotheses about the general human condition. Their personal experiences led the theorists to look in some places rather than in others, and to be likely to see some things rather than others. Thus, for example, I will argue that Freud's personal life experiences made him particularly attuned to unconscious mental events, whereas Skinner's personal life experiences tuned him into behavioral events instead. Coming to their professional work with these respective sympathies, it is not at all surprising that Freud chose to study nocturnal dreams, the mental activity that occurs when conscious thought and behavioral activity are shut down, whereas Skinner chose to study rats, which are behaviorally demonstrative but can give no report of their mental life. I do not think that either man could have taken much interest in the topic of study of the other. Their personal concerns led them to make certain types of professional observations and to extract from those observations certain types of theories.

In the context of discovery, then, subjectivity plays a role in any science. But the goal of science is to discover a pattern that truly exists in the world; thus, even in the context of discovery the theorist is governed in important ways by the phenomenon he or she is observing as well as by his or her own personal ways of looking. Kekulé's visions were not solely a function of his past experience with architecture but were informed as well by what he studied of organic compounds, as Freud's theories would be informed by the nature of the nocturnal dreams he studied; and Skinner's, by the nature of the rats he studied. Furthermore, in the next stage of science the hypotheses formed in the first stage must be submitted to rigorous empirical testing, and here objectivity is paramount. It is in this context of justification that the validity of a scientific theory is tested. I will turn to this stage in the final chapter, by exploring some empirical evidence for the theories submitted by our three psychologists. But the point I wish to make now is that the existence of subjectivity in the development of a hypothesis does not mean that the hypothesis must be invalid, as the later confirmation of the validity of Kekulé's theory demonstrates.

So, my goal in uncovering the personal sources of these theories is not to show that the emperor is wearing no clothes. I do not believe that these theories are simply expressions of individual self-delusions into which the public has bought. The evidence to be reviewed in our last chapter supports the validity of many of these ideas. But I also think it is important for us to recognize that the emperor's personal body provides the underlying framework over which the clothes were fashioned. This will allow us to understand why the clothes have taken on a certain shape and not others, and to explain why in psychology we have three differently shaped theories. I hope by such an analysis to contribute to the study of what has been called "the psychology of knowledge" (Tomkins, 1965; Stolorow and Atwood, 1979).

METHOD OF ANALYSIS

At this point, let me turn to discuss the method of analysis I use in the upcoming chapters to identify relationships between our theorists' personal lives and their professional works. At the most basic level, my method is that of *pattern matching*. That is, similarities are sought between patterns displayed in a psychologist's theoretical writings and those in his personal life experiences. Many have warned of the potential pitfalls of this method of pattern matching. Donald Spence (1976), in his article on "Clinical Interpretation," offers one of the most articulate critiques of this method as it is employed in the context of psychotherapy.

A psychoanalyst listens to the flow of images a patient recounts in stories about past and present life experiences. From out of this flow the analyst begins to extract patterns: For example, "the anxiety that the patient is now expressing upon hearing that I will be going on vacation is like the fear she felt at the age of five upon hearing that her father was leaving the family." But are these two experiences of the patient indeed a match? They may look similar to the analyst, but it is Spence's argument that this link may be imposed by the analyst rather than being inherent in the patient's own imagery. By its nature, narrative material is both rich and ambiguous. An analyst will be actively looking to extract patterns of similarity from this narrative material, and the richness and ambiguity of the material assures that with this goal in mind he or she will always be able to find something. In fact, Spence argues, the number of potential matches that could be identified is virtually infinite. To illustrate this idea in a particular case, let us look at a psychological analysis made of the artist Vincent Van Gogh.[1]

In his book *Stranger on the Earth*, Albert Lubin (1972) devotes a chapter to uncovering the origins of a single but dramatic event in Van Gogh's life. Late in the evening on December 23, 1888, when he was 35 years old, Van Gogh cut off the lower half of his left ear and took it to a brothel where he asked for a prostitute named Rachel, and handed her the earlobe with the words "keep this object carefully." After introducing this extraordinary event to the reader, Lubin considers the possible origins for the act in earlier events that show a match with this one. Over the course of his chapter he offers more than a dozen candidates. Here are just a few.

1. In the months preceding this episode, Jack the Ripper had mutilated a series of prostitutes in London's East End. Among the various organs he removed from his victims, the ear was occasionally his choice. His crimes gave rise to various emulators at the time and Van Gogh was one such emulator. But Van Gogh was a masochist rather than a sadist, and so he reversed the act by mutilating his own ear and giving it to a prostitute.

2. In the region where Van Gogh lived, bullfighting was a compelling cultural activity. In this drama a matador who has vanquished a bull is given the bull's ear as an award; upon receiving the ear the matador tours the arena with his prize and then gives it to the lady of his choice. Van Gogh was identifying with both the victorious matador and the vanquished bull when he cut off his own ear that night and gave it to the lady of his choice.

3. The advent of Christmas evoked Van Gogh's religious imagery and his identification with the martyred Christ. In cutting off his ear he was symbolically reenacting the seizure of Christ at the Garden of Gethsemane, identifying in that one act with Simon Peter, who cut off the ear of the servant who came to seize Christ, with Malchus the servant, whose ear was severed, and with Christ, who was seized to be killed. In giving his ear to the prostitute Rachel, he was then symbolically reenacting the mourning over the dead Christ at Calvary, with Rachel representing both the Virgin Mary mourning over her son and the biblical Rachel, who mourned the death of her children when Herod slaughtered infant sons in his attempt to kill Jesus.

4. During the day of December 23, Van Gogh had had a fight with fellow painter Paul Gaugin and had attempted to assault him with a razor. When Gaugin overpowered him, Van Gogh later turned the razor against himself. His conflict with Gaugin was

based on his childhood oedipal hostility toward his father, with whom he competed for his mother, in part because Gaugin was much superior with the local prostitutes. In cutting off the lower part of his ear and giving it to a prostitute, Van Gogh was symbolically trying to possess his mother sexually, for in his native Dutch the word for earlobe (lel) resembles a slang word for penis (lul).

In each of these accounts we can recognize a match with the two essential elements of Van Gogh's act: cutting off his ear and giving it to a prostitute. But in each the matching element is found in a quite different source. The cutting of the ear is modeled variously on Jack the Ripper's mutilation of prostitutes, the matador's victory over his bull, Simon Peter's attack on Malchus, and a symbolic castration due to oedipal rivalry. Offering the ear to a prostitute is modeled in turn on reversing Jack the Ripper's crimes against prostitutes, the matador's gift to his lady, Mary and Rachel's mourning for their dead children, and a symbolic sexual possession of the mother. What, then, are we to make of these various patterns? Are each of these four (and indeed the many others that Lubin proposes) actual sources for Van Gogh's act that evening, serving as independent streams that united into a river whose course was overpowering? Or are none of these matches a real source of Van Gogh's behavior, each being an imposter for the truth?

It is Spence's argument that we have no way of answering this question. Because of the richness and ambiguity of life history material, an unlimited number of constructions can be placed on that material with each having just as much intrinsic plausibility. But because the pattern we are trying to match is in the historical past, we have no way of reconstructing the original source and determining the validity of any one formulation over another. Furthermore, the analyst's experience of comfort with a match, the feeling that it is a natural fit rather than one that was worried into position, is no criterion for evaluation. Each analyst has his or her own personal beliefs and concerns that serve as templates for resolving ambiguity, and the comfort that he or she feels with an interpretation will be a function of its resonance with these personal themes. That resonance will make it feel, as Michelangelo felt about his creation of "David," as if the form were inherent in the material all along just waiting to be uncovered; but it is instead the analyst's own creation. Spence's conclusion, then, is that we should give up the goal of discovering the true pattern inherent in an individual's experience, and in its place pursue the goal of discovering which pattern is most therapeutically useful. That is, in the context of psychotherapy, the question should not be which interpretation is correct but which interpretation helps the patient.

Sadly, this solution is of no help to us. For our task is not to help an individual who sits before us now, but rather to understand an individual who has long since passed away. But happily for us, Spence's solution to the problem is not the only one. Although there may be an unlimited number of interpretations possible, actually they are not all equally plausible; and although subjective resonance may be a compelling criterion for evaluating the validity of an interpretation, there are better criteria available to us.

I agree with Spence that individuals have their own personal beliefs and concerns that will direct their ways of understanding others. In fact, it is this assumption that underlies my argument for the personal sources of the psychological theories of Freud, Skinner, and Rogers. But people's views are not determined solely by a blind application of these personal beliefs onto a reality they do not fit (unless of course the person is psychotic, which by definition means that they are unable to test their inner experiences against outer reality). People build their personal beliefs from past experiences, and they use these beliefs to guide their understanding of similar experiences met in the future. Thus, perception involves a dialog between observations of actual phenomena in the world and the mental structures by which we can give these observations meaning. The task for a psychological theorist, for a psychoanalyst, or for me when trying to understand another individual, is to make sure that the interpretations made reflect patterns that come from that other individual rather than simply from ourselves.

So, to my mind, the most important criterion to use in forming valid interpretations is that they derive explicitly from the imagery of the individual being studied. If we apply this first criterion to the interpretations of Van Gogh previously reviewed, we can evaluate some as being less plausible. Let us look at the last one, which proposes that Van Gogh's oedipal rivalry was acted out in an assault on Gaugin (as father substitute) and the gift of his earlobe (a penis substitute) to a prostitute (a mother substitute).

This interpretation is built on a number of premises that we know to derive not from Van Gogh himself, but rather from elsewhere.

For example, the concept of oedipal rivalry derives from Sigmund Freud. As I show in the next chapter, the idea of oedipal rivalry finds support in personal life experiences that Freud himself had. But we have no evidence of the existence of such experiences in Van Gogh's life. In Freud's case, for instance, we have a letter he wrote in which he remembers being sexually aroused by his mother as a young child; nothing like this was found in Van Gogh's personal recollections. Second, the attempt to assault Gaugin with a razor also appears nowhere in Van Gogh's own accounts. It comes from an account given by Gaugin 15 years after Van Gogh's self-mutilation. But Gaugin did not make any mention of such an assault back in 1888, when he gave a detailed description of Van Gogh's fit to fellow artist Emile Bernard shortly after it had happened. It is likely that Gaugin fabricated Van Gogh's assault on him years later, in order to justify the fact that he had abandoned Van Gogh and returned to Paris when his friend was in the midst of this personal crisis. There is also nothing from Van Gogh's own imagery to indicate that he saw Gaugin as like his father, the prostitute as like his mother, or an earlobe as like a penis (although the basis of this association in his native language is better than nothing). Altogether, then, this particular interpretation shows no basis in Van Gogh's own imagery and so is not justifiable.

In my own analyses, in order to assure that the patterns I am extracting come from the individual's own imagery, I rely on primary sources. The theorist's work is drawn from his own theoretical writings, and his life experiences are drawn from his letters, diaries, and autobiographies. In the case of Skinner, we have a three-volume autobiography that needs no supplementing. Both Freud and Rogers wrote only brief autobiographical reports, however; so in these cases I draw as well on authoritative biographies, although relying most heavily on the man's letters and diaries reported in those biographies.

This is a beginning. But as Spence has pointed out, this type of material is a richly woven tapestry, and many threads could be followed. How can we know which are important to the individual himself rather than to us as observers? Let us return to the interpretations of Van Gogh. The first posits that Van Gogh was unconsciously emulating Jack the Ripper, and there is evidence in one of his letters that Van Gogh read the newspapers in which these crimes were reported. The second posits that he was emulating a matador, and Van Gogh's letters mention his attending bullfights. The third posits his emulating Christ at Gethsemane and Calvary, and here, too, his letters indicate awareness of these scenes. But was the exposure to any of these events important enough in Van Gogh's psychological life to motivate his behavior? In the first case it is most doubtful, because none of Van Gogh's letters mention Jack the Ripper's crimes. Using this criterion of importance, the third is most promising (although it may be problematic by other criteria). Van Gogh was the son of a Christian clergyman, and religion had been important enough to him that he initially studied theology and entered missionary school before becoming an artist. Specifically in the year of his self-mutilation, he had twice painted the Gethsemane scene, and had mentioned it in his letters. And after he had recovered from his attack, he referred to it as having an absurd religious character. Greater justifiability is found, then, when there is evidence of the importance of a particular pattern to the individual being studied. What we need are rules for identifying this importance.

A set of rules for identifying salient imagery has been offered by Irving Alexander (1990) in his book *Personology*. Alexander argues that we can avoid imposing our own a priori assumptions if we examine another's imagery not by searching for particular contents, but instead by focusing on the manner in which the information is conveyed. Topics that are important to an individual will be signaled by the way they are expressed. Drawing on 40 years of clinical experience as well as on the psychological literature on perception, learning, personality, and psychotherapy, Alexander has identified nine such *identifiers of salience*. According to the identifier of *primacy*, what appears first is significant in serving as a foundation stone or key to unfolding meaning. The identifier of *frequency* signals the importance of that which recurs. In *uniqueness*, what is singular or odd is found to have significance. In *negation*, what is actively denied or opposed is flagged as having special consequence. *Emphasis* calls attention to that which is obviously accented or underlined; underemphasis can be as salient as overemphasis. With *omission* we are given notice of the importance of that which is missing. In *error* or *distortion* a mistake indicates the presence of revealing material. The indicator of *isolation* is a signal of salience to that which does not fit or stands alone. Alexander's last indicator is *incompletion*, which calls attention to the significance of that which is left unfinished.

In my analysis of our three theorists, I use these identifiers of salience to extract from their writings those issues that are important to the theorists themselves. For example, in looking at Freud's work I focus on a close examination of his "Dream of Irma's Injection," because there are numerous identifiers that tell us that this dream is salient. Primacy is one: It is the first dream that Freud ever submitted to a comprehensive analysis. Frequency is another: It is referred to in six of the seven chapters of his major psychological work, *The Interpretation of Dreams*, and the index of that work reveals that more pages are devoted to this dream than to any other. Emphasis is a third: Freud reported having the fantasy that a marble tablet would be placed some day on the house where he had the dream, marking its date as the moment when the secret of dreams was revealed to him. By these three identifiers, we find Freud signaling the importance of the Irma dream.

Other identifiers seem to signal importance in less conscious ways, and an example is found in an incident I closely analyze from Skinner's life. When Skinner was 19, his younger brother Ebbe died suddenly of a brain aneurism. This is the type of event that we could identify as significant by an a priori judgment of its content, which would presumably have a powerful effect on anyone. But the particular nature of its effect on Skinner is made salient by a number of identifiers in his way of talking about it. One is negation: In an autobiographical chapter he wrote in his early 60s, Skinner reported about the event, "I was not much moved. I probably felt guilty because I was not." Another is error, for a decade later in a full-volume autobiography, Skinner contradicted this account and wrote that Ebbe's death had had a devastating effect on him, and that he had been "far from unmoved" (itself a double negation: "far from" and "un"). His account is also salient by isolation, for in both the autobiographical chapter and the full autobiography, he immediately followed his statement about being moved by Ebbe's death with a childhood memory of striking his brother with an arrow, and then isolated some lines from *Hamlet* about disavowing evil intent in hurting his brother with an arrow. Incompletion is a final signal of salience here, for he never explained this association to *Hamlet* and its relevance to his brother's death; in the autobiographical chapter, his next words after the quotation began a new paragraph describing the town where he grew up! These indicators signal that there is much more going on here that demands further scrutiny.

My primary means for avoiding the pitfalls that Spence has highlighted, then, are to draw patterns from the theorist's own imagery and to focus on those things that are flagged by the theorist himself as being significant to him. Of course, even these methods may not fully protect against my imposing my own presumptions. For example, I was concerned when I found myself discovering that rivalry with a younger brother was important in the lives of both Freud and Skinner. Seeing the same thing in two different lives could reflect a correspondence in the person who is doing the perceiving rather than in the persons being perceived. In this case, I reviewed the evidence again to make sure that there was a basis for the idea in salient imagery from the theorists themselves; in this case also, I knew that it could not be a simple projection of my own literal theme, because I have no younger siblings. I have tried to evaluate each of my interpretations in this way. Perhaps more importantly, I have asked some colleagues to read my interpretations and to tell me when they felt any to be unfounded. I invite the reader to ask the same question while reading.

An even more rigorous method would be to have two interpreters independently analyze all of the material and then to have other judges evaluate the correspondence of these interpretations. I have done this with success in a project of much more limited scope, comparing Skinner's first research studies and the first volume of his autobiography (Demorest & Siegel, 1996). To do this for a project of the present magnitude was just not possible. Still, I hope that in the end enough of the particular interpretations here are justifiable and that the general argument of life–work relationships proves to be well substantiated. You should be the judge of that.

To this point I have focused on evaluating an interpretation by the criterion of its basis in the experience of the person who is being analyzed. Although I think this to be the first and most important criterion, it is certainly not the only one to apply in evaluating an interpretation. In his book on *Life Histories and Psychobiography*, William McKinley Runyan (1982) outlines a number of criteria that we should employ in evaluating psychobiographical interpretations. Among those he reviews, the following seem particularly relevant to the present task of pattern matching: (a) Is the interpretation logically sound? (b) Does it account for puzzling aspects of the case that are otherwise hard to explain? (c) Is it consistent with the full range of available evidence from the case itself? (d) Is it consistent with more general knowledge about human functioning? While analyzing the material, I have tried to keep each of these questions in mind as well.

Finally, let me be explicit about the theoretical assumptions I am employing in undertaking my analysis. Earlier, I took issue with applying Freud's theory of oedipal rivalry to understand Van Gogh. If I do not apply Freud's theory, what theory do I apply? I see my approach as falling within the tradition of *personology* (Alexander, 1990; Carlson, 1971; McAdams, 2000; Murray, 1938; Tomkins, 1979; White, 1975). The personological approach was launched by Henry Murray with his call for the detailed study of individual lives in all of their complexity. According to this tradition, each person is unique in the way they have lived and understood their own life. Thus, in order to understand any one individual most fully, we should not be imposing a theory that was derived from elsewhere, but rather should attempt to understand that individual's own view of life.

Adopting this personological approach, I assume that it is part of human nature to extract personal beliefs or themes to explain the way life works. We all do this so that we can understand and deal with emotionally significant experiences in life. But because these themes are formed from our own personal experiences, and because we are born into different worlds and have different personal endowments, the particular contents of these themes will not be the same across people. Freud's concept of the oedipus complex would constitute the identification of one potential theme an individual can hold—and presumably one that fits with Freud's own personal experiences. But it would not be presumed that other people hold the same theme unless they have had similar experiences to make these issues salient to them as well.

Approaching the analysis of our three theorists with this personological stance, then, I employ from the outset principles about shared psychological structures and processes. I assume that all three of our theorists have personal themes, that these themes have been derived from the theorists' life experiences, and that they play a role in determining the theoretical models that these men developed. I also employ other principles about shared psychological processes, such as the idea that people manipulate their beliefs in order to manage their emotions. For example, you will see me occasionally offering an analysis characterizing the individual as trying to master or to ward off unpleasant thoughts. But although such a process is most readily associated with Freud's theory of defense mechanisms, we will see that all three of our theorists identified this universal human process. The personological approach means employing general psychological knowledge about mental structure and process, then, but it is does not impose general proposals about psychic content. Rather, it seeks to let the individual identify what content is important to him or her.

I hope that enough has now been said to clarify my method of analysis. Finally, let me anticipate for the reader the organizational structure of the upcoming chapters. I consider each of our three theorists in each of the next three chapters: Sigmund Freud, B. F. Skinner, and Carl Rogers. In each chapter, I begin with a brief introduction to the theorist by sketching what led him to the problem he first chose to confront in his work. I then dive into a detailed case study from his first major work. For Freud, this means a close analysis of his own "Dream of Irma's Injection," which has a prominent place in his major psychological treatise, *The Interpretation of Dreams*. For Skinner, this means a close examination of his first laboratory experiments with rats, which led to the findings he published in *The Behavior of Organisms*. For Rogers, this means a close inspection of the transcript of the psychotherapy of "Herbert Bryan," whose case Rogers fully reported and evaluated in his book *Counseling and Psychotherapy*.

There are two different reasons why I begin each chapter with these case studies. The first is that I think this type of reading most successfully conveys the man's theoretical ideas to the reader: It brings the ideas to life, shows from what professional observations they derived, and illuminates how they are played out in a concrete case. A more general summary of the theoretical ideas then follows the case study. But I have a second aim in mind, too, with this approach. It is from a close reading of these professional observations that I uncover the first signs of the personal concerns that underlie them. If primacy is a signal of salience, then the first problems to which these men gave their close attention should provide clues to the themes that are important to them. My other goal in starting with this type of reading, then, is to identify what it is we will seek to explain by a study of the man's life. An exploration of the theorist's personal life then follows the summary of his theoretical ideas, as I look for the sources of those ideas in his personal experiences.

I am hoping to play the role of Sherlock Holmes to the reader, first setting out the mystery that needs to be solved through an analysis of the work, and then revealing the solution through an analysis of the life, all by use of the methods outlined in this chapter. Indeed, Holmes used some of the very same principles that Alexander has identified for targeting salient information. Consider, for example, the following exchange between Holmes and the outmatched Inspector Gregory in "Silver Blaze". While the two are musing over the case of the theft of the horse, Silver Blaze, Gregory asks:

"Is there any point to which you would wish to draw my attention?"
"To the curious incident of the dog in the night-time."
"The dog did nothing in the night-time"
"That was the curious incident," remarked Sherlock Holmes.[2]

This is the use of omission to identify something noteworthy. In this case, the dog's lack of commotion when the horse was stolen from his stable indicated that the culprit was an insider well known by the dog.

Thus, our analysis proceeds by first examining the work closely to extract clues about salient themes, and then examining the life closely to identify the origins for these themes. After this method is applied in the chapter on Freud, perhaps in the chapters on Skinner or Rogers, the reader will notice the clues before I identify them, and anticipate what life sources might be found to explain the mysteries that have thus been signaled. In this way, I hope in this book to illustrate not only the claim of life–work relationships but also a method by which such thematic relationships can be discovered.

NOTES

1. This case study was first used by William McKinley Runyan to address the issue of evaluating multiple interpretations, although Runyan's use of the material is different from my own. See his *Life Histories and Psychobiography* (New York: Oxford University Press, 1982).

2. A. Conan Doyle (1901). *Memoirs of Sherlock Holmes* (p. 22). New York: Harper & Brothers. (Original work published 1893)

REFERENCES

Alexander, I. E. (1990). *Personology: Method and Content in Personality Assessment and Psychobiography*. Durham: Duke University Press.

Carlson, R. (1971). Where is the person in personality research? *Psychological Bulletin, 75*, 203–219.

Demorest, A., & Siegel, P. (1996). Personal influences on professional work: An empirical case study of B. F. Skinner. *Journal of Personality, 64*, 243–261.

Hanson, N. R. (1972). *Patterns of Discovery: An Inquiry into the Conceptual Foundations of Science*. Cambridge: Cambridge University Press.

Hein, G. E. (1966). Kekulé and the architecture of molecules. In O. T. Benfey (Ed.), *Advances in Chemistry* (Series No. 61). Washington, DC: American Chemical Society.

Holton, G. (1973). *Thematic Origins of Scientific Thought*. Cambridge: Harvard University Press.

Lubin, A. J. (1972). *Stranger on the Earth: A Psychological Biography of Vincent Van Gogh*. New York: Holt, Rinehart & Winston.

McAdams, D. P. (2000). *The Person: An Integrated Introduction to Personality Psychology* (3rd ed.). Hoboken, NJ: Wiley.

Murray, H. A. (1938). *Explorations in Personality*. New York: Oxford University Press.

Pagels, H. R. (1982). *The Cosmic Code: Quantum Physics as the Language of Nature*. New York: Simon & Schuster.

Reichenbach, H. (1938). *Experience and Prediction*. Chicago: University of Chicago Press.

Runyan, W. M. (1982). *Life Histories and Psychobiography*. New York: Oxford University Press.

Spence, D. P. (1976). Clinical interpretation: Some comments on the nature of the evidence. In T. Shapiro (Ed.), *Psychoanalysis and Contemporary Science* (Vol 5). New York: International Universities Press.

Stolorow, R. D., & Atwood, G. E. (1979). *Faces in a Cloud: Subjectivity in Personality Theory*. Northvale, NJ: Aronson.

Tomkins, S. S. (1965). Affect and the psychology of knowledge. In S. S. Tomkins & C. E. Izard (Eds.), *Affect, Cognition, and Personality*. New York: Springer.

Tomkins, S. S. (1979). Script theory: Differential magnification of affects. In H. E. Howe & R. A. Dienstbier (Eds.), *Nebraska Symposium on Motivation, Vol. 26*. Lincoln: University of Nebraska Press.

White, R. W. (1975). *Lives in Progress* (3rd ed.). New York: Holt, Rinehart & Winston.

Ziman, J. (1978). *Reliable Knowledge*. Cambridge: Cambridge University Press.

2

THE PSYCHODYNAMIC APPROACH: SIGMUND FREUD

Sigmund Freud was just over 40 when he conceived of writing the book that would become *The Interpretation of Dreams*. By all accounts it was his greatest work, introducing a model of the human psyche that was to profoundly change the way that later generations would think about themselves and their world. Although the book appeared in print in November 1899, the publication date printed on the title page was 1900, as if to lay claim to the emergence of a new era. Freud himself wrote of it in his 1931 preface to the third English edition: "It contains, even according to my present-day judgement, the most valuable of all the discoveries it has been my good fortune to make. Insight such as this falls to one's lot but once in a lifetime."[1] But at the dawn of the 20th century, an analysis of dreams would seem an unlikely topic for an important work, especially for a man who considered himself a scientist, not a mystic. So it is worth asking what led Freud to undertake such a thing. Before we look directly at the book itself and the theory it presents, let us see what led Freud to the study of dreams.

In the late 1890s Freud held a medical degree from the University of Vienna and had set up practice in Vienna as a specialist in neurology. As a specialist of physical disorders in the nervous system, in this time and place, the most frequent illness that he encountered in treatment was *hysteria*. Hysteria was an astonishing syndrome that baffled the medical community. It was characterized by various physical problems that on superficial analysis seemed to be based in neurological damage: problems such as blindness, deafness, paralysis, or anesthesia of limbs. But fuller examination would reveal the impossibility of a physical cause. For one thing, it was not uncommon for the symptoms to move from one part of the body to another. A patient might first show signs of blindness, then weeks later appear with loss of hearing, later with paralysis in a leg, and later still with lack of feeling in a hand.

One account tried to explain this by viewing hysteria as resulting from a generally weak nervous system that produced random effects. But there was a further problem: Some of the symptoms made no sense neurologically. Take one common symptom of hysteria, *glove anesthesia*, which involves loss of feeling in the hand. Anatomically, there are three separate nerves that run the length of the arm from shoulder to fingertips, and this means that damage to any one would result in partial loss of feeling in the whole arm. Despite its psychological reasonableness, there is no way to account neurologically for total loss of feeling in the hand only.

An alternative explanation of hysteria, proposed by confused and no-doubt frustrated practitioners, held that the syndrome was just an expression of malingering, intentional fakery by the patient in order to get attention or to avoid responsibility. Support for this account could be inferred from another feature of the disorder, this one involving mental functioning. Patients with hysteria often alternated between two different states of consciousness: one a normal state and the other a hallucinatory state. In the hallucinatory state, patients would behave as if experiencing events that were not actually occurring, and would fail to experience events that were occurring in front of their eyes. A woman might carry on a conversation with an imaginary figure, but make no response to her husband despite his attempts to get through to her.

But there was also counter-evidence to the account of intentional fakery to explain hysteria. For example, some patients appeared with hysterical pregnancies that involved actual physical changes, such as swelling of the stomach and breasts, which could not be faked. In other patients, symptoms such as partial blindness were discovered in the course of a medical examination that had not been noticed previously by the patient or by others in her life.

In the midst of these flailing attempts to come to terms with this remarkable disorder, there was one man in Vienna who had suggested a wholly new approach to hysteria. This innovative thinker, Josef Breuer, was a renowned researcher and a highly esteemed clinician. Freud was a medical student when he first met Breuer, and he was fascinated when Breuer told him of his treatment of a hysterical woman whose case has since become famous under the pseudonym of "Anna O."

Anna O. was 21 when she first developed symptoms of hysteria, after nursing her father for months through what was to be a fatal illness for him. Over the course of her hysteria she developed a host of symptoms: paralyses and anesthesias in her arms, legs, and neck; deafness and visual disturbances; the loss of ability to speak her native German. (For a period she spoke only in English, without knowing that she was doing so, having disputes with her nurse who could not understand a word.) She also experienced a delirious state in which she had hallucinations, at one point in her illness hallucinating day after day the actual events that had occurred exactly 1 year before. At first Breuer was unable to make any sense of Anna O.'s hallucinations, for she was unable to relate to him while in her delirious state, and was unable to recall her hallucinations when she returned to a normal state of consciousness. But one day he discovered that she could answer his questions about the hallucinations if she was in a state of hypnosis.

What he learned from her answers was that her hallucinations were always related to her current symptom. Further, he was astonished to discover that if she was given the opportunity to talk out all memories associated with the symptom she was experiencing at the time, that symptom would suddenly disappear when the final memory was recounted. For example, in the course of her illness she developed a visual disorder in which she saw objects as large and blurred. Under a state of hypnosis, she recounted to Breuer a series of memories of times when she had visual difficulties, until finally arriving at one that originated from early in her father's illness. In this memory she sat by her father's sickbed, crying while he slept. When her father awoke and asked her the time, she swallowed her sobs and tried to blink back her tears so that he would not know she was crying. To answer his request she had to bring the clock close to her face to read it through her tears. This made the timepiece looked large and blurred, as all objects looked in the symptom that developed after this experience. But as soon as she recounted her memory of this experience to Breuer with its associated feelings, her visual symptom suddenly disappeared.

According to the story that Breuer told to the transfixed young Freud, each of Anna O.'s symptoms was cured one by one as she was able to recall emotionally disturbing memories that were associated with the symptoms. Each ultimately went back to a memory of her time nursing her fatally ill father. This suggested to Breuer that hysteria was both caused and cured by psychological processes. It was not, as most physicians assumed, a disorder caused by physical damage to the nervous system to be cured by physical intervention. Nor was it, as others proposed, a sham to get attention that should be dismissed as a nonillness. Rather it was an illness in which pathological processes took place in a mental domain rather than in a physical one.

Breuer's proposal was that hysteria results when psychologically traumatic events create an excess of emotion that cannot be expressed. As a result, the unexpressed emotional experiences find symbolic expression in physical symptoms. In Anna O.'s case, the trauma of the fatal illness of her beloved father led to painful but censored emotional experiences (e.g., she sought to hide her tears while crying at her father's sickbed). These found symbolic expression in symptoms that related to her emotionally disturbing memories of his illness (e.g., her visual disturbance). If the experiences could be remembered and their associated emotions expressed, there would no longer be any need for the symbolic symptoms. It was a radical conceptualization of the disorder in psychological terms, requiring a psychological treatment.

Freud was deeply impressed by Breuer's work, and as he set up his own medical practice in Vienna he was determined to take a psychological approach to hysteria. But there was a challenge to identifying the psychological origins of a patient's disorder, for Breuer had found that they could not be recalled in a normal waking state. Freud originally began his treatment of hysteria by trying Breuer's method of hypnosis. He found hypnosis unsatisfactory, however, partly because he was never very good at it. And so he began to search for other ways to access information that his patients seemed to know at some level, but were unable to report in a normal waking state. In pursuing this search, Freud came to the study of dreams. In his patients' dreams Freud was able to find clues to the meanings of their symptoms. It was with the goal of finding the meaning and cure of this remarkable syndrome of hysteria, then, that Freud first came to the analysis of dreams.

As it turns out, however, it was not only in his work with patients that Freud found the fruitfulness of dream analysis. In the 1890s, he also began to analyze his own dreams. For Freud himself suffered from a neurosis. This neurosis was most pronounced during the years 1897 to 1900, when he pursued his self-analysis most systematically and wrote the book on dreams at the same time. Although Freud at times referred to his neurosis as "hysteria," he probably meant *anxiety hysteria,* a disorder different from that described earlier and what today would probably be called *panic disorder.* His primary symptoms were mood related, involving a change of mood from periods of elation to periods of anxiety and depression; in particular, he suffered fears about dying (what he called "death deliria") and about traveling by train ("travel anxiety"). A heart arrhythmia was probably also a neurotic symptom, which he described as "the most violent arrhythmia, constant tension, pressure, burning in the heart region; shooting pains down my left arm . . . and with it a feeling of depression, which took the form of visions of death and departure."[2] He also suffered from gastrointestinal problems or *irritable colon,* which is common in people with panic disorder.

So Freud had turned to dream analysis in part to find the meaning of his own neurosis, and the discoveries that he reported in *The Interpretation of Dreams* are discoveries that had revealed to him the source of this disturbance. A hint of the source of Freud's neurosis can be found in two events in the late 1890s that coincided with the worsening of his symptoms. Both events involve the loss of intimate male authority figures: his mentor Josef Breuer through estrangement and his father through death. For over a decade, Josef Breuer was not only Freud's collaborator in studying hysteria but also a supportive mentor with whom Freud shared an affectionate relationship. Breuer had provided Freud friendship and advice, as well as substantial financial loans. Yet by the 1890s this relationship began to deteriorate, primarily because of a disagreement over how hysteria should be conceptualized. In 1896 there was such bad feeling between them that Freud would write to a friend "I simply can no longer get along with Breuer at all; what I had to take in the way of bad treatment and weakness of judgement that is nonetheless ingenious during the past months finally deadened me, internally, to the loss."[3] But despite this claim, Freud continued to be deeply affected by their break, and he wrote to the same friend only one week later "I would like indeed to have Breuer's letter; in spite of everything, I find it very painful that he has so completely removed himself from my life."[4]

It was also in 1896, in the latter part of the year, that Freud's father died. Freud himself gave this event a decisive role in prompting both his self-analysis and his writing of the dream book. In the preface to the second edition of the book in 1908 he wrote: "the book has still another subjective meaning which I could comprehend only after it had been completed. It proved to be for me a part of my self-analysis, a reaction to the death of my father—that is, to the most significant event, the deepest loss, in the life of a man."[5] We find, then, that the death of Freud's father and the estrangement of his mentor coincided with the rise of his neurotic symptoms, which centered on fears of death and departure, and that his self-analysis in the midst of these symptoms led to the discoveries reported in *The Interpretation of Dreams*. A clearer case of personal experiences leading to professional ideas could hardly be found. Let us turn now to those professional ideas.

WORK

Early Case Study

The Interpretation of Dreams is an extraordinary synthesis, a scientific treatise documented with the data of personal confessions. The first chapter presents a scholarly review of the previous professional literature on dreams, and the next dives headlong into a detailed analysis of one of Freud's own dreams to reveal its intimate meanings. Freud described the plan of the book to a sympathetic colleague as follows: "The whole thing is planned on the model of an imaginary walk. At the beginning, the dark forest of authors (who do not see the trees), hopelessly lost on wrong tracks. Then a concealed pass through which I lead the reader—my specimen dream with its peculiarities, details, indiscretions, bad jokes—and then suddenly the high ground and the view."[6] This specimen dream is analyzed more thoroughly than any other in the book, and it not only constitutes the bulk of the second chapter but is referred to in each of the following five chapters of the book as well. We learn from a footnote appearing right before the dream is presented that it is the first dream Freud ever analyzed completely, and he wrote of the dream in 1900: "Do you suppose that someday one will read on a marble tablet on this house: Here, on July 24, 1895, the secret of the dream revealed itself to Dr. Sigm. Freud."[7] There is no better place to begin an understanding of Freud's ideas than with this "Dream of Irma's injection."

Freud introduces the dream with a preamble explaining the circumstances under which it was dreamt. He had been treating a young female hysteric, Irma, who was on very friendly terms with him. The treatment had been only partially successful, however, and Freud had proposed a solution to Irma that she was unwilling to accept. They had stopped treatment for the summer vacation in this state of disagreement. On the day before the dream, Freud was visited by a colleague, Otto, who had been visiting with Irma's family just previously. When Freud asked him how he had found Irma, Otto responded that she was better but not fully well. Freud thought he heard a reproach in Otto's tone, but he did not say anything to Otto about it. Instead, that night he wrote out Irma's case history with the thought of giving it to Dr. M., the leading figure in their circle, to justify himself. The dream he had afterwards is reproduced in the following in full:

> A great hall—many guests whom we are receiving—among them Irma, whom I immediately take aside, as though to answer her letter, to reproach her for not yet accepting the "solution." I say to her: "If you still have pains, it is really only your own fault." She answers: "If you only knew what pains I now have in the neck, stomach, and abdomen; I am drawn together." I am frightened and look at her. She looks pale and bloated; I think that after all I must be overlooking some organic affection. I take her

to the window and look into her throat. She shows some resistance to this, like a woman who has a false set of teeth. I think anyway she does not need them. The mouth then really opens without difficulty and I find a large white spot to the right, and at another place I see extended grayish-white scabs attached to curious curling formations, which have obviously been formed like the turbinated bone—I quickly call Dr. M., who repeats the examination and confirms it. . . . Dr. M.'s looks are altogether unusual; he is very pale, limps, and has no beard on his chin. . . . My friend Otto is now also standing next to her, and my friend Leopold percusses her small body and says "She has some dullness on the left below," and also calls attention to an infiltrated portion of the skin of the left shoulder (something which I feel as he does, in spite of the dress). . . . M. says: "No doubt it is an infection, but it does not matter; dysentery will develop too, and the poison will be excreted." . . . We also have immediate knowledge of the origin of the infection. My friend Otto has recently given her an injection with a propyl preparation when she felt ill, propyls. . . . Propionic acid . . . Trimethylamin (the formula of which I see printed before me in heavy type). . . . Such injections are not made so rashly. . . . Probably also the syringe was not clean.[8]

Now, this dream seems like pure nonsense: For example, Irma is sick because of a shot Otto gave her and she will be made well by diarrhea. But rather than dismiss the dream as drivel, Freud adopts the assumption that it is neither nonsensical nor randomly generated, but rather that it has a meaning, if its language can only be deciphered. He analyzes the dream by following his own associations to each of the different elements of the dream. From these associations there emerges a story of the dream's meaning, and more generally, a set of proposals about the content, dynamics, and structure of the human psyche. We consider here only a portion of the dream analysis, but enough to lay the groundwork for Freud's claims about the nature of the psyche.

"I immediately take [Irma] aside . . . to reproach her for not yet accepting the 'solution.' I say to her: 'If you still have pains, it is really only your own fault.'" In looking at these elements at the beginning of the dream, Freud notices that his words show him to be anxious not to be responsible for the pains Irma still has. He blames Irma for her symptoms; if they are her fault they cannot be his. "I am frightened and look at her. . . . I think that after all I must be overlooking some organic affection." Considering these dream elements, Freud finds himself suspicious of the alarm expressed. He notes that this organic trouble too may be an expression of his wish not to be responsible for Irma's incomplete cure. For his treatment was designed to cure hysterical pains, not those of organic origin. If her problem is an organic one, he could not be blamed for her continuing illness.

"'If you only knew what pains I now have in the neck, stomach, and abdomen'. . . I take her to the window and look into her throat." In his associations to this part of the dream Freud notes that these are not symptoms Irma actually has, and he recalls that he has never had any occasion to look into her throat. Freud is reminded instead of another woman who suffered from choking symptoms and who was examined by a window. In the dream he apparently has replaced Irma's characteristics with those of this other woman. This woman is a friend of Irma's who was not a patient of Freud's, but rather was a patient of M.'s. Freud reports that he has a very high opinion of this other woman and has previously had the wish that she would seek his medical services. He now suspects that these elements of the dream express his wish to replace Irma, who had not yielded to his solution, with this more appealing patient who would have yielded to him more readily. In this series of associations to dream elements involving Irma, then, Freud finds the expression of a wish not to be at fault for Irma's continuing illness, and a wish to replace Irma with a better patient.

"M. says: 'No doubt it is an infection, but it does not matter; dysentery will develop too, and the poison will be excreted.'" Freud's first association to this element of the dream suggests that he may have been feeling guilty in his dream and seeking to make amends. The dream had been trying to shift the blame for Irma's illness away from himself, but in the process it had invented a severe organic illness for Irma. M. is brought in to assure that all will be well in the end. But this could not be the whole story, for why is M.'s consolation so nonsensical? To claim that a toxic infection can be relieved by diarrhea is foolish. Freud is then reminded of two other physicians who had made foolish diagnoses, and he concludes that this dream element serves to make fun of M. by portraying him as similar to these other two physicians in his ignorance. Freud now recalls that he has reason to suspect that the appealing patient of M., whom Freud wishes to have as his own, is herself a hysteric and that M. is ignorant of this. But why, Freud wonders, would he wish to treat M. so badly in his dream by making him out to be a fool? He suddenly understands that the reason he treated M. badly in the dream, by making him a fool, is the same as that which led him to treat Irma badly, by replacing her with a better patient. Just as Irma had rejected Freud's proposed solution for curing her hysteric symptoms, M. too had recently rejected Freud's solution to the problem of hysteria.

"We also have immediate knowledge of the origin of the infection. My friend Otto has recently given her an injection with a propyl preparation when she felt ill. ...Such injections are not made so rashly." In reporting his associations to this dream element, Freud recounts that when Otto had visited the day before the dream he had brought as a gift a bottle of liqueur. When Freud's wife opened the bottle that evening it gave off such a strong smell of fusel oil that Freud refused to touch it. In his dream the propyl represents this distasteful smell. But another insult from Otto was the basis for the accusation in the dream, that Otto had been careless in making such an injection. Freud recalls that he had formed the idea that Otto was careless on the previous day, when Otto had told him that Irma was not fully well. Hearing an accusation in Otto's tone, Freud judged that Otto had probably been too easily influenced by Irma's family to side against him, and had rashly jumped to the conclusion that Freud had mishandled Irma's treatment. In the dream, then, Freud takes revenge on Otto for criticizing his treatment of Irma by throwing the blame back on Otto: Irma's illness has been caused by Otto's injection.

Although Freud's full analysis of the dream of Irma's injection is much more complex and intricately woven than I have elaborated here, we now have before us sufficient information from which to extract the conclusions he derived about mental life. What, first, does the analysis tell us about the content of mental life? What is the dream about? A common thread can be extracted from the tapestry of associations that Freud makes to the different elements in the Irma dream. Freud was not to blame for Irma's pains, for she herself was at fault for not accepting his solution. Freud could not be blamed for her lack of cure, for the problem was organic and not amenable to psychological treatment. Freud need not worry about her continued pains, for all would be well once the toxin is eliminated. And it is not Freud, but Otto, who had caused her trouble by carelessly injecting her with an unsuitable drug. Could it be that this wish to be relieved of responsibility for Irma's continued illness is the reason why the dream was dreamt? This is what Freud concludes. An event from the day before the dream, Otto's report that Irma was not fully well and the apparent reproach in his words, had prompted in Freud a wish to be relieved of blame. Freud concludes: "The dream acquits me of responsibility for Irma's condition by referring it to other causes, which indeed furnish a great number of explanations. The dream represents a certain condition of affairs as I should wish it to be; *the content of the dream is thus the fulfilment of a wish; its motive is a wish.*"[9]

And a second set of wishes is expressed in the dream as well. Irma, who had rejected Freud's solution, has been replaced by a more favorable patient. M., who himself had rejected Freud's solution, is made to look like a fool. Otto, who had seemed to blame Freud for Irma's continuing troubles, is himself found to blame for Irma's illness. Thus, the dream also fulfills a wish to get vengeance on those who had questioned Freud's treatment: by replacing them, making fun of them, and throwing the accusation of mistreatment back on them. And it is this wish for revenge that accounts for the nonsensical elements in the dream. Irma looks different in the dream from the way she does in real life because of Freud's wish to replace her with another who would be more congenial. The nonsensical statement by M. about dysentery relieving a toxin is an expression of Freud's wish to make fun of M. The odd injection of propyl expresses Freud's wish for vengeance on Otto for blaming him for Irma's illness. But why does this wish for revenge get expressed by such nonsensical elements?

Freud argues that a dream appears odd or nonsensical because it expresses a wish that is not acceptable to consciousness and so has been distorted. He introduces a distinction between the *manifest content* and the *latent content* of a dream. In the Irma dream, manifest elements such as Irma's looks, M.'s assurance, and Otto's injection are expressions of a latent wish for vengeance. The wish for revenge on a patient or on colleagues for expressing doubt about his treatment was certainly not an acceptable wish in Freud's mind. Yet it was felt at some level, and sought expression. The manifest dream provided a way of expressing this wish in disguised form, so that it was unrecognizable and so allowable to consciousness. Thus, Freud argues, the dream is a compromise between an unconscious wish that seeks expression and a censoring force that judges it as unacceptable.

In this analysis of the Irma dream, Freud has introduced the basic scaffolding for a general model of psychic content, dynamics, and structure. In the next 40 years of his life he was to build on this scaffolding but never to dismantle the basic foundation. In all mental life, as in dreams, he would claim, wishes are the basic content. The dynamics of mental life involve a conflict between wishes seeking expression and judging forces seeking to censor those wishes, with the result representing the compromise struck by these conflicting forces. The mental structure consists of distinct regions, one manifest or conscious and another latent or unconscious.

This is an image of the psyche that envisions an intriguing mystery hidden under what is apparent, one that infers powerful forces battling unseen within us. Our familiarity with these notions today should not blind us to their novelty at the time Freud introduced them and to the incredible daring of his book. In studying dreaming he had turned an inquisitive eye on an experience so common as to be overlooked as unimportant by most people, and he had found in it the key to understanding the human psyche. Just as most people would never infer the relative speeds of light and sound from their common experience of seeing lightning before they hear thunder, they would never infer the important psychological laws that underlie their common experience of dreaming. It took Freud to unearth these laws. It is still a matter of debate how valid his particular principles are, but the enduring power of the overall vision is indisputable.

The Theory

The basic principles of psychic content, dynamics, and structure were revealed to Freud in the dream of Irma's injection, but he elaborated on this basic foundation in later chapters of *The Interpretation of Dreams* and in other works in later years. Let us explore how.

The dream of Irma's injection is a wish-fulfillment, but what is the evidence that all dreams are wish-fulfillments and that more generally, as Freud was to claim at the end of the dream book, nothing but a wish can set our mental apparatus in motion? In particular, consideration of nightmares would seem to provide a challenge to the idea that all dreams represent wishes. But Freud insisted that the claim applies to these dreams as well. He demonstrated this through the analysis of many such dreams by others. His analysis of one of his own dreams is particularly illustrative, because it falls into a class that he regarded as "typical dreams": dreams of the death of a loved relative.

Freud reported that he himself had not had a true anxiety dream in dozens of years, but he remembered an especially vivid one he had in his seventh or eighth year. In the dream, he saw his mother with a peculiarly peaceful sleeping expression being laid on her bed by two people with birds' beaks. He woke up screaming and in tears, and he interrupted his parents' sleep to make sure that his mother was not dead. Now it hardly seems that this dream could express a wish on Freud's part. But we must remember the difference between the manifest and latent content of dreams, and that if the latent wish motivating a dream is unacceptable it will be distorted before finding expression in the manifest content.

Freud examined his associations to the oddest manifest image of this dream, that of two people with birds' beaks. He was led first to a memory of an illustration of Egyptian gods with falcons' heads from the Philippson's Bible he had in childhood. From this recollection he was led to another childhood memory of a boy named Philipp who first taught him the slang term for sexual intercourse. In German, this sexual term shares the root of the word for "bird." His final interpretation of the dream was that it expressed in disguised form a sexual wish for his mother, disguised because of the abhorrence he would have felt on acknowledging such a wish consciously. In fact, in a long section in the dream book on dreams of the death of a loved one, by far the longest section in his consideration of typical dreams, Freud developed the argument that such unacceptable cravings are typical in children. Not surprisingly, many of his readers found this idea abhorrent.

After analyzing the anxiety dreams of a number of his patients, Freud wrote:

> According to my experience, which is now large, parents play a leading part in the infantile psychology of all later neurotics, and falling in love with one member of the parental couple and

hatred of the other help to make up that fateful sum of material furnished by the psychic impulses...But I do not think that psychoneurotics are here sharply distinguished from normal human beings...It is far more probable, as is shown also by occasional observation upon normal children, that in their loving or hostile wishes towards their parents psychoneurotics only show in exaggerated form feelings which are present less distinctly and less intensely in the minds of most children. Antiquity has furnished us with legendary material to confirm this fact.[10]

The legendary material to which he refers is the story of Oedipus. The Greek tragedy tells of the child of Laius, King of Thebes, and his wife Jocasta. The oracle foretold to Laius that his newborn son, Oedipus, would kill him and marry Jocasta, and so Laius ordered the child to be put out to die. But Oedipus was rescued and raised in an alien court. When he came of age, Oedipus too learned from the oracle that he was destined to kill his father and marry his mother. And so he left the family he knew. On the road he met a man whom he slew in a quarrel, and when he traveled on he came to the town of Thebes, whose king had just been slain on the road. The town was suffering under the spell of a sphinx, and when Oedipus was able to remove the spell, he was rewarded by the Thebans by being made their king, and given for his bride their queen Jocasta. To the ignorance of all, the oracle was fulfilled.

The drama of Oedipus as written by Sophocles portrays the gradual revelation of the truth to Oedipus, to his eventual horror. It was Freud's contention that the power of this drama from Greek to modern times results from the fact that it expresses impulses that the audience shares with Oedipus, but of which they, too, are ignorant and would be horrified to learn. In later years Freud gave the term *oedipus complex* to this pair of impulses he thought universal in children: love toward the opposite-sex parent and hostility toward the same-sex parent as a rival for that love. As humans, Freud argued, we are born with impulses toward sexuality and aggression, and these impulses find infantile expression in our earliest relations with the figures closest and most important to us.

In developing this theory Freud would eventually propose that these impulses of sexuality and aggression are expressions of two basic classes of instinct with which we are innately endowed. In his early theory, Freud classified the two classes of instinct as *species-preservative* and *self-preservative*, and he argued that these two classes of instinct are inherently in conflict with one another. Later in his theory, however, he merged the species-preservative and self-preservative instincts into one category, the life or *libidinal* instincts, which seek the preservation of life. Thereafter he proposed a new opposing category of instincts, the *death* or destructive instincts. His argument now held that as well as being motivated toward individual survival and species reproduction, we are also inherently motivated toward our own death and destruction. Just as there are biological processes of growth and development underlying the psychology of the life instinct, there is a biological imperative to return eventually to an inorganic state underlying the psychology of the death instinct. This astonishing concept of an impulse toward death is one that Freud himself admitted to be a product of "far-fetched speculation"[11] when he first proposed it. It remains the one thesis that even Freud's most loyal followers have had trouble adopting.

According to Freud, the innate sexual and aggressive impulses are the basis for all psychic activity and the motivators of all behavior. Yet, not only are they inherently in conflict with each other, but also from their earliest expressions in childhood they come into conflict with environmental forces. The child's attempts to satisfy sexual and aggressive impulses are punished and censored by the parents as socializing agents of society. Eventually, by virtue of his or her identification with the parents, the child comes to internalize what was originally external censorship and to censor these impulses himself or herself. Freud gave the term *repression* to the process by which an individual keeps his or her own unacceptable sexual or aggressive impulses from becoming conscious, so that the individual is not even aware of having the impulses. This, Freud argued, is the fate of our oedipal impulses, leaving us as unaware as Oedipus of what we have wished in relation to our parents.

But repression cannot be the final fate of these impulses, because they are the basis for all psychic activity and seek a way to be expressed. In *The Interpretation of Dreams*, Freud identified a number of unconscious processes by which these unacceptable impulses can find expression in distorted form so as to be acceptable to consciousness. He gave the term *dreamwork* to the processes by which latent wishes motivating the dream are transformed into manifest dream images. The primary dreamwork process he identified is *displacement.* In displacement, unacceptable wishes find distorted expression in the manifest dream content by allying themselves with innocuous material. According to Freud's analysis, unconscious sexual and aggressive wishes of infantile origin are always on the alert, looking for an opportunity to be expressed. They find this opportunity via displacement when they can attach themselves to innocuous images that are symbolic of them. In Freud's anxiety dream, for example, a latent sexual wish for his mother was symbolized by a manifest dream image of bird-beaked figures laying her on her bed. Because of the association in Freud's mind between the word for bird and a slang term for sex, the image of bird-beaked figures served as a displacement for his wish for sex.

In later writings, Freud generalized this process of displacement and other dreamwork processes, seeing them as being expressed not only in dreams but in all mental products and behavioral actions people display. He now argued that everything we do as adults, not only in dreaming but also in patterns of work or romantic involvement, represents a symbolic expression of repressed sexual and aggressive impulses originating in childhood. He gave the name *defense mechanisms* to the various processes by which these unacceptable wishes can find expression in consciousness in distorted form.

Freud retained the term of *displacement* to refer to the process by which an impulse is transferred from an original, psychically valued object onto a substitute object that is symbolically related to the original. In displacement, for example, hostility that is unconsciously felt toward the father can be consciously experienced as hostility toward a boss who symbolizes the father. He gave the term *reaction-formation* to a process by which the impulse itself is turned into its opposite. For example, hostility unconsciously felt toward the father can be consciously experienced as exaggerated love toward the father. In *projection*, an impulse that is unacceptable to the self is seen as belonging to someone else instead. For example, hostility unconsciously felt by the self toward the father can be experienced consciously as hostility felt by the father toward the self. In these ways and others, powerful impulses that are truly felt but that cannot be accepted by the individual are kept out of awareness but find a symbolic expression in unrecognizable form.

This phenomenon, Freud argued at the end of *The Interpretation of Dreams,* implies that the psyche consists of multiple levels of awareness. First, there is the *conscious* level, which in dreaming is shown in the manifest content of the dream that is available to us after waking. But the discovery of the latent content of dreams, of wishes we cannot admit to ourselves, reveals the existence of another level, which is *unconscious.* At this level reside psychic contents that cannot be allowed into consciousness because of their social unacceptability, that is, the sexual and aggressive impulses. A third level is further implied by the observation that there is a screen between the unconscious and the conscious levels, a filter through which unconscious impulses must pass and be subjected to censorship if they are to reach consciousness. Freud labeled this the *preconscious* system.

In later years, Freud elaborated on the notion of distinct mental structures, identifying not only these three levels of awareness but also three distinct psychic agencies that negotiate the dynamic conflict between an impulse seeking expression and a censoring force denying expression. The names he gave to these three psychic agencies have come to be known in English as *id, ego,* and *superego.* But it is worth noting that in Freud's original German, he chose to use the familiar terms for "it," "I," and "over-I."[12]

The id is the mental agency that harbors the innate sexual and aggressive impulses that are the source of energy for all mental activity. Freud referred to this mental system as the "it" because we come to find these impulses unacceptable and so we experience this part of our psyche as foreign to us. The superego is the mental agency that has the function of self-observation, of watching over us to determine that morally good behaviors are enacted and morally bad behaviors avoided; thus its name, "over-I." This part of the psyche judges the sexual and aggressive impulses of the id as unacceptable and seeks to censor them. The ego is the mental agency that must negotiate between these conflicting demands of the id and superego. It is the ego that employs defense mechanisms to allow expression of id impulses in a form that is both acceptable to the superego and realistic within the context of the external world. Freud called this mental system the "I" because it is that part of the psyche with which we identify.

To summarize Freud's final model, then, all psychological activity is motivated by sexual and aggressive wishes. These impulses are with us from the first years of life and are experienced in childhood in the form of the oedipus complex. But sexual and aggressive impulses toward parents are unacceptable and must be repressed, to find only distorted expression after being subjected to defense mechanisms. Our adult activities are thus disguised fulfillments of these childish wishes, compromises providing satisfaction for conflicting forces in the unconscious mind.

A Return to the Irma Dream

Before we leave our consideration of Freud's work, let us see how these final theoretical proposals compare with his interpretation of the dream of Irma's injection, from which he felt he had discovered the secret of dreams. Freud analyzed the dream of Irma's injection at the beginning of his dream book, using it to put forth the conclusion that dreams are wish-fulfillments. The primary wish he identified was the wish to be absolved of guilt for Irma's continuing illness; secondarily he identified a wish for revenge against those who had doubted his treatment. But these are contemporary wishes based on current adult events, and the first is presumably also a conscious wish, because Freud reported writing out Irma's case the night before the dream in an effort to justify himself.

By the end of the dream book, Freud had come to the conclusion that a contemporary and conscious wish is never the true motivator of a dream. Rather, the true wish motivating a dream is invariably a childish and unconscious one. Through the process of displacement, a repressed sexual or aggressive wish of infantile origin finds expression by attaching itself to a conscious and contemporary wish. What are we to make of this apparent inconsistency or error? Could it be that the classic dream of Irma's injection does not itself support Freud's final theoretical conclusions? Or is it that the analysis he gave the reader of the Irma dream was not a complete one?

If we turn back to look again at the Irma dream, we find that in fact in a number of asides, thus made salient by both frequency and isolation, Freud indicates that the interpretation he has given of the dream is not complete. First in a footnote that appears just before he introduces the dream he writes: "I am obliged to add, however, by way of qualification of what I have said above, that in scarcely any instance have I brought forward the *complete* interpretation of one of my own dreams, as it is known to me."[13] Later, having just completed the analysis of the dream, he writes again in a footnote: "Though it will be understood that I have not reported everything that occurred to me during the process of interpretation."[14] And finally in the main text, to begin the last paragraph of the chapter, he writes "I will not pretend that I have completely uncovered the meaning of this dream."[15] So Freud tells us explicitly that his interpretation of the Irma dream is incomplete (itself an indicator of salience). A number of indicators of salience signal to us that there is something important to be found here, that to uncover a fuller interpretation of the Irma dream will be to uncover deeper sources of the subjective origins of Freud's theory. And so let us fortify ourselves for a journey into these deeper layers of the dream of Irma's injection.

Our question is whether uncovering the material Freud censored will resolve the inconsistency we found: Are the wishes that Freud identified really displacements of repressed sexual or aggressive wishes from childhood? A promising place to begin is with the second wish Freud identified: the wish for revenge against those who had doubted his treatment. Although a contemporary wish, this probably represents an aggressive impulse that was unconscious before Freud undertook the dream analysis.

One target of this aggressive impulse is the figure whom Freud calls "Dr. M." in the dream; Freud's hostility toward M. is displayed when M. is made to be a fool by claiming that dysentery would relieve Irma's illness. In his preamble to the dream Freud had identified M. as the leading figure in his circle for whom he had written out Irma's case. Now the leading figure at the time Freud had this dream was actually his mentor, Josef Breuer. In his associations to the dream, Freud had reported that he was angry at M. for not accepting his solution to the problem of hysteria. Thus, the dream represents what we already know to have been an important conflict between Freud and Breuer. Their disagreement over how hysteria should be conceptualized was a source of tension by the time the Irma dream was dreamt, and the break in their relationship as a result of this disagreement was complete by the time the dream book was written. In part, then, the Irma dream appears to express Freud's contemporary hostility at Breuer for rejecting his solution to the problem of hysteria.

Is there any evidence that this adult hostility to Breuer was displaced from a childhood hostility to an earlier figure in Freud's life? Freud says he is not giving the full interpretation of the Irma dream, and so we should not expect to find a thread leading explicitly to this endpoint. The following suggestive leads are worth noting, however. First, we know that Breuer had acted as a father figure to Freud, providing him professional, personal, and financial support. We also know that Freud had a neurosis that emerged in fullest force after his split with Breuer and the simultaneous death of his father, and that his neurosis centered on fears of departure and death. These observations indicate that there may have been an association in Freud's own mind between Breuer and his father, and thus that Freud's adult hostility to Breuer may be a displacement of a childhood hostility to his father.

What's more, Freud does explicitly link Breuer with a male family member in one of his associations to the Irma dream. This association appears to a dream image that is nonsensical, which according to Freud means that it has undergone distortion because of the need for censorship. In the dream M. looks different than usual: He walks with a limp and has no beard. Freud reports that these features actually belong instead to his elder brother, and that the dream image has fused the characters of M. (Breuer) and this brother. Freud then reports that he is also in ill-humor with his brother because he, too, had rejected a proposal Freud had recently laid before him. Thus, we find Freud explicitly comparing his hostility to Breuer with his hostility to an elder male family member.

In our earlier examination we saw that Otto too is a target for Freud's aggressive impulse in the dream. This hostility is displayed in the dream when Otto is blamed for causing Irma's illness by giving her an injection. Freud's associations had previously led to his anger at Otto for bringing a foul-smelling gift and for questioning Freud's treatment of Irma. But there is another nonsensical element that we have yet to consider: The injection was finally found to be of "trimethylamin." What is the meaning that this odd image disguises? When Freud considers the word trimethylamin in his associations he writes:

> The formula is printed in heavy type, as if to lay special stress upon something of particular importance, as distinguished from the context. To what does this trimethylamin lead, which has been

so forcibly called to my attention? It leads to a conversation with another friend who...had just informed me of some of his ideas about sexual chemistry, and had mentioned, among others, that he thought he recognized in trimethylamin one of the products of sexual metabolism. This substance thus leads me to sexuality.[16]

This means that Otto has injected Irma with a sexual substance. Now we might wonder if Freud's hostility toward Otto is also in part a competition with Otto over his sexuality toward Irma. After all, Freud had described Irma as being on very friendly terms with him, and Otto had just come from a stay with her. Does this dream reflect not only hostile impulses toward Breuer and Otto but also a sexual impulse toward Irma?

In our previous review we saw that Irma is actually the third figure who seems to be a target of Freud's aggressive impulse; his hostility toward Irma is displayed in the dream by replacing her with a more appealing patient. But in his associations, Freud tells us that his complaint against Irma is that she did not yield to him, and in the dream he faults her for not having accepted his "solution." Now as we look closer we notice that Freud himself has isolated the word "solution" in quotation marks when he reports the dream. Why does he do this? One possibility is that the quotation marks signal that the word has a double meaning. In German as in English, solution (losüng) can be a slang term for male sexual fluid.[17]

But this implied sexual content is not all. There is also a nonsensical dream image regarding Irma that we have not yet examined. This is the image of Freud looking into Irma's throat and seeing curly structures modeled after the turbinated bones of the nose. In his associations to this image Freud recalls a friend who is a nose specialist, and he says of this friend that he "has revealed to science several highly remarkable relations of the turbinated bones to the female sexual organs (the three curly formations in Irma's throat)."[18] So in looking into Irma's throat, Freud is looking at something symbolic of Irma's sexual organs. And when Freud complains of Irma's resistance in not opening her mouth properly, he is complaining of her not yielding her sex organs to him. These images suggest that the Irma dream represents an unconscious sexual impulse toward Irma as well as the unconscious aggressive impulses previously identified.

Is there any evidence of an infantile source of this sexual impulse, which in contemporary form is directed toward Irma? Previously we acknowledged that because Freud did not provide a full interpretation of this dream, an explicit indication of the childish origins should not appear. Yet we did find hints that the contemporary hostility to Breuer is a displacement of Freud's childhood hostility toward his father. Are there clues that Irma too symbolizes a childhood figure? Some suggestive leads are provided in Freud's associations to the distorted appearance of Irma.

Remember that Irma in reality did not have choking symptoms, and that the appearance of these symptoms in the dream indicates that she is being substituted by someone else. That someone else is a patient of Breuer's who had those symptoms in reality. In his associations, Freud expresses a wish that he could have this patient of Breuer's as his own, thinking she would have yielded more readily to his solution. If Breuer symbolizes Freud's father, then it is possible that this patient that belongs to Breuer could symbolize Freud's mother. Irma's looks are distorted in the dream in yet other ways, for Freud tells us that it also was not characteristic of Irma to look bloated or to have abdominal pains. We need to look to a footnote to discover the third figure who is being represented by these symptoms: It is Freud's own wife. Although Freud tells us in the isolated form of a footnote that these symptoms represent his wife, he omits telling us why his wife was bloated and had stomach pains. The historical record tells us, however, that his wife was pregnant at the time of the Irma dream. So these symptoms, too, could represent a mother figure.

Finally at the end of his analysis of Irma's distorted appearance, Freud compares the three women, Irma, Breuer's patient, and Freud's wife, in terms of their willingness to yield to him. He then concludes rather abortedly with another footnote: "I had a feeling that the interpretation of this part of the dream was not carried far enough to make it possible to follow the whole of its concealed meaning ... There is at least one spot in every dream at which it is unplumbable—a navel, as it were, that is its point of contact with the unknown."[19] Thus there is an unknown (repressed unconscious) source to which these three women refer that Freud represents as being contacted by the imagery of a navel. A navel, of course, is the point of attachment of a fetus to its mother.

Although Freud did not provide the full interpretation of the Irma dream when he introduced it to his readers, we now have found a number of clues as to what a fuller meaning of the dream might be. The dream appears to express hostile impulses toward male colleagues (Breuer and Otto) as well as sexual impulses toward female patients (Irma and Breuer's appealing patient). Furthermore, there are signs that these contemporary figures are substitutes for Freud's father and mother, and therefore that these contemporary impulses are displacements of childish ones. But if this is right, why did Freud not give this full interpretation to the reader when he introduced the dream? There are likely multiple reasons.

One is a pragmatic consideration of how best to present his novel ideas. The dream of Irma's injection is the first dream Freud analyzes for his readers, and he uses it to illustrate the conclusion that dreams are wish-fulfillments. It is two chapters later that Freud takes on the topic of distortion in dreams, and here he brings in new dreams to illustrate this point. In the next chapter he introduces the oedipus complex; in the following one, the topic of displacement; and finally in the last chapter he explicitly states that the true motive of a dream is always in the end an infantile one, in each case bringing in new dreams to convey his point. It takes time for Freud's theory to unfold, and given its complexity it could not be effectively told in full at the outset.

But a second reason is more personal. According to Freud, to uncover the secret of our dreams is to uncover things we do not want to know about ourselves, let alone admit to others. So he was understandably hesitant to reveal to his readers the deepest meanings of his dreams, as is evident in the three caveats he made about his interpretation of the Irma dream. "I am not telling all I know," he kept saying. He was well aware that some readers might delight in learning of unsavory details about his personal life without paying any mind to the important theoretical proposals that were his purpose in revealing them, and even worse that other readers might use these revelations to discredit his theory as the product of a warped personality. But he presumably also knew that those who took his manuscript seriously and studied it closely would be able to return to the Irma dream and extract its fuller meanings, and he did not begrudge this to the serious student of his work. For after all, what is thus revealed are the kinds of wishes and self-deceptions he believed common to all of us, which he felt the honest reader would recognize in himself or herself as well. The fuller interpretation reveals a man who has retained from childhood sexual impulses toward his mother and hostile impulses toward his father, who has found it necessary to deny these wishes to himself while they continue to live on within him secretly, and whose adult relationships are colored by these secret impulses and serve as displacements for them. This fuller meaning, of course, is quite consistent with Freud's final theory. Let us turn now to Freud's personal life to see if it provides evidence for these patterns.

LIFE

I have said that the most valuable source of information for understanding an individual's life experiences is his or her own writings. Unfortunately, Freud systematically destroyed almost all letters, diaries, notes, and manuscripts in his possession at two different times in his life, at the ages of 28 and 51. Surprisingly, the first time he did so he had us in mind. He wrote to his fiancée at the time:

> I have just carried out one resolution which one group of people, as yet unborn and fated to misfortune, will feel acutely. Since you can't guess whom I mean I will tell you: they are my biographers. I have destroyed all my diaries of the past fourteen years, with letters, scientific notes and the manuscripts of my publications. Only family letters were spared . . . Let the biographers chafe; we won't make it too easy for them. Let each one of them believe he is right in his 'Conception of the Development of the Hero': even now I enjoy the thought of how they will go astray.[20]

It is hard not to be amused by Freud playing this trick on us. It is also hard not to be struck by his hubris, for if he was kidding it seems only partly so. How could he, a young physician largely unknown, envision himself as a "hero" whom biographers would so hunger to know that they could be distressed by his act? But he was right, of course.

Luckily, plenty of material has survived to allow a fairly rich picture of Freud's life to emerge. Not only are there the family letters he kept, and letters from after the second purge, but also many of the letters he had written early on were kept by his correspondents. There are also accounts of Freud's life experiences in his professional writings, especially so in *The Interpretation of Dreams.* Ironically, Freud revealed more personal information in some of his professional pieces than in a piece he wrote and titled "Autobiography." The title is misleading, because that work is more a history of Freud's psychoanalytic ideas than of his personal life. Beyond these primary sources written by Freud himself, there is an authoritative three-volume biography of Freud written by a man who was part of Freud's intimate professional circle for 40 years, Ernest Jones. Jones' book provides invaluable information about events during Freud's life, along with letters and memories from family members and colleagues that were not otherwise published. From these sources and various others, Freud's life can be known.

Childhood

Sigmund Freud was born on May 6, 1856, in Freiberg, Moravia, a small town located about 150 miles northeast of Vienna. He was born into a family of an unusual configuration. His father Jakob, a Jewish merchant, was 40 years old at his birth, whereas his mother, Amalie Nathansohn, was 20. Jakob had been married previously and had two grown sons from his first marriage, Emanuel and Philipp. Emanuel and his family lived close by, and Philipp, a bachelor, lived across the street. Freud's half-brothers were closer to his mother's age than was his father, Emanuel being 24 and Philipp 20. As a child he felt some confusion as to whether his mother belonged with Philipp or with Jacob. To further tax the young boy's mind, Freud's half-brother Emanuel had a son John, who was Freud's primary playmate in his first 3 years of life. But although Freud was John's uncle, John was the elder by a year. This unusual family constellation proved vexing to the young Freud, and called his attention to the distinction between what appears to be true and what actually is true. In this we might find one source for his later theory discriminating manifest appearance from latent truth.

Freud was born of his mother's first marriage and was her first child. It was a relationship of mutual adoration from the beginning. He was born in a caul, the fetal membrane surrounding his head, which was thought to prophesy future fame and happiness. This prophesy was further reinforced when one day an old woman who met the young mother and son in a pastry shop declared that Freud's mother had brought a great man into the world. His mother referred to him throughout her life as "mein goldener Sigi."[21]

This love she felt for him was reciprocated by an equally strong love on his part for her, and in his case the feeling even took on an explicitly erotic tone. In a remarkable letter written to a confidant in 1897 when his self-analysis was bearing rich fruit, Freud reported that when he was 2 years old his "libido toward *matrem* was awakened, namely, on the occasion of a journey with her from Leipzig to Vienna, during which we must have spent the night together and there must have been an opportunity of seeing her *nudam*."[22] (italics in original) It is likely that the event he recalls actually occurred when he was almost 4, because at that time the family moved from Leipzig, where they lived for a brief period, to Vienna, traveling by train and probably sharing a sleeping compartment. Nevertheless, it is a remarkable memory for its content, the experience of sexual feelings toward his mother in early childhood. It is likewise remarkable for its manner of expression, with the words for "mother" and "nude" uniquely expressed in Latin. This uniqueness serves to make salient his experience of his mother's nudity; to report her nudity in Latin probably represents a distancing or defensive maneuver against this powerful experience. Thus, the memory gives evidence of a precocious and powerful sexual impulse on Freud's part. This impulse would later find a place in his theory of the importance of infantile sexual impulses in psychic life, and of the sexual component of the oedipus complex in particular.

Despite the close attachment Freud shared with his mother, he felt deeply a number of threats of being displaced from this all-important relationship. When he was only 11 months old, his mother had a second son, Julius, and then five daughters followed in turn until the last child, another son, was born when Freud was 10. The arrival of the first intruder came as a great shock. In the same letter in which Freud reported having sexual feelings for his mother as a child, he reported that he had greeted this brother's arrival with jealousy and ill wishes. Julius died 8 months after being born, when Freud was 19 months old. Julius' death had a

momentous impact on Freud as well, for the same letter continues that this death "left the germ of [self-]reproaches in me."[23]
This too is a striking memory, then, both for its content, that he
felt jealousy, ill-wishes, and guilt by 19 months of age, and for its
manner of expression, with "self-reproach" being mistakenly written as "reproach." Freud's infantile feelings of anger are thus made
salient in this memory, and they may well be one source for his
later theoretical proposition of the import of infantile aggressive
impulses. Furthermore, his feeling of self-reproach upon Julius'
death indicates that at some level the young Freud blamed his own
ill wishes for his brother's death. This primitive belief in the power
of his wishes later found a place in his theory that wishes are the
fuel in psychic life. His belief that such wishes have the power to
kill, and the guilt that he felt upon the realization of this, may
also be a source for the attention paid in his theory to the need to
censor or repress unacceptable impulses.

Freud was also disturbed by the birth of his mother's next child,
Anna, when he was $2\frac{1}{2}$. He decided at that point that his brother
Philipp had colluded with his mother to bring this intruder into
the family. He reports the discovery of this in a letter written in
1897, less than 2 weeks after the one previously cited. The discovery resulted from his analysis of a memory that was salient by
frequency, because it had occurred to him recurrently since childhood, although he had never been able to understand it. In the
memory, his mother was nowhere to be found and he was crying in
despair. He stood before a cupboard demanding that his brother
Philipp unlock it for him, and when he found that his mother
was not inside it he howled still more. Then suddenly his mother,
looking slim and beautiful, came into the room and his anxiety
was allayed.

His analysis of this memory reveals that it referred to events
around the time of his sister's birth. While his mother was pregnant
with Anna, Freud's nursemaid had been caught stealing from the
family. It was Philipp who had called in a policeman to apprehend
her, and she was sent to jail for 10 months. With his mother con-
fined in her pregnancy, the nurse had been a surrogate mother
for Freud, and so her sudden disappearance was a painful loss
at a difficult time. He had asked Philipp where she was, and his
brother had replied in an elusive and punning manner that was
characteristic of him: "She's boxed up." Although an adult would

have understood this to mean she had been locked up in prison, Freud's young mind took it literally. One day some months later, just after Anna's birth, Freud was anxiously missing his mother. He suspected that Philipp had done the same thing to her that he had done to the nurse, and so he turned to Philipp and begged him to release her from the cupboard. In this early memory, important enough in Freud's psychic life to have recurred frequently, we have a vision of the young Freud wrestling with the anguish of the loss of his nurse and subsequent absence of his mother, and turning to his brother Philipp for the key to their return. What he got from Philipp was a cryptic response, a pun in which the literal words were not the truth that Philipp knew, which failed to satisfy his need. This experience too, then, may have provided a basis for Freud's later belief that true meaning lies in what is latent rather than what is manifest.

Freud continued his analysis of this memory to uncover a deeper layer of meaning:

> Anyone who is interested in the mental life of these years of childhood will find it easy to guess the deeper determinant of the demand made on the big brother. The child of not yet three had understood that the little sister who had recently arrived had grown inside his mother. He was very far from approving of this addition to the family, and was full of mistrust and anxiety that his mother's inside might conceal still more children. The wardrobe or cupboard was a symbol for him of his mother's inside. So he insisted on looking into this cupboard, and turned for this to his big brother, who (as is clear from other material) had taken his father's place as the child's rival. Besides the well-founded suspicion that this brother had had the lost nurse 'boxed up', there was a further suspicion against him—namely that he had in some way introduced the recently born baby into his mother's inside... His great satisfaction over his mother's slimness on her return can only be fully understood in the light of this deeper layer.[24]

Freud's use of third-person pronouns such as "the child" and "he" in this account is surprising, given that in the previous paragraph he clearly claimed this memory as his own. This inconsistency makes salient the fear of displacement that is being reported, and his choice to use the third person here may represent a distancing or defensive maneuver similar to that found in his earlier account of seeing his *matrem nudam*. His fear of displacement by rivals thus appears to be as powerful as the sexual longing that is threatened by this displacement. This recurrent experience with rivals, then, may be a source for Freud's theoretical proposals about the psychic process of displacement, making him sensitive to the ways that one figure can be substituted for another. Further, it is intriguing to consider that the proposal of displacement may also serve as a way to relieve Freud of his anxieties about rivals. Recall that displacement is a process of transferring powerful impulses from the important figure in one's life onto less important figures. By theorizing that it is the original figure who is really wanted and that others are only lesser substitutes, Freud assures that it is he as first-born whom his mother really loves above all others.

In the memory cited here, Freud indicates that his brother Philipp had taken his father's place as the primary rival for his mother's love and was seen as the one to blame for the appearance of further rivals. We might also remember in this connection that the name Philipp appeared in Freud's associations to the anxiety dream that revealed his sexual longing for his mother: Philipp was the name of the boy he reports to have taught him the slang term for sexual intercourse. But what of Freud's attitude toward his father Jakob? In the same letter where he first records the preceding memory, he also first reports his discovery of the oedipus complex, saying "I have found, in my own case too, being in love with my mother and jealous of my father."[25] Thus, although he may have consciously thought of Philipp as the man who shared a special intimacy with his mother, at some level he recognized that Jakob enjoyed this kind of relationship with her. There probably were signals of this in regular daily occurrences, such as whom his mother slept with at night.

Two of Freud's rare early memories involve his inappropriate intrusion into his parents' bedroom and his father's angry rejection of this initiative. These rare memories, salient by their uniqueness, give evidence of his oedipal rivalry with his father. The first is a memory whose salience is further indicated by the fact that Freud frequently found it referred to in his dreams even in adulthood. One evening when he was 7 or 8 years old, he urinated in his parents' bedroom in front of them. His father responded by harshly reprimanding him and declaring that he would amount to nothing. The evidence that this memory represents a sexual rivalry with his father is found in *The Interpretation of Dreams*. In his dream book, Freud recounts this memory as an association to a particular dream image: Freud is standing in a railway station with an elderly gentleman who is blind in one eye, and Freud hands the man a urinal so that he can urinate into it. According to Freud's interpretation of this dream scene, the elderly gentleman represents his father who had glaucoma in one eye. Freud further interprets the dream image as representing an act of revenge in reversing the roles between his father and himself, because his father is doing the shameful urinating in the dream whereas Freud himself had done so in reality. In fact, Freud interprets the whole dream as an expression of rebellion against his father. Although he goes no further in making an explicitly oedipal interpretation, he alludes to the sexual basis of this hostility against his father by indicating that he will not give the full interpretation of the dream because he is compelled to suppress sexual material.

For the second of Freud's childhood memories he puts forth an explicitly oedipal interpretation. In this memory he forced his way into his parents' bedroom one night out of sexual curiosity and was thrown out again by his father. This memory too appears as an association to one of Freud's dreams in the dream book. The contemporary instigator of the dream was this: Freud was traveling by train, and in entering his sleeping compartment he found an elderly couple who treated him cooly. He imagined that their annoyance resulted from the fact that his arrival had prevented the intimate exchange they had been preparing for that night. Freud saw this contemporary interruption and unfriendly response as an analogy to the childhood one he now recalled. After going to sleep that night, he had a dream in which he was sleepwalking. In interpreting this dream Freud reports an association to a patient who had developed the idea that he was committing murders while sleepwalking. Freud writes: "I knew that hostile impulses towards his father from the time of his childhood, in connection with sexual material, had been at the root of his illness. By identifying myself with him [by sleepwalking in the dream], I wanted to make an analogous confession to myself."[26] The memory, dream, and associations, then, portray his sexual interest in his mother, his aggressive wish to displace his father, and his father's rejection of this effort. Thus, we can find in these two rare early memories a basis for many of Freud's later theoretical propositions: the role of sexual and aggressive impulses, the view of these impulses as unacceptable and requiring censorship, and of course the oedipus complex itself.

The other important relationship to consider from Freud's early childhood is that with his older nephew John, who lived nearby during Freud's first 3 years before the family moved to Leipzig. According to his descriptions in *The Interpretation of Dreams*, theirs was a relationship that was both intense and ambivalent. Freud reports that they were inseparable, and that they both loved each other and fought with each other. With John being the elder of the two he won their physical battles, and Freud paints a picture of John treating him badly on occasion and of himself standing up courageously to his tyrant. He imagines his childhood thoughts pursuing the following lines: "It serves you quite right if you had to vacate your place for me; why did you try to force me out of my place? I don't need you, I'll soon find someone else to play with."[27] These feelings toward John seem to echo both the hostility of a battle for primacy that he felt with other family members ("It serves you quite right if you had to vacate your place for me; why did you try to force me out of my place?") and the pain of loss of intimacy that he felt with his mother ("I don't need you, I'll soon find someone else to play with."). Both love and hate were felt toward the same person in this inseparable playmate of his earliest years. Perhaps this relationship, then, poignantly impressed upon Freud that conflict rages within an individual between two driving impulses of love and hate, the sexual impulses and the aggressive impulses.

Childhood Patterns Revisited in Adulthood

Thus, personal experiences that Freud had in these early years appear to have had an impact on the psychological theory he subsequently developed. But we should look as well at the influence of adult life experiences on Freud's theory, for *The Interpretation of Dreams* was written when he was over 40. One of the most striking things we find when we turn to his adulthood, however, is the extent to which his adult relationships repeat the same dynamic we saw in his early years. This repetition gives a further personal source for his theoretical concept of displacement, in which powerful impulses of infantile origin are redirected toward other figures later in life. The dynamic that recurs, of course, is that of the oedipus complex: a passionate longing for a loved other and the need to fight rivals to secure exclusive ownership of that other. We first see this dynamic at play during Freud's courtship and betrothal with his future wife, Martha Bernays.

Martha as the Mother

Freud was 25 when he met Martha and she was 20 (the age of his mother at the time of his birth); they became engaged 2 months later. Freud did not yet have the financial resources to establish a family, because he had only just received his medical degree the year before. As a result, Freud and Martha were engaged for 4 years before they could marry, and for 3 of those years they lived in distant cities. The luck in this for biographers of Freud, if not for Freud himself, is that there is a record of these years in the many letters totaling over 900 that Freud wrote to his betrothed. Ernest Jones was allowed by the family to read the full set of letters and was deeply impressed by what he described as Freud's "grande passion." Jones wrote that the letters reveal "above all how mighty were the passions that animated Freud ... He was beyond doubt someone whose instincts were far more powerful than those of the average man."[28] Freud's passion was expressed most fully when he felt keenly his separation from Martha or when he worried about her ill heath, which preoccupied him to an unrealistic degree. In one letter, for example, he wrote about his longing to be with her as "a frightful yearning—frightful is hardly the right word, better would be uncanny, monstrous, ghastly, gigantic; in short, an indescribable longing for you,"[29] and elsewhere when anxious about her health: "I really get quite beside myself when I am disturbed about you. I lose at once all sense of values, and at moments a frightful dread comes over me lest you fall ill. I am so wild that I can't write much more."[30]

It was not only their physical separation or the thought of losing her from ill health, however, that disturbed him. As in his relationship with his mother, he also was deeply fearful of rivals. The first potential rival appeared in the form of a man named

Fritz Wahle. Freud had heard that Fritz had the reputation of being able to steal a woman away from another man. But Fritz was a close friend of Freud's, and had been a brotherly friend to Martha for many years before Freud and Martha met. What's more, he was engaged to marry Martha's cousin by the time Freud began to court Martha. As it turns out, however, Fritz's feelings for Martha were apparently more than fraternal, for when he heard of her engagement to Freud he broke down crying. When he and Freud met shortly thereafter, he threatened to shoot Freud, and then himself, if Freud did not make Martha happy. Freud tried to laugh off the threat, but Fritz then declared that if he wrote Martha telling her to dismiss Freud she would, and he immediately penned such a letter, using phrases such as "beloved Martha" and "undying love." Taking him quite seriously now, Freud tore the letter into pieces. The next day Freud, still much upset, said "He is no longer my friend, and woe to him if he becomes my enemy. I am made of harder stuff than he is, and when we match each other he will find he is not my equal . . . '*Guai a chi la tocca.*' [Woe to him who touches her.] I can be ruthless."[31]

Despite this confident assertion, Freud began to doubt his hold on Martha and to suffer an appalling dread. This was made worse by Martha's reaction to the situation, writing Fritz a letter assuring him that their friendship could continue unchanged. Freud was so enraged by the letter that he wrote to Martha: "I lose all control of myself, and had I the power to destroy the whole world, ourselves included, to let it start all over again—even at the risk that it might not create Martha and myself—I would do so without hesitation."[32] When they next saw each other, Freud told Martha that she must reject all contact Fritz attempted with her. After many talks about the matter in which Martha was evasive, she finally agreed. Later in their relationship, Freud told her more than once that if she had not agreed then, they would have had to part forever.

Now it is worth asking whether this rivalry with Fritz over Martha's love is a true example of displacement. Are Freud's powerful feelings of rivalry with Fritz an expression of his childhood hostility toward rivals for his mother's love? In this case it is hard to know, for the reality of the adult situation might justifiably call up these same feelings without their having any childhood basis. Fritz did have a reputation for stealing women away from other men, and his reaction to Martha's engagement to Freud certainly sounds like more than a feint in that direction. So in this case we cannot be sure. But there were other instances when Freud experienced revivals of this same dynamic when their basis in reality was by no means so clear. One occasion emerged shortly after Freud's successful defeat of Fritz, when he now became fearful of another competitor for Martha's love. This time the competitor was Martha's own brother, Eli Bernays.

Eli was a friend of Freud's and indeed of the whole Freud family. He became engaged to Freud's sister Anna around the same period that Sigmund and Martha were engaged, and he had taken on the youngest Freud, Alexander, as an apprentice. Yet Freud stated soon after his engagement to Martha that Eli was his "most dangerous rival."[33] He seemed to seize the first opportunity he found for drawing the battle lines. Alexander at age 16 was being apprenticed to Eli without pay. Although this was customary, Freud told Alexander after 2 months that he should ask Eli for a salary and quit if not given one immediately. The dutiful younger brother asked as he was told, and Eli said he would begin paying him at the arrival of the new year, which was 2 months away. Because the salary was not to be given immediately, Alexander quit. Eli was exasperated and complained to Freud about the situation, but Freud was unmoving. Freud insisted that Martha side with him on the matter and against her brother, and she did. As in the case of Fritz, Freud later told her that if she had not done so, he would have broken things off with her.

Other opportunities for conflict with Eli emerged and were taken up over the course of Freud's engagement to Martha, until the final months when they were securing sufficient funds to finalize their wedding date. It turned out that Martha had given half of her dowry to Eli, who as a businessman would know how to invest it wisely. Freud, however, knew nothing about investing and assumed that the cash was locked away in a safe. At the point when Freud told Martha to retrieve the money, Eli had overinvested his funds and could not easily lay his hand on ready cash, so he attempted to delay his fulfillment of Martha's request. This elicited Freud's mistrust and fury once again, probably because in withholding the money Eli was withholding what to Freud was his means for marrying Martha. Freud wrote Martha a number of frenzied letters denouncing Eli as a thief and telling her to insist that Eli return the money immediately, but Martha replied that she trusted her brother and resented Freud's harsh words against him. Freud then took the matter into his own hands and wrote Eli directly, at which point the hurt Eli somehow got cash to send to Martha the next day, along with a note expressing his innocence and pain at Freud's brutal words. When Martha wrote Freud rebuking him, his reply said that she should not write him again until she had promised to break off all relations with Eli! This tested Martha's love to the fullest. But in the end they weathered this storm as they had weathered previous ones, and Freud emerged feeling victorious over his rival, even at the cost of Martha's feeling utterly shattered and drained.

Although Freud's feeling of rivalry with Fritz Wahle can be seen as justified and might have been felt by many men in his situation, his feeling of rivalry with Eli Bernays is hard to see as warranted and probably constitutes an error or distortion. That he viewed Eli in this way when there was not good basis for this view suggests that he was displacing onto this adult relationship expectations that were derived from an entirely different source in childhood. But perhaps the most surprising displacement of Freud's childhood oedipus complex in adulthood was one that was played out on another stage entirely. It appears that Freud's attitude toward his professional work was also modeled after his childhood attitude toward his mother, and that in this case, too, he saw rivals. Yet when we remember that Freud argued in his theory that work serves as an object of displacement of one's sexual or aggressive impulses, this should not be so surprising after all.

There are a number of clues that Freud displaced his sexual interest for his mother onto his work. Consider his decision to study medicine in the first place. On graduating from secondary school, Freud was still undecided about his future career, drawn both to law and to medicine. According to his autobiography, he decided on medicine immediately after hearing Goethe's essay on Nature read aloud at a popular lecture. Jones describes this essay as "a romantic picture of Nature as a beautiful and bountiful mother who allows her favorite children the privilege of exploring her secrets."[34] That Freud took from this an erotic meaning is affirmed by a passage he wrote years later in *The Interpretation of Dreams*. Discussing the case of a man who had broken down in a frenzy crying "Nature! Nature!," Freud wrote: "The physicians in attendance thought that the cry was derived from reading Goethe's beautiful *essay*, and that it pointed to overwork in the patient in the study of natural philosophy. I thought rather of the sexual sense in which even less cultured people with us use the word 'Nature'."[35] And consider his imagery over a decade later, when shortly after receiving his medical degree he applied for a postgraduate grant. On the night before the committee was to meet to decide who would get the grant, Freud dreamt that his recommender on the committee told him he had no chance because there were seven other competitors. Freud knew that in reality there were only two others, whereas the number seven represented instead the number of siblings in his own family of origin. This indicates that he experienced competition in his medical pursuits as akin to competition for his mother.

Breuer as the Father

As a young professional Freud's work came to be psychoanalysis, and he came to view his mentor Josef Breuer as a rival for it. We have seen that Breuer served as a father figure to Freud when Freud was establishing his career as a young physician, providing emotional, intellectual, and financial support. Most importantly for our current concern, Freud went so far as to characterize Breuer as the founder of psychoanalysis when he was first invited to the United States in 1909 to give a series of lectures on the psychoanalytic movement. But by 1914 when Freud wrote his "History of the Psycho-Analytic Movement" he explicitly retracted his earlier view. The reasons he gave for rejecting Breuer as the founder of psychoanalysis now appear to reflect a displacement of his oedipal rivalry with his father onto Breuer.

Freud's 1914 paper begins by pointing out that in 1909 he had attributed the founding of psychoanalysis to Breuer but that friends complained that the credit belonged to him. His initial method of deciding the question is quite unusual: Freud claims that the ownership of psychoanalysis must be his because he himself has met with great hostility whereas Breuer has met with none. In the first paragraph he writes: "I have never heard that Breuer's great share in psycho-analysis has earned him a proportionate measure of criticism and abuse. As I have long recognized that to stir up contradiction and arouse bitterness is the inevitable fate of psychoanalysis, I have come to the conclusion that I must be the true originator of all that is particularly characteristic in it."[36] This peculiar reasoning sounds as if it is modeled on an oedipal dynamic: The true owner of psychoanalysis (mother) will elicit hostility (jealous rivalry) from others.

His account next turns to the reason why psychoanalysis has met with such hostility: its assertion of the centrality of sexual impulses in psychic life. He claims that Breuer had experienced the importance of sexuality in the classic case of Anna O. out of which psychoanalysis grew, but that Breuer had repudiated the role of sexuality in hysteria and in psychic life more generally. Having rejected this essential tenet of psychoanalysis, Freud's argument goes, Breuer cannot be seen as its true originator. A review of the evidence, however, suggests that Freud's characterization is distorted in a number of ways. And it appears that the cause of this distortion is a displacement onto Breuer of Freud's childhood sexual rivalry with his father.

Recall that Anna O. was a hysterical patient of Breuer's who, according to Breuer's report of the case, was cured of her disorder when she was able to remember emotionally disturbing memories associated with the fatal illness of her father. Breuer saw her hysteria as resulting from these disturbing emotions brought up by her father's illness, and in his report of the case he explicitly said of Anna O. that "the element of sexuality was astonishingly undeveloped in her."[37] But Freud believed that this was not the full story. After each of Anna O.'s symptoms had been relieved, Freud now claimed, there emerged at the end of her treatment a final symptom that Breuer had never reported: a hysterical pregnancy in which she claimed to be carrying Breuer's baby. According to Freud, Breuer did not want to admit to such a distasteful revelation, and so he did not report this symptom in his case study and denied a role for sexuality in causing Anna O.'s hysteria. But Freud saw in Anna O.'s hysterical pregnancy the basis for understanding the true meaning of her illness. Freud's reinterpretation of the case was that the source of Anna O.'s illness lay specifically in sexual impulses for her father. These sexual impulses, which had been repressed since childhood, were reawakened while she was caring for her father at his sickbed, and displaced onto Breuer as a father-substitute.

There is a problem with Freud's reinterpretation of Anna O.'s case, however. It is based not on actual evidence as Breuer reported it to Freud, but rather is a result of what Freud himself inferred. What Freud actually writes in his 1914 report is that "I have strong

reasons for *suspecting* that after all her symptoms had been relieved Breuer *must have* discovered from further indications the
sexual motivation ... *He never said this to me in so many words* but
he told me enough at different times to justify this *reconstruction*
of what happened."[38] (emphases added) This means that Freud's
alternative story of the case of Anna O. is formed via inference
and is therefore quite subject to the expectations Freud would be
bringing to it. If this is so, then it may be a displacement of his
oedipus complex that led Freud to infer that there was something
sexual going on between Breuer and Anna O. in the case that
originated psychoanalysis.

In all published accounts Freud indicates that this reinterpretation of Anna O.'s case is derived by inference, but there is one
personal letter he wrote quite late, in 1932, which claims that
Breuer explicitly reported to him Anna O.'s hysterical pregnancy.
In this letter Freud writes:

> What really happened with Breuer's patient I was able to guess
> later on, long after the break in our relations, when I suddenly
> remembered something Breuer had once told me in another
> context before we had begun to collaborate and which he never
> repeated. On the evening of the day when all her symptoms had
> been disposed of, he was summoned to the patient again, found
> her confused and writhing in abdominal cramps. Asked what
> was wrong with her, she replied: "Now Dr. B.'s child is coming!"
> At this moment he held in his hand the key that would have
> opened the "doors to the Mothers," but he let it drop.[39]

It is hard to believe that Breuer would have reported such an
event to Freud early in their relationship, when they were just
getting to know one another, but not later once they were intimate
colleagues studying hysteria together. It is also hard to believe that
Freud would have forgotten such an important event initially, not
been reminded of it when he read Breuer's report of the case of
Anna O. in the book they co-authored on hysteria in 1895, and
yet spontaneously recalled it many years later. All this is possible,
of course, but it is more likely that Freud's 1932 account of the
events involves a memory distortion itself, because false memories
can be created as easily as true ones can be forgotten. Even in this
account, he refers to having "guessed" at what really happened,

and his reference to Breuer having the means to open the "doors to the Mothers" does not exactly relieve the suspicion of an oedipal displacement!

There is also evidence against the view that Breuer rejected Freud's sexual theory of hysteria because he found it distasteful. In fact, Breuer had claimed that although Anna O.'s illness was not based in sexuality, he had other patients in whose illnesses sexuality played a major role. Indeed, in the theoretical chapter Breuer wrote for the 1895 book on hysteria that he co-authored with Freud, *Studies on Hysteria*, Breuer had spent many pages addressing the role of sexuality in hysteria. He began this review with the statement: "We are already recognizing sexuality as one of the major components of hysteria. We shall see that the part it plays in it is very much greater still and that it contributes in the most various ways to the constitution of the illness."[40] His review ended with the conclusion: "It is self-evident and is also sufficiently proved by our observations that the non-sexual affects of fright, anxiety and anger lead to the development of hysterical phenomena. But it is perhaps worth while insisting again and again that the sexual factor is by far the most important and the most productive of pathological results."[41] Breuer was therefore far from rejecting sexuality as a cause of hysteria, or even as the most important cause. What he rejected was Freud's claim that it was the only cause. He characterized his view of this divergence with Freud in a personal letter written in 1907 after their break. "Freud is a man given to absolute and exclusive formulations: this is a psychical need which, in my opinion, leads to excessive generalization."[42]

Surprisingly, Freud seems to have held this same interpretation of Breuer's complaint against him at the time of their break in 1896, when he wrote to a confidant about Breuer: "I believe he will never forgive that in the *Studies* I dragged him along and involved him in something where he unfailingly knows three candidates for the position of *one* truth and abhors all generalizations, regarding them as presumptuous."[43] It is after 1896 that Freud developed the view that Breuer rejected him because of his sexual claims. In this reinterpretation we can see that Freud was now viewing Breuer as like his own father who had rejected his sexual assertions.

Freud's 1914 account of the history of psychoanalysis, therefore, may have served to assert his sole possession of the work that had come to symbolize his mother. But the break between Freud and Breuer occurred in 1896, and by 1914, Breuer had long since fallen out of involvement with psychoanalysis. What, then, prompted Freud to write this historical account to assert his primacy at this particular time? In fact, the early 1910s marked the time of Freud's struggle with another rival for the ownership of psychoanalysis, and his historical report was written primarily to assert his claim against this potential usurper. But in this case too, the evidence suggests that Freud's adult rivalry was not justified by contemporary events, but rather represented a displacement of a childhood family dynamic. The rival this time, apparently representing Freud's younger brother Julius rather than his father Jakob, was his younger colleague Carl Jung.

Jung as the Brother

Jung had been at his first post as an assistant physician at the Burghölzli Mental Hospital in Switzerland when he read Freud's *Interpretation of Dreams* soon after it was published. In 1906 Jung sent to Freud his own book, *Diagnostic Association Studies,* which cited Freud's theory and provided empirical support for it. With this there began an intense relationship between the two men, Freud very quickly embracing the younger Jung as his successor and "crown prince." By 1908, Freud had arranged that Jung would be the editor of the first psychoanalytic journal, the *Jahrbuch für psychoanalystische und psychopathologische Forschungen,* and when in 1910 the International Psychoanalytic Association was founded, Freud designated Jung as its president. But it was not long before Freud began to worry about the man he had identified to take over the psychoanalytic movement after him.

Two incidents between them are particularly worth reviewing because in both Freud displayed what was for him a unique neurotic symptom: He fainted. The first occurred in 1909, when G. Stanley Hall, then president of Clark University, invited both Freud and Jung to America to mark Clark's 20th anniversary and to receive honorary degrees. Freud considered this a momentous event for his work, because it was his first invitation to speak about psychoanalysis in public and his first invitation to be honored in a foreign country. In his autobiography, written years later, he wrote that "it seemed like the realization of some incredible daydream."[44] That Jung was invited as well may have provoked Freud's competitive feelings. Before Freud departed for the trip his travel anxiety was apparently in full force, for he took out life insurance worth 20,000 marks and slept poorly on the overnight train to Bremen, Germany, where he would meet Jung to board a ship for America. Freud and Jung dined together in Bremen, and Jung began expounding on his interest in corpses that he heard were perfectly preserved in the peat bogs in the area. Freud was visibly disturbed by the topic and kept asking Jung why he was so concerned with these corpses. As Jung continued on the topic, Freud suddenly fell unconscious. After he had revived, Freud told Jung that he was sure Jung's great interest in the corpses represented a death wish against him; the interpretation left Jung dumbfounded.[45]

Three years later, a second fainting episode occurred while Freud, Jung, and a few others were having lunch in Munich, Germany. A discussion arose about a paper one had recently written about the Egyptian pharaoh Amenophis IV. The paper argued that the pharaoh's destruction of the name of the god Amon from all records was motivated by his oedipal hostility against his father Amonhotep. Freud suddenly took this occasion to begin reproaching Jung for failing to mention Freud's name in recent articles Jung had written about psychoanalysis in Swiss journals. Then, as before, he fell down in a faint. Presumably, as before, he was feeling that Jung had death wishes against him. A month later, however, Freud wrote to another colleague that he had successfully analyzed his fainting attacks, and had found their source in the death of his younger brother Julius.[46] This suggests that Freud's own childhood death wishes against Julius had been displaced onto Jung. Then, because Freud could no more accept a hostile impulse against Jung than he could a hostile impulse against Julius, he had further defended against this impulse by projecting it onto Jung and seeing it as being felt by Jung rather than by himself.

In reality, the evidence does not appear to justify Freud's fear of Jung as a rival wishing to destroy him to steal psychoanalysis. In the earliest letter that survives from Jung's correspondence with Freud, Jung expressed his inability to fully adopt Freud's psychoanalytic theory because of its excessive emphasis on sexuality. A dozen years later, at the meeting in Munich, Jung was expressing this same aversion. During their discussion of the pharaoh Amenophis IV, Jung argued that the important thing to understand about Amenophis was not his sexual rivalry with his father, but rather how it was that he had accomplished the profound religious achievement of establishing a monotheistic religion. In his own work Jung was led to elaborate the role of spirituality in psychic life. He was fiercely independent about pursuing his own ideas; he had no wish to steal Freud's. When conflicts with Freud escalated, Jung resigned his editorship of the *Jahrbuch* in 1913, and his presidency of the International Psychoanalytic Association in 1914. It was in the latter year that Freud began his "History of the Psycho-Analytic Movement," published in the *Jahrbuch*, with the following preamble:

> No one need be surprised at the subjective character of the contribution I propose to make here to the history of the psycho-analytic movement, nor need anyone wonder at the part I play in it. For psycho-analysis is my creation . . . Although it is a long time now since I was the only psycho-analyst, I consider myself justified in maintaining that even today no one can know better than I do what psycho-analysis is . . . In thus repudiating what seems to me a cool act of usurpation, I am indirectly informing the readers of this *Jahrbuch* of the events that have led to the changes in its editorship.[47]

With Jung having voluntarily given up his roles as editor of the journal and president of the international society, it is unlikely that Freud's characterization of Jung as a usurper was justified by Jung himself. More likely Freud was displacing his childhood rivalry with Julius onto this adult situation.

We have seen, then, that many of Freud's adult relationships were colored by a displacement of dynamics set up in his childhood. This suggests a personal basis for his theoretical concept of displacement. Other examples too could be elaborated. In *The Interpretation of Dreams*, Freud himself attributes a pattern in his adult relationships with friends and foes to his childhood relationship with his nephew John. He writes:

> My friendships as well as my enmities with persons of my own age go back to my childish relations with my nephew, who was a year older than I. . . . We lived together inseparably, loved each other, and at the same time, as statements of older persons testify, scuffled with and accused each other. . . . An intimate friend and a

hated enemy have always been indispensable requirements for my emotional life; I have always been able to create them anew, and not infrequently my childish ideal has been so closely approached that friend and enemy coincided in the same person, not simultaneously, of course, nor in repeated alterations, as had been the case in my first childhood years.[48]

One individual who probably served as a displacement for John is Wilhelm Fleiss, who was Freud's confidant during his self-analysis and while he was writing the dream book, but with whom Freud later had a falling out. There were events from Freud's adulthood that were specific to that time of life, however, which also had their influence on his theoretical ideas. Let us now turn to examine some of these.

Adulthood

One set of events that Freud himself attributed importance to consists of his experiences with anti-Semitism. Before seeing how these experiences entered Freud's life as a young man, we should review the historical context of anti-Semitism in Austria. Freud's father, Jakob, was born in a small town in Galacia, the region where the majority of the Jewish population of Austria lived at the time. The Jews in Galacia primarily worked as traveling merchants, craftspeople, innkeepers, and farmers. Although they were on good terms with their non-Jewish neighbors, their economic activities were closely regulated and monitored by government officials. When at the age of 20 Jakob moved to Moravia to establish himself as a wool merchant, he was exposed to even greater restrictions. Jews in Moravia were not allowed to settle permanently but required a residency permit that had to be renewed every 6 months, and their residency was restricted to certain inns unless they paid a special tax to stay in private dwellings. Their relations with non-Jews in Moravia were also worse, and Jakob once told his son that as a young man he had been approached in the street by a Christian who knocked his new fur cap into the mud and shouted "Jew, get off the pavement!" Familiar with such anti-Semitic postures and gentle by temperament, the young Jakob responded by quietly going into the roadway to pick up his cap. His son Sigmund would be exposed to a different history and would display a different temperament.

By the time of Freud's birth in 1856, a period of liberalism had begun in Austria, and Jews were beginning to enjoy equal rights with Christians, a policy made official in 1867 when they were awarded full citizenship. Anti-Semitism also receded and many Jews migrated to the cities. Vienna, where the Freuds had moved in 1860, saw an increase in its Jewish population from a few hundred in the early 1800s to over 100,000 by the late 1800s. Many Jews developed reputations as lawyers, doctors, and scientists; a substantial portion of the medical faculty and students at the University of Vienna were Jews when Freud enrolled in 1873. But it was in this same year that the situation began to reverse.

On May 9, 1873, the Austrian stock market crashed; this was followed by bank failures, mass bankruptcies, and a deep economic depression. Jews were readily targeted as the scapegoat, and after a long lull, anti-Semitism burst out again. In his *Autobiographical Study* Freud writes:

> When, in 1873, I first joined the University, I experienced some appreciable disappointments. Above all, I found that I was expected to feel myself inferior and an alien because I was a Jew. I refused absolutely to do the first of these things ... I put up, without much regret, with my nonacceptance into the community ... These first impressions at the University, however, had one consequence which was afterwards to prove important; for at an early age I was made familiar with the fate of being in the Opposition and of being put under the ban of the "compact majority." [49]

Freud himself thus indicates that anti-Semitism was important in making salient to him the problems of being in the opposition and of being banned. These experiences may have found expression in his theoretical proposal that there will be conflict between an individual's impulses and social forces, because Freud as an individual had felt in conflict with the social majority, as well as in the related concept of the repression of impulses as a result of socialization pressures, because Freud himself had felt put under a ban by the social majority.

There are a variety of social factors from Freud's adult years that also may have informed his specific ideas on the basic nature of instincts. Remember that Freud was consistent in thinking that there are two general categories of instinct that are inherently in conflict with each other. Freud changed in how he characterized these two classes of instinct, however. Initially he labeled them self-preservative versus species-preservative, but later he identified them as life versus death. Because this change occurred during his adult years, between 1910 and 1920, we might infer that the reasons for the change rest in influences from those years. Further, because the concept of a death instinct was one that Freud himself regarded as highly speculative, and because it is the one concept that even his most loyal followers failed to adopt, this concept in particular may be suspected to have its origins in Freud's subjective experiences.

One source for Freud's early classification of self-preservative versus species-preservative instincts is probably Darwin's theory of evolution, which had an overwhelming impact on scientific thought in the late 1800s. In his autobiography, Freud cites Darwin's theory as the other major influence in his decision to study medicine along with Goethe's essay on Nature. But there also may have been personal reasons why the young Freud was attracted to this dichotomy between self and species. We have already seen that as a Jew Freud felt in opposition to the majority culture. Further, Freud wrote in his autobiography of his early years as he was developing his theory: "For more than ten years after my separation from Breuer I had no followers. I was completely isolated. In Vienna I was shunned; abroad no notice was taken of me."[50] In 1897, Freud was nominated for the respected title of associate professor but failed to be granted the position in that and the subsequent 4 years; in 1900 his was the only name proposed that was not ratified. What's more, despite the enormous long-term impact of *The Interpretation of Dreams*, his major treatise was initially met with barely a glance; it was 8 years before the 600 copies of its first edition were sold. Freud might well have been aware of the contrast with Darwin's comparable monument, *The Origin of Species*, whose first edition of 1,250 copies sold out by the evening of its day of release. Thus, in his early career, the image of a lone pioneer at odds with the larger society was foremost in Freud's existence, and to such a loner the dichotomy between self and species may have made great sense.

But by 1910 things had begun to change. A group of followers collected around him in Vienna, instituting weekly meetings to discuss his theories. He was invited to the United States to present his theories there, and there grew sufficient interest in his work by professionals in various countries to merit the founding of an international society. The distinction between self and species no longer found an echo in Freud's personal experience, and it made sense rather to see the two as united in a creative enterprise that would be captured in his theory of the life instincts.

Soon other events appeared to suggest an antagonistic force to this one, however. In the early 1910s conflict emerged with Jung, as well as with other disciples such as Adler and Stekel, and Freud experienced these conflicts as potential threats to the future of psychoanalysis itself. In 1914 the world around him erupted in the massive destruction that was World War I. His oldest and youngest sons saw active service, the youngest narrowly escaping death when the rest of his platoon was killed, the oldest not being heard of for months and ending up in an Italian hospital as a prisoner of war. Death itself visited the family when Freud's half-brother Emanuel died in a train accident in 1914. Also in 1914, Freud had such severe gastrointestinal problems that his physician advised a rectoscopy, after which Freud was congratulated so warmly that he concluded the physician must have suspected a malignant tumor. In 1917 Freud himself suspected he had cancer when he experienced a painful swelling in his palate. These events together gave him personal experience with destructive forces that he would give a place to in his theory of the death instinct.

Freud himself suggests that there were personal sources for the concept of a death instinct when he writes:

> It is impossible to pursue an idea of this kind except by repeatedly combining factual material with what is purely speculative and thus diverging widely from observation... Unfortunately, however, people are seldom impartial where ultimate things, the great problems of science and life, are concerned. Each of us is governed in such cases by deep-rooted internal prejudices, into whose hand our speculation unwittingly plays."[51]

At another point he even provides the motive for this particular prejudice:

> We have drawn far-reaching conclusions from the hypothesis that all living substance is bound to die from internal causes.

We made this assumption thus carelessly because it does not seem to us to *be* an assumption. We are accustomed to think that such is the fact, and we are strengthened in our thought by the writings of our poets. Perhaps we have adopted the belief because there is some comfort in it. If we are to die ourselves, and first to lose in death those who are dearest to us, it is easier to submit to a remorseless law of nature . . . than to a chance which might perhaps have been escaped.[52]

CONCLUSION

In May of 1933, the Nazi party, which had recently taken control of Germany, set to flames massive numbers of books in town and city squares. Among those books were the writings of Sigmund Freud. Five years later the Nazis took Vienna, and Freud escaped to England barely in time to die a year later, on September 23, 1939, at the age of 83. But Freud's work is far from forgotten more than 60 years later. His impact on contemporary thought is enormous, as his ideas have spread from the field of psychology to the arts and humanities and the lay culture. The compelling effect of his model rests in its full-bodied portrait of the human psyche, embracing the passions, conflicts, and irrationalities of humanity and providing a systematic and synthetic analysis of their origins and consequences. With remarkable elegance and power, this model has been applied to account for a wide range of human phenomena, from dreams and mental disorders to psychotherapy and parenting, artistic and literary creations, religion and war.

Yet criticism of the theory emerged from the outset, and has not abated with time. Among early psychoanalysts who studied with Freud, there were those such as Carl Jung and Alfred Adler who objected to Freud's overwhelming emphasis on the biologically based sexual impulse, and maintained that there are also innate impulses of a spiritual or social nature. Later theorists who also worked within the psychoanalytic context, such as Karen Horney and Harry Stack Sullivan, took issue with Freud's claim that wishes are the only psychic motivator and argued that anxiety is a more powerful impetus in psychic life. Still others, such as Erik

Erikson, Heinz Hartmann, and the Object Relations theorists, felt that too much focus is given in Freud's theory to the conflictual id impulses, to the detriment of understanding the role of the adaptive and relational capacities of the ego. A large body of work has emerged from these critiques in the form of alternative theories that broaden or shift the focus of Freud's model without rejecting its basic claims. These various psychodynamic theories share a family resemblance and cluster around some core ideas that are Freud's legacy. They all envision a mental apparatus in the human psyche with unconscious as well as conscious realms, within which unconscious dynamic forces are constantly engaged in the process of finding ways of conscious expression.

But another whole body of critiques has attacked Freud's theory from without rather than from within, and not rarely with a flavor of contempt. Among these critiques are those that take issue with Freud's model because of the methods by which it was derived. Despite his claims to the contrary, it is argued, Freud was no scientist, or at best a poor one. His observations were made on a small and nonrepresentative sample of the human population; his information was not collected in a controlled manner but rather with Freud the observer also an active participant, not only in producing his own dreams but also in affecting what his patients said to him as their therapist; his interpretations were presented as conclusions without explicating the line of reasoning by which they were derived or checking them against the independent interpretations of other analysts; patterns of findings were asserted through examples or analogies without any quantitative measures testing their significance. Even his first collaborator Josef Breuer worried over Freud's tendency toward excessive generalizations. With these many faults in his scientific method, it is argued, Freud developed a model that is purely a reflection of his own subjective prejudices rather than a reflection of objective reality. What's more, some have argued that the theory is not even capable of being scientifically tested, because its hypotheses are too vague to be empirically verified or too ambiguous to be empirically falsified.[53]

There are many ways to respond to these critiques. Some defenders have dismissed them from the outset with the claim that the traditional methods of empirical science are inappropriate for the study of the human psyche. They argue that it is only through the intimate and long-term relationship found in clinical work that the complexity of human nature is revealed. To try to isolate psychological phenomena in synthetic laboratory situations is to lose them entirely. Some argue further that it is not appropriate to appraise the truth of Freud's theory by traditional scientific standards; rather its truth should be appraised by standards used in interpretive disciplines such as history or literary criticism. Employing such criteria as "coherence," "consistency," and "configuration" to evaluate Freud's theory reveals its verity.[54]

Among those who view the scientific method as a promising means for understanding human psychology, and thus who take the critiques to heart, two primary approaches have been taken. Those who find Freud's vision of humanity a compelling one would argue that his theoretical concepts should be considered as hypotheses quite appropriate to the initial stage of the scientific enterprise. As one of the first systematic investigators of psychology working over a century ago, Freud did not employ the types of controls that are standard in psychological research today. But he did develop and modify his hypotheses out of close observation of various psychological phenomena. The validity of his ideas can now be assessed by empirical work. Although it is difficult to conceive of empirical tests for Freud's "metapsychological" propositions, such as the proposal of life and death instincts, it is possible to design tests whereby the large body of "empirical" propositions can be verified or falsified.[55] This is the approach taken in this book, and in the last chapter we will review some empirical tests of Freud's model.

A wholly different response is to say that we must reject the foundation Freud's theory offers and begin anew, using the most rigorous standards of scientific method to build a valid understanding. This is the approach taken by B. F. Skinner in his behavioral theory, which we turn to in the next chapter. In his effort to assure a purely objective approach to psychology, Skinner not only employed rigorous scientific methods but also directed those methods exclusively to observable behavior. To establish itself as an objective science, he argued, psychology must give up all unavoidably futile attempts to examine an imagined "inner psyche" and must focus squarely on behavior. But we will find that despite Skinner's resolute advocacy of objectivity, his theory, too, would be vulnerable to subjective influences.

SUGGESTED READINGS

Primary Sources

Freud, S. (1965). *The Interpretation of Dreams.* New York: Avon Books. (Original work published 1900)

Freud, S. (1965). *The Psychopathology of Everyday Life.* New York: Norton. (Original work published 1901)

Freud, S. (1966). *Introductory Lectures on Psycho-analysis.* New York: Norton. (Original work published 1917)

Freud, S. (1950). *Beyond the Pleasure Principle.* New York: Liveright. (Original work published 1920)

Freud, S. (1962). *The Ego and the Id.* New York: Norton. (Original work published 1923)

Freud, S. (1963). *An Autobiographical Study.* New York: Norton. (Original work published 1925)

Freud, S. (1965). *New Introductory Lectures on Psychoanalysis.* New York: Norton. (Original work published 1933)

Biographical Sources

Clark, R. W. (1980). *Freud: The Man and the Cause.* New York: Random House.

Gay, P. (1988). *Freud: A Life for Our Time.* New York: Norton.

Jones, E. (1953–1957). *The Life and Work of Sigmund Freud* (Vols. 1–3). New York: Basic Books.

Schur, M. (1972). *Freud: Living and Dying.* New York: International Universities Press.

Other Suggested Readings

Alexander, I. E. (1990). The Freud-Jung relationship: The other side of Oedipus and countertransference. In *Personology: Method and Content in Personality Assessment and Psychobiography.* Durham: Duke University Press.

Bettelheim, B. (1983). *Freud and Man's Soul.* New York: Knopf.

Ellenberger, H. F. (1970). *The Discovery of the Unconscious: The History and Evolution of Dynamic Psychology.* New York: Basic Books.

Elms, A. C. (1980). Freud, Irma, Martha: Sex and marriage in the "Dream of Irma's Injection." *The Psychoanalytic Review, 67,* 83–109.

Erikson, E. H. (1954). The dream specimen of psychoanalysis. *Journal of the American Psychoanalytic Association, 2,* 5–56.

Grinstein, A. (1968). *On Sigmund Freud's Dreams.* Detroit: Wayne State University Press.

Monte, C. F. (2000). *Beneath the Mask: An Introduction to Theories of Personality* (7th ed.). Hoboken, NJ: Wiley.

Sulloway, F. J. (1979). *Freud: Biologist of the Mind.* New York: Basic Books.

NOTES

1. Sigmund Freud (1955). *The Interpretation of Dreams* (p. xxxii). New York: Basic Books. (Original work published 1932)

2. Jeffrey M. Masson (Ed. & Trans.). (1985). *The Complete Letters of Sigmund Freud to Wilhelm Fliess, 1887–1904* (p. 67). Cambridge, MA: Harvard University Press.

3. Masson, ibid., 170.

4. Masson, ibid., 172.

5. Sigmund Freud (1913). *The Interpretation of Dreams* (p. viii). New York: Macmillan. (Original work published 1900)

6. Masson, op. cit., 365.

7. Masson, ibid., 417.

8. Freud (1913). *The Interpretation of Dreams* (pp. 89–90). New York: Macmillan. (Original work published 1900)

9. Freud, ibid., 100.

10. Freud, ibid., 221.

11. Sigmund Freud (1950). *Beyond the Pleasure Principle* (p. 27). New York: Liveright. (Original work published 1920)

12. Bruno Bettelheim (1983). *Freud and Man's Soul* (pp. 53, 58). New York: Knopf.

13. Freud (1955). *The Interpretation of Dreams* (p. 105). New York: Basic Books. (Original work published 1932)

14. Freud, ibid., 118.

15. Freud, ibid., 120–121.

16. Freud (1913). *The Interpretation of Dreams* (p. 98). New York: Macmillan. (Original work published 1900)

17. Alan Elms (1980). Freud, Irma, Martha: Sex and marriage in the "Dream of Irma's Injection." *The Psychoanalytic Review, 67,* 100.

18. Freud (1913). *The Interpretation of Dreams* (p. 99). New York: Macmillan. (Original work published 1900)

19. Freud (1955). *The Interpretation of Dreams* (p. 111). New York: Basic Books. (Original work published 1932)

20. Ernest Jones (1953). *The Life and Work of Sigmund Freud, Vol. 1* (pp. xii–xiii). New York: Basic Books.

21. Jones, ibid., 3.

22. Masson, op. cit., 268.

23. Masson, ibid., 268.

24. Sigmund Freud (1965). *The Psychopathology of Everyday Life* (pp. 51–52, n. 2). New York: Norton. (Original work published 1901)

25. Masson, op. cit., 272.

26. Freud (1913). *The Interpretation of Dreams* (p. 364). New York: Macmillan. (Original work published 1900)

27. Freud, ibid., 386.

28. Jones, op. cit., 138.

29. Jones, ibid., 169.

30. Jones, ibid., 132.

31. Jones, ibid., 112.

32. Jones, ibid., 114–115.

33. Jones, ibid., 117.

34. Jones, ibid., 29.

35. Freud (1913). *The Interpretation of Dreams* (p. 346). New York: Macmillan. (Original work published 1900)

36. Sigmund Freud (1914). On the history of the psycho-analytic movement. In James Strachey (Ed.). (1981). *The Standard Edition of the Complete Psychological Works of Sigmund Freud, Vol. XIV* (p. 8). London: Hogarth Press.

37. Josef Breuer & Sigmund Freud (1955). *Studies on Hysteria* (p. 21). New York: Basic Books. (Original work published 1895)

38. Freud, On the history of the psycho-analytic movement. In James Strachey (Ed.). (1981). *The Standard Edition of the Complete Psychological Works of Sigmund Freud, Vol. XIV* (p. 12). London: Hogarth Press.

39. Ernst L. Freud (Ed.). (1975). *Letters of Sigmund Freud* (p. 413). New York: Basic Books.

40. Breuer & Freud, op. cit., 244.

41. Breuer & Freud, ibid., 246–247.

42. Paul F. Cranefield (1958). Josef Breuer's evaluation of his contribution to psycho-analysis. *International Journal of Psycho-analysis, 39,* 320.

43. Masson, op cit., 175.

44. Sigmund Freud (1963). *An Autobiographical Study* (p. 99). New York: Norton. (Original work published 1925)

45. C. G. Jung (1965). *Memories, Dreams, Reflections* (p. 156). New York: Vintage.

46. Eva Brabant, Ernst Falzeder, & Patrizia Giampieri-Deutsch (Eds.). (1993). *The Correspondence of Sigmund Freud and Sandor Ferenczi, Vol. 1, 1908–1914* (p. 440). Cambridge, MA: Harvard University Press.

47. Freud, On the history of the psycho-analytic movement. In James Strachey (Ed.). (1981). *The Standard Edition of the Complete Psychological Works of Sigmund Freud, Vol. XIV* (p. 7). London: Hogarth Press.

48. Freud (1913). *The Interpretation of Dreams* (pp. 384–385). New York: Macmillan. (Original work published 1900)

49. Freud (1963). *An Autobiographical Study* (pp. 14–15). New York: Norton. (Original work published 1925)

50. Freud, ibid., 91.

51. Freud (1950). *Beyond the Pleasure Principle* (pp. 81–82). New York: Liveright. (Original work published 1920)

52. Freud, ibid., 59.

53. For example, see E. Nagel (1959). Methodological issues in psychoanalytic theory. In S. Hook (Ed.), *Psychoanalysis: Scientific Method and Philosophy* (pp. 38-56). New York: Grove Press; & K. Popper (1963). *Conjectures and Refutations.* London: Routledge & Kegan Paul.

54. For example, see J. Habermas (1971). *Knowledge and Human Interests.* Boston: Beacon Press; G. Klein (1976). *Psychoanalytic Theory.* New York: International Universities Press; P. Ricoeur (1974). *Hermeneutics and the Human Sciences.* New York: Cambridge University Press; & D. Spence (1982). *Narrative Truth and Historical Truth: Meaning and Interpretation in Psychoanalysis.* New York: Norton.

55. For example, see S. Fischer & R. Greenberg (1996). *Freud Scientifically Reappraised: Testing the Theories and Therapy.* New York: Wiley; P. Kline (1981). *Fact and Fantasy in Freudian Theory.* London: Methuen; J. Masling & M. Schwartz (1979). A critique of research in psychoanalytic theory. *Genetic Psychology Monographs, 100,* 257–307; D. Rapaport & M. Gill (1959). The points of view and assumptions of metapsychology. *International Journal of Psychoanalysis, 40,* 153–162; L. Silverman (1976). Psychoanalytic theory: "The reports of my death are greatly exaggerated." *American Psychologist, 31,* 621–637; & R. Wallerstein (1986). Psychoanalysis as a science: A response to new challenges. *Psychoanalytic Quarterly, 55,* 414–451.

3

THE BEHAVIORAL APPROACH: B. F. SKINNER

When Burrhus Frederic Skinner entered graduate school in psychology at Harvard University in 1928, he had never taken a psychology course before. He had backed into the field of psychology as a way to back out of his previously chosen pursuit of literature. Indeed, the future behavioral psychologist, whose theory would de-emphasize the inner world of thoughts and feelings and wishes, is hardly recognizable when as a young man he is deeply involved in being a writer. But in his sudden shift from literature to psychology a great deal is foreshadowed about the kind of psychologist Skinner would become. Let us look briefly at how this shift came about before turning to Skinner's early work as a psychologist and the theory that emerged from it.

Skinner entered Hamilton College in Clinton, New York, at the age of 18 and immediately gave himself over to literature as if having found the love of his life. Although he had written little before college, in his freshman year at Hamilton he began producing volumes of poetry. He reproduced a number of examples

in the autobiography he wrote more than 50 years later.* Here are
two:

> The wind is sad —
> Mournful is the wind.
> In the silver night
> Swift, winding veils of streaming snow
> Enshroud the trees.
> Caught in the agonies of death,
> They stretch
> Their arms to heaven,
> And are wrapped
> In sifting shrouds.[1]

> If I could understand
> The molten blood
> That drips from the ladle of the moon,
> Or the voiceless mists that rise
> From a frozen sea;
> Then, Helen,
> Might I understand thee, too.[2]

By his junior year, Skinner's poems and short stories were appearing regularly in the *Hamilton Literary Magazine* and the *Royal Ga-
boon* and he had earned a reputation on campus as a "writer." An
alumnus told him about the Bread Loaf Summer School of English where he applied and was accepted to study the following
summer. At Bread Loaf he met such literary giants as Carl Sandburg and Robert Frost, and Frost invited Skinner to send him some
of his writing. Skinner sent Frost three of his short stories upon
returning to Hamilton his senior year. In the spring semester a
supportive letter from Frost decided him on a literary career.

Armed with Frost's support, Skinner convinced his dubious parents to put him up at home for a year after college during which he
would try to write a novel. But the year proved to be a turning point.
Suddenly the fount from which his college writing had drawn was

---

*From *Particulars of My Life* by B. F. Skinner, copyright ©1976 by B. F. Skinner.
Used by permission of Alfred A. Knopf, a division of Random House, Inc; extract
from *Particulars of My Life* by B. F. Skinner published by Jonathan Cape. Used by
permission of the Random House Group Limited.

dried up, and he found that he had nothing to say. After building himself a study in the attic of his parents' house, he sat at his desk with an empty filing cabinet beside it in which to put his new manuscripts, but, as he put it, "nothing happened." During the long days he would occupy himself by reading in his study or playing music on the family piano or building a model ship on the workbench in the garage. In the painfully long evenings sitting in the library with his parents he found himself displaying a curious "symptom," sitting completely motionless in a dull stupor for long periods of time. When his father called attention to this behavior one evening Skinner said that he thought he should see a psychiatrist. His father dismissed the idea, saying that an old friend of his had once spent a lot of money on a psychiatrist and gotten nothing out of it. Skinner was forced to endure without help what he later came to call "The Dark Year."

At the end of the disastrous year he was faced with a poignant problem. He had agreed with his parents in arranging the year at home that if by the end of it he had nothing to show, he would admit failure and give up on writing. But failure was hard to admit, and he needed a way to justify himself. Skinner found a solution in blaming literature itself. Recounting this period years later in an autobiographical chapter, he wrote: "I had failed as a writer because I had nothing important to say, but I could not accept that explanation. It was literature which must be at fault."[3] A friend had said to him that science was the art of the 20th century, and Skinner modified this to claim: "Literature as an art form was dead; I would turn to science."[4] The science he turned to was psychology, but it was a very different form of psychology than we have seen in the work of Sigmund Freud. It was a psychology that bypassed the inner world of thoughts and feelings and desires and saw human behavior as being controlled entirely by environmental forces. It was a psychology that would allow Skinner to blame his failure as a writer externally on literature itself rather than on any deficiency in his own inner qualities, and he embraced it like a drowning man grasping a life jacket. This was the psychology of behaviorism.

Toward the end of the Dark Year, Skinner was, as he wrote in his autobiography, "floundering in a stormy sea and perilously close to drowning, but help was on the way."[5] This help came in his discovery of the work of John B. Watson. Watson was an American psychologist who was a flagrant maverick in his personal life as well as in his professional theories. In his young adulthood he had secretly married one of his students over the objections of her brother, who knew of Watson's reputation as a womanizer. Less than 2 decades later he was involved in a nasty divorce trial that included such highlights as the publication in the newspaper of one of his love letters to a current student, which had been stolen by his wife from the student's home. He was subsequently expelled from his university position and found no other academic institution willing to take him on. It was shortly after this expulsion, however, in 1924, that Watson published his book *Behaviorism*, which made him the most influential psychologist in America. In the book Watson disparaged psychology's previous focus on mental states and argued that the true object of study for psychology must be that which can be observed: behavior. He showed particular scorn for Freud's thesis that unconscious sexual impulses are the basis for conscious anxiety and pathological behavior. In fact, he had conducted a study that he believed demonstrated conclusively that fearful feelings and phobic behavior result not from unconscious desires but rather from environmental *conditioning*. It was a study that would never pass ethics approval these days.

The study was conducted on an infant boy to whom Watson gave the pseudonym of "Albert." Albert was a healthy child who had been raised in a children's hospital where his mother worked as a nurse, which is what allowed Watson access to him. When Albert was 9 months old, Watson tested the boy's reactions to a range of stimuli: a ball of white cotton wool, a fur coat, a rabbit, a white rat. Albert's general reaction to the stimuli was one of curiosity; he showed no fear and never cried. Two months later, when Albert was 11 months old, Watson began his conditioning experiment. He knew that infants are innately disposed to respond to a sudden loud sound with a fear reaction of crying and avoidance. In the language of behaviorism, a sudden loud sound is an *unconditioned stimulus* (that is, it is innate or unlearned) that reliably elicits crying and avoidance as unconditioned responses. Watson decided to pair the loud sound, a stimulus that innately elicits fear, and another stimulus that is not innately frightening to infants. In this case he chose the white rat that Albert had previously responded to with curiosity rather than with fear.

The rat was put before Albert, and just as the boy reached forward to touch the animal Watson loudly struck a metal bar with a hammer right behind Albert's head. Albert responded by jumping violently and burying his face. Over a series of similar pairings of the rat and loud noise, Albert showed a consistent fear reaction, whimpering and withdrawing his body. Then Watson presented the rat alone without any loud sound. He discovered that Albert now responded with the same kind of fear reaction that he had originally shown to the sound, even though the sound was no longer present. Whereas the rat had innately been a neutral stimulus to which Albert had responded with curiosity, after being paired with the loud sound it now was a *conditioned stimulus* (that is, it was learned), to be responded to with a conditioned response of fear. What's more, Watson found that when he presented other stimuli that were in ways similar to the rat but that had never themselves been paired with the loud sound, such as a fur coat or a ball of wool, Albert now responded with fear to these as well by virtue of *stimulus generalization*. Because the fur coat and ball of wool were stimuli that shared similar qualities with the white rat, they too had acquired a fear response. From this research Watson would argue that basic emotional reactions such as fear are acquired from exposure to environmental contingencies. And to explain pathological behaviors such as phobias that appear irrational, we do not need to engage in Freud's mental gymnastics and infer an unconscious conflict between sexual impulses and censoring forces. Rather, we can explain them by an unfortunate conditioning history with stimulus generalization.

In Watson's book, *Behaviorism* (1924) that Skinner read at the end of the Dark Year, Watson made this bold claim: "Give me a dozen healthy infants, well-formed, and my own specified world to bring them up in and I'll guarantee to take any one at random and train him to become any type of specialist I might select—doctor, lawyer, artist, merchant-chief and, yes, even beggar-man and thief, regardless of his talents, penchants, tendencies, abilities, vocations, and race of his ancestors."[6] It was a promise that held great appeal for the young Skinner. Not only did it provide a justification for blaming his failure as a writer on literature rather than on himself, but also it gave the hope of full control of behavior in the future. Even before he had taken a single course in psychology, Skinner had become a self-proclaimed champion of the behaviorist system.

WORK

When Skinner entered graduate school in 1928, he brought with him certain starting assumptions. He believed first that psychology is a science. The value of science, he argued, as distinct from other enterprises such as poetry or art, is in its cumulative progress over time. Our contemporary artists are not more effective than Michelangelo, yet our contemporary scientists are certainly more effective than those of Michelangelo's day; our high school students know more about the natural world than did the greatest scientists of Michelangelo's time. Skinner claimed that this progress was a result of the scientist's search for order and lawful relations among events. But according to Skinner, the discovery of order is not the end of science but only the means to the final goal of control.* "What we call the scientific conception of a thing is not passive knowledge . . . When we have discovered the laws which govern a part of the world about us, and when we have organized these laws into a system, we are then ready to deal effectively with that part of the world. . . . We not only predict, we control."[7]

It is worth pausing at this point to examine the themes that underlie Skinner's assumptions about science. Because he brought these assumptions with him before undertaking any formal study of psychology, we can expect to find later that these themes have a source in his personal life experiences. Many probably find an echo in the experience that brought him to psychology, his failure as a writer. In distinguishing science from poetry and art, Skinner focuses on the theme of progress; indeed his own efforts in literature during the Dark Year had led him nowhere. He then attributes progress to the ability to achieve order and to control. We might expect that these themes will also be found to be important in Skinner's personal life, although their role in the Dark Year is not yet fully apparent. A final pair of themes that occurs in Skinner's description of science is a distinction between passivity and activity. Skinner writes that science does not consist of "passive knowledge" but rather of the ability to "deal effectively" with the

---

*From B. F. Skinner (1983), *Science and Human Behavior*. Used by permission of the B. F. Skinner Foundation, Cambridge, Massachusetts.

world. These themes too should play a role in his life, and hints of their significance during the Dark Year are found in his experience that "nothing happened" in the days when he tried to write, as if he was waiting passively for something, and in his motionless stupor in the evenings.

The second set of assumptions Skinner brought with him to graduate school had to do with the science of psychology in particular. To be a science, he argued, psychology must give up its past efforts to study the human mind and focus squarely on behavior. He contrasted the study of the mind as a "passive" kind of knowing, focusing on thoughts, needs, or emotions that occur to people, with the study of behavior as the study of what people actively do. Furthermore, he argued, our inclination to attribute active causal status to thoughts, needs, or emotions is totally misguided. He wrote:

> Every science has at some time or other looked for causes of action inside things it has studied. ... The motion of a rolling stone was once attributed to its *vis viva*. The chemical properties of bodies were thought to be derived from the *principles* or *essences* of which they were composed. Combustion was explained by the *phlogiston* inside the combustible object. Wounds healed and bodies grew well because of a *vis medicatrix*. It has been especially tempting to attribute the behavior of a living organism to the behavior of an inner agent... [A] common practice is to explain behavior in terms of an inner agent which lacks physical dimensions and is called "mental" or "psychic." The purest form of the psychic explanation is seen in the animism of primitive peoples. From the immobility of the body after death it is inferred that a spirit responsible for movement has departed. The *enthusiastic* person is, as the etymology of the word implies, energized by a "god within." It is only a modest refinement to attribute every feature of the behavior of the physical organism to a corresponding feature of the "mind" or of some inner "personality". ... In all this it is obvious that the mind and the ideas, together with their special characteristics, are being invented on the spot to provide spurious explanations. A science of behavior can hope to gain very little from so cavalier a practice.[8]

In this passage, Skinner first draws an explicit parallel between psychology's study of human behavior and physics' study of a rolling stone, and he ends by making the astonishing claim that attention to internal states is no more relevant to the former than it is to the latter. The study of humans can proceed along the same lines as that of physical objects. With this claim he is making two assumptions for which we should seek a personal source. First, he assumes that what we want to understand about people is their "action" or "behavior," whether it is lacking after death or it is energized in enthusiasm. Second, he assumes that human behavior, like the behavior of a rolling stone, is caused by external forces and that inner causes are a fiction.

Skinner stopped short of Watson's extreme claim that environmental factors are the sole forces over behavior to the exclusion even of genetic endowment. Watson might have had an easier time raising someone to be a thief who was endowed with a body that was small and agile rather than large and clumsy. But Skinner argued that an analysis of genetic factors is of no use to the study of behavior because, in a return of a theme we saw earlier, such factors cannot be controlled after the individual has been born. Thus, in his effort to develop a science of psychology, Skinner sought to identify the laws by which the environment influences human behavior.

Early Case Study

Although he entered graduate school with these basic assumptions, Skinner's lack of formal background in the field meant that he could build his research program from scratch and explore freely. Many years later, for his Presidential Address to the Eastern Psychological Association, he wrote up the series of studies he undertook at Harvard. The major point of this paper was that he had never behaved as "Man Thinking." He did not begin with a hypothesis that he conceptualized how to test. He simply operated on the materials available in his environment and pursued those things that yielded an effect. For his subjects he chose rats because they were cheap to buy and keep, they occupied little space, and they could be submitted to experimental control of their routine of living. For his experimental apparatus he manipulated various materials available to him in the department's machine shop, and for his experimental design he followed what struck him.*

> My first gadget was a silent release box, operated by compressed air and designed to eliminate disturbances when introducing a rat into an apparatus. I used this first in studying the way a rat adapted to a novel stimulus. I built a soundproofed box containing a specially structured space. A rat was released, pneumatically, at the far end of a darkened tunnel from which it emerged in exploratory fashion into a well-lighted area. To accentuate its progress and to facilitate recording, the tunnel was placed at the top of a flight of steps, something like a functional Parthenon. The rat would peek out from the tunnel, perhaps glancing suspiciously at the one-way window through which I was watching it, then stretch itself cautiously down the steps. A soft click (carefully calibrated, of course) would cause it to pull back into the tunnel and remain there for some time. But repeated clicks had less and less of an effect. I recorded the rat's advances and retreats by moving a pen back and forth across a moving paper tape.
>
> The major result of this experiment was that some of my rats had babies.[9]

After watching with curiosity the behavior of the baby rats, Skinner designed a second experiment:

> If you hold a young rat on one hand and pull it gently by the tail, it will resist you by pulling forward and then, with a sudden sharp spring which usually disengages its tail, it will leap out into space. I decided to study this behavior quantitatively. I built a light platform covered with cloth and mounted it on tightly stretched piano wires ... When the tail of a young rat was gently pulled, the rat clung to the cloth floor and tugged forward. By amplifying the fine movements of the platform, it was possible to get a good kymograph record of the tremor in this motion and then, as the pull against the tail was increased, of the desperate spring into the air.[10]

---

*From "A case history in scientific method" by B. F. Skinner, 1956, *American Psychologist, 11*, p. 221–233. Copyright 1956 by American Psychological Association. Reprinted with permission.

A third design brought back elements of the first (e.g., the click) as well as adding new ones (e.g., food):

> But if this technique would work with a baby, why not try it on a mature rat? To avoid attaching anything to the rat, it should be possible to record, not a pull against the substrate, but the ballistic thrust exerted as the rat runs forward or suddenly stops in response to my calibrated click . . . I threw away the piano-wire platform, and built a runway, eight feet long . . . The runway became the floor of a long tunnel, at one end of which I placed my soundless release box and at the other end myself, prepared to reinforce the rat for coming down the runway by giving it a bit of wet mash, to sound a click from time to time when it had reached the middle of the runway, and to harvest kymograph records of the vibrations of the substrate . . . In this way a great many records were made of the forces exerted against the substratum as rats ran down the alley and occasionally stopped dead in their tracks as a click sounded.[11]

In reporting this series of studies Skinner sought to demonstrate that his method of exploration was entirely a function of environmental factors: He manipulated materials available to him and pursued whatever had an effect. But was this manipulation and pursuit as free of internal direction as it first appears? There are many things that one could study about a rat, but Skinner had focused on some things in particular. In his first design, he released a rat into a tunnel and watched it advance out of the tunnel in the context of clicking noises. In the second design, he pulled a rat by the tail and recorded its tug forward until it sprung into the air. In the third design, he set up a runway for a rat to run toward food in the context of periodic clicks. Across these three designs there are recurrent elements that reflect those things for which Skinner himself showed concern.

One element represents a theme we have noticed before: progress. In the first design Skinner's focus is on the rat's "advances," and he constructs a flight of steps explicitly "to accentuate its progress." The second design is also concerned with how the rat "tugged forward," and the third design provides a runway in which the rat "runs forward." There is a second element common to all three designs that appears to be a new theme: The progress emerges out of a context of restraint. In the first design this appears in the form of a "release box, operated by compressed air," which is at "the far end of a darkened tunnel" out of which the rat emerges. Restraint appears in the second design in the "pull against the tail" that the rat tries to "disengage." In the third design, we find Skinner concerned to "avoid attaching anything to the rat," but the release box returns. A third element worthy of note is the animal's experience of a potential threat. This is especially surprising because Skinner appears to attribute fearful emotions to his rats despite his discounting of human emotions. Skinner introduces a threatening click in the first design and he describes the rat as advancing "suspiciously" and "cautiously." In the second design, the pull against the tail seems to be a threat because Skinner characterizes the rat's spring into the air as "desperate." When in the third design the click returns, it leads the rat to stop "dead" in its tracks.

Thus, although a host of experimental designs might be imagined, Skinner's all involve the behavior of progress in the context of a restraining and threatening environment; indeed in this context the behavior takes on a dimension not only of progress but also of escape. That Skinner had chosen to focus on these elements in particular may be a result of personal concerns that he brought with him to graduate school. And now we might begin to wonder if his design of a rat emerging from a "darkened tunnel" is more than coincidentally reminiscent of the "Dark Year" out of which he had just emerged.

It was at the point of his third research design, however, that the force of environmental effects began to play a more decisive role. Skinner got tired of having to carry the rat back to the beginning of the runway after each run. He therefore modified the design from a one-way tunnel to a quadrangular tunnel with four legs, so that after eating the food at the end of the first leg the rat could run around three other legs to bring itself again to the beginning of the first runway. In this way the rat could run itself. But now came an unexpected event that was the key to Skinner's future research program. After eating the food, the rat would sometimes wait a long time before continuing around the tunnel for another run. At first Skinner was annoyed at this. But when he timed the delays with a stopwatch and plotted them, he found them to show orderly changes. His analysis revealed that the rat's rate of running around the runway was a square function of the time elapsed since it last got food. Here was the order that he had been looking for: It was in the effect of the presentation of food on the animal's rate of behavior. Skinner had discovered a mathematical law to account for a pattern of animal behavior as reliably as the law of gravity can account for the movement of physical objects. What we might intuitively believe to be "voluntary" behavior was found to be determined by lawful effects of environmental conditions.

Focusing now on the rate of behavior yielding food, Skinner realized that he needed neither the runway nor the clicking noise that his personal predilections had first led him to. He built a new apparatus in which the rat was required to press a lever to initiate the mechanical discharge of a food pellet and he began to record lever-pressing behavior. This lever-pressing behavior had the advantage of not being in the innate repertoire of a rat, as opposed to the running behavior of his previous design. The mechanical discharge of the food had the advantage of saving Skinner the work of distributing the food himself, and this proved to be the source of his second discovery. The mechanical discharge of food was conducted by a food magazine that he had fashioned from a disk of wood he had found discarded in the department's store room. One day the food magazine jammed and stopped distributing food. Rather than immediately fixing it, Skinner decided to record the rat's lever-pressing behavior after food was no longer presented, and he discovered an orderly process of extinction of the behavior. For a short time the rat pressed the lever at a high rate, but then its behavior began to fall off, and when Skinner plotted the decline of the behavior he found that it showed a logarithmic course. Here was a second mathematical law of animal behavior.

A final group of findings emerged again as a result of environmental events rather than from his premeditated pursuit of a hypothesis. Skinner himself had made not only the mechanical apparatus for this research but also the food pellets that were delivered by it. Making the pellets was a time-consuming process, requiring him to mix a formula of wheat, corn, flax seed, bone meal, and salt and to cook it in a double boiler; the mixture was then put in a grease gun to deliver it in a long thin rope of paste, which was scored lightly by razor blades and, once dried, broken up into cylindrical pellets. One pleasant Saturday afternoon Skinner found that he was low in his supply of pellets and would have to spend the rest of the afternoon and evening making them to keep up his experiments into Monday. Not wanting to give up the beautiful day to that activity, he wondered why a food pellet had to be delivered with every press of the lever by the rat. Instead he tried reinforcing lever-pressing only once every minute. When he compared the rat's rate of responding under this condition of periodic food with that under the condition of continuous food, he found systematic differences. Under continuous reinforcement the rat's rate of behavior was high and constant; when food was given once a minute the rat's behavior slowed down after reinforcement, but then quickened as the end of the minute interval approached. However, the rat's behavior under periodic reinforcement was remarkably stable and more resistant to extinction than that built by continuous reinforcement. Skinner had now discovered that different schedules of reinforcement would yield different rates of behavior, and the basic principles of his life's work had been established.

The Theory

Skinner published the series of studies he had conducted at Harvard, first as a graduate student and later as a Junior Fellow, in his 1938 book *The Behavior of Organisms*. In over 400 pages the book reports his research in laborious detail with such heavy-going sentences as: "The completed chain may be written: sSD: visual lever. R: lifting → sSD: tactual lever. R: pressing → sSD: tray SD: sound of magazine. R: approach to tray → S: food. R: seizing, where the second arrow is understood to connect the response with SD: sound only."[12] It is not the kind of narrative to titillate the heart or mind, and it is not surprising that the book left most readers cold. But a foreshadowing of Skinner's later ability to affect his readers is found in his boldly choosing a broad title for the book, for the only "organism" Skinner had studied was the white rat. Skinner firmly believed that the principles of animal behavior he had discovered in his work with rats could be effectively applied to understand all organisms, including people.

In 1953 when Skinner explicitly extrapolated his findings to a systematic treatment of human behavior in *Science and Human Behavior*, he had found a way to stir the pulse of psychologists, although as often in an expression of alarm and ire as of excitement. When he wrote a similar analysis for the lay reader in his 1971 book *Beyond Freedom and Dignity*, he had succeeded in arousing the general public. His picture appeared on the cover of *Time* magazine under the heading "B. F. Skinner Says: We Can't Afford Freedom," and the article inside introduced him as "the most controversial contemporary figure in the science of human behavior, adored as a messiah and abhorred as a menace."[13] We will have to wade through the thick waters of his basic conditioning principles to come to understand his provocative application of these principles to the study of people, but the effort will be well worth it.

What, then, are the basic principles of Skinner's model? Skinner first proposes a distinction between two kinds of behavior, *respondents* and *operants*. Respondents are behaviors that are elicited in response to an environmental stimulus. For example, an eyeblink is a respondent elicited by a burst of air in the eye. But according to Skinner the majority of behavior by any adult organism, and the most complex and important type, is in the form of operants. Operants are not elicited by an environmental stimulus, but rather are enacted by the organism to operate on the environment. Once enacted, however, their environmental consequence will determine the probability that they will recur in future. For example, a wink is an operant that, once enacted, will be more likely to recur in future if it results in a smile from the other being winked at, and less likely to recur if its consequence is a scowl from the other. According to Skinner, complex patterns of human behavior, such as the constellations of behavior that make up a romantic involvement or professional pursuit, are also operants whose maintenance is a function of their consequences, such as affection from the partner or praise from the boss.

Intuitively, we distinguish between a respondent such as an eyeblink and an operant such as a wink by calling the former "involuntary" and the latter "voluntary." But Skinner would assert that we are entirely wrong if we mean to imply by this that whereas respondents are not under the organism's control, operants are. Both operants and respondents are fully under the control of the environment, not of the organism. It is simply that the nature of that control differs, making it less apparent in the case of operants. In the case of respondents, the environmental stimulus occurs before the behavior, and it reliably elicits that behavior for all organisms in all situations because this has proven to be adaptive for survival. A burst of air in the eye reliably elicits blinking because that blinking protects the eye from foreign matter that could interfere with vision. In the case of operants, on the other hand, the environmental stimulus occurs after the organism's behavior, and the relationship between behavior and environmental consequence is not constant across organisms or situations. A wink has consequence for people but not for rats; a person may draw a smile when he winks at his spouse and a scowl when he winks at his boss. Because of this variability, the environmental control of operants is less apparent than that of respondents. But it is no less a fact: Operant behaviors are fully controlled by their environmental consequences, not by the organism. Skinner asserted that the idea of "self-determination" or "free will" is a fiction that has no place in the science of psychology. It was one of the claims that engendered alarm in many of his readers.

According to Skinner there are three major processes by which operants are controlled by their environmental consequences: *reinforcement, extinction,* and *punishment.* Reinforcement is the process by which a behavior increases in frequency or is more likely to occur. An operant behavior will increase in frequency if it is followed by the presentation of something favorable or by the removal of something unfavorable. Thus, Skinner's rat increased lever-pressing when that behavior was followed by a food pellet. Likewise a spouse will be more likely to be an attentive listener when that behavior is followed by affection from their partner, and a worker will be more likely to persist at a task when that behavior is followed by praise from their boss. A behavior will decrease in frequency as a function of extinction or punishment. In extinction, a reinforcing consequence no longer follows from the behavior and so the behavior drops off. Skinner's rat showed a decline in lever-pressing when the food magazine jammed and stopped delivering food for it. In punishment, a behavior decreases in frequency because it is followed by the presentation of something unfavorable or by the removal of something favorable. A child will be less likely to say a dirty word if the consequence of that behavior is to get a spank or to lose television privileges.

Skinner felt that punishment is the more commonly employed method of human control, but he persistently argued against its use. He had two primary complaints against punishment as a technique. For one, according to Skinner, punishment does not really work. The immediate effect of punishment is that the unwanted behavior is reduced, but the behavior will simply reappear when the punishing consequences are removed. For another, punishment has unfortunate by-products in the form of negative emotions, such as fear and rage.

But now we might be surprised to find Skinner using such language as "fear" and "rage." We have understood him to focus exclusively on observable behavior and the environmental stimuli that control it. Does he not entirely deny the existence of inner states such as emotions, needs, and thoughts? Actually it is not so much that Skinner denies the existence of such states; rather he denies that they have any causal status in motivating human behavior. They are neither necessary nor useful as scientific explanations. As to whether they exist at all, Skinner does address such phenomena as emotions, needs, and thoughts, and indeed even takes on such Freudian concepts as the superego and repression. Using his model he re-defines these phenomena in behavioral terms.

Let us look at his analysis of emotions, for example. Although our intuitive understanding of emotions may be based primarily on our subjective experience of them, Skinner claims that emotions can be usefully defined solely from the perspective of an objective observer. An emotion can be understood not as an inner state but instead as a predisposition to act in certain ways.

> The "angry" man shows an increased probability of striking, insulting, or otherwise inflicting injury and a lowered probability of aiding, favoring, comforting, or making love. The man "in love" shows an increased tendency to aid, favor, be with, and caress and a lowered tendency to injure in any way. "In fear" a man tends to reduce or avoid contact with specific stimuli—as by running away, hiding, or covering his eyes and ears; at the same time he is less likely to advance toward such stimuli.[14]

The behaviors that co-vary in an emotion do so because they result in common environmental consequences. For example, behaviors that are stronger or more frequent in anger, such as striking or insulting, have the common consequence of damaging a person or object. The evolutionary basis for this is that it is biologically useful to inflict this damage when the individual is in competition with another for resources or when struggling with the inanimate world. A number of behaviors that are probable in anger are innately determined; others, however, are learned or conditioned.

> For example, if an angry child attacks, bites, or strikes another child—all without prior conditioning—and if the other child cries or runs away, then these same consequences may reinforce other behavior of the angry child which can scarcely be innate— for example, teasing the other child, taking toys away from him, destroying his work, or calling him names.[15]

Emotions thus consist of a class of behaviors that are associated because they result in similar environmental consequences. If an individual finds another person cutting in line in front of him, that individual may strike the other, yell at the other, or insult the other, all with the consequence of removing the other and regaining his place in line.

It is common for people to infer an internal link between the preceding event and the operant behavior of an emotion, and to give that internal link a causal status. We say that being cut in front of made a man feel angry, and that the angry feeling then made the man yell. But according to Skinner the inferred feeling state is a useless fiction. How do we know that the man felt angry? If we judge this from the fact that he yelled, then we cannot use the angry feeling as an explanation for the yelling, for that would be circular. If we judge that the man felt angry from the fact that he was cut in front of, then the feeling state is of no use in the explanation of the behavior, for it is the external event that has provided the explanation.

> As long as we conceive of the problem of emotion as one of inner states, we are not likely to advance a practical technology. It does not help in the solution of a practical problem to be told that some feature of a man's behavior is due to frustration or anxiety; we also need to be told how the frustration or anxiety

has been induced and how it may be altered. In the end, we find ourselves dealing with two events—the emotional behavior and the manipulable conditions of which that behavior is a function—which comprise the proper subject matter of the study of emotion.[16]

At this point we might be inclined to protest Skinner's analysis of emotions. "I myself experience emotions such as anger and love and fear," we might say, "as well as other internal states such as needs and thoughts. I know they exist as inner states because of my experience of them, and an understanding of these experiences is essential to an understanding of what it is to be human." In fact, Skinner does acknowledge that there is a part of our world that is private in the sense of being accessible only to us. For example, we may be in a privileged position to report the "thought": "I'm thinking of going home" This is because we have access to information unavailable to others: to covert movements on our part that anticipate this behavior perhaps, or to our past history of heading home when it starts to get dark out. But, Skinner argues, in identifying this thought we are only making a judgment of the probability of a behavior using the same criteria an observer would use when judging probability from publicly observable events. What's more, we would never have come to recognize such a private experience in the first place if our environment had not taught us to do so. Our parents taught us to recognize thoughts and needs and emotions by attending to our behavior and the events that control it. For example, when they saw us crying they said "Are you feeling sad because your best friend just moved away?" Without this training from the external environment, Skinner argues, we would never come to "experience" sadness in the first place. "Strangely enough," he writes, "it is the community which teaches the individual to 'know himself.' "[17] Strange indeed. Skinner's model takes familiar ideas and turns them inside-out.

Let us turn now to Skinner's analysis of Freudian concepts. Freud posited three distinct personality structures: the id, which consists of innate, socially unacceptable impulses; the superego, which consists of moral imperatives learned via socialization; and the ego, that part of the psyche that must realistically balance the opposing demands of id and superego as well as of the external world. Skinner believes that Freud has invented different inner structures to account for certain patterns of behavior that are a function of different conditioning histories. He writes:

> Freud conceived of the ego, superego, and id as distinguishable agents within the organism. The id was responsible for behavior which was ultimately reinforced with food, water, sexual contact, and other primary biological reinforcers ... On the other hand, the controlling behavior engendered by the community consists of a selected group of practices evolved in the history of a particular culture because of their effect upon anti-social behavior. To the extent that this behavior works to the advantage of the community—and again to this extent only—we may speak of a unitary conscience, social conscience, or superego.[18]

Skinner accepts the observation that people commonly display the distinct patterns of behavior that Freud identified, but he does not accept Freud's explanation of these patterns as being caused by distinct psychic structures. Rather, the behavior patterns are a result of distinct contingencies of reinforcement and punishment in the environment. The id represents those behaviors controlled by biological reinforcers, the superego represents those behaviors controlled by social punishment, and the ego represents those behaviors controlled by practical contingencies.

Freud's model further proposes a dynamic process whereby wishes in the id seek expression but are censored because of their unacceptability to the superego. Skinner's alternative account runs as follows:

> Let us consider the apparent result of the struggle of a wish to express itself. An example which permits us to observe the principal Freudian dynamisms is sibling rivalry. Let us say that two brothers compete for the affection of their parents and for other reinforcers which must be divided between them. As a result, one brother behaves aggressively toward the other and is punished, by his brother or by his parents. Let us suppose that this happens repeatedly. Eventually any situation in which aggressive action toward the brother is likely to take place or any early stage of such action will generate the conditioned aversive stimulation associated with anxiety or guilt. This is effective from the point of view of the other brother or the punishing parent because

it leads to the self-control of aggressive behavior; the punished brother is now more likely to engage in activities which compete with and displace his aggression. In this sense he "represses" his aggression . . . The same punishment may lead the individual to *repress* any knowledge of his aggressive tendencies. Not only does he not act aggressively toward his brother, he does not even "know" that he has tendencies to do so.[19]

Thus repression can be understood as a decrease in aggressive behavior as a consequence of the punishment that followed such behaving. It can also involve a decrease in activities associated with the aggressive behavior and therefore with the punishment, such as the earliest preparatory stages of this behavior that the individual recognizes in the activity of thinking. What Freud conceived of as a dynamic intrapsychic conflict is, for Skinner, a behavior pattern that results from conflicting contingencies of biological reinforcement and social punishment.

To summarize then, Skinner's model claims that psychology can provide a useful understanding of people if it will give up the study of inner states and focus exclusively on observables: human behavior and the environmental events of which it is a function. Behavior is not under the control of the person or his or her "psyche," it is under the control of the environment. We can talk about wishes or emotions, and also about the superego or repression, but only if we understand that these terms refer to patterns of behavior that occur as a function of contingencies of reinforcement and punishment. By studying such contingencies we can reliably predict and control behavior, as behavior is increased through reinforcement and decreased through punishment or extinction.

This is an image of people in action like rolling stones, pushed and pulled to behave as they do by lawful external forces. Skinner's model is as daring as Freud's surely, but where Freud's model gains its power from a rich complexity, Skinner's gains its power from an elegant simplicity. It is by his confident assertion that the inner world can be comfortably ignored that Skinner was able to lay bare the mathematical lawfulness of relationships between human behavior and the environment. Even those who are disturbed rather than comforted by ignoring the inner world may view with some measure of admiration the airtight account that Skinner's model is able to achieve.

Because of its resolute stand of objectivity, observing the human being from the outside and denying subjective motivations, Skinner's model offers a special test of the proposal that a psychological theory is influenced by the subjective experiences of its theorist. Freud explicitly used self-observation to form his theory when he systematically analyzed his own dreams. But Skinner did no such thing, and the research he did conduct was not even undertaken on humans but rather on rats and pigeons. Does this mean that his behavioral theory is distinctly free of subjective influences? Not at all. We have noted that Skinner began with certain assumptions even before he undertook his first study, and that these assumptions are likely to reflect themes derived from personal experiences. In his characterization of science in general he showed a concern with progress, with order and control, and with activity versus passivity. In his characterization of psychology in particular he demonstrated a focus on action or behavior, an assertion of the importance of the external environment, and a call to avoid the inner world. Furthermore, although Skinner claimed that his first studies were determined solely by environmental effects, we found that they too showed patterns that suggested personal predilections. His first three designs all showed a concern with the issues of progress and escape in the context of restraint and threat.

We might also find further clues to subjective sources of Skinner's work in places we have not yet looked. It should be worthwhile to pay attention to points in Skinner's work where his claims are inconsistent: with what he has said elsewhere, with what other behavioral analysts have said, or with what empirical research has demonstrated. Such an inconsistency may signal that his claim results from a personal concern on his part rather than from "objective evidence." Let us examine one example of each kind of inconsistency.

When Skinner first addresses the issue of inner states in his book *Science and Human Behavior* (1953), he shows inconsistency within himself as to whether such states exist. He first writes that in focusing on inner states psychologists "continue to look for something which may not exist."[20] Only four pages later he writes that "the objection to inner states is not that they do not exist, but that they are not relevant."[21] We will want to look for personal sources of this ambivalence over the existence of inner states. Skinner makes a claim inconsistent with many other behavioral analysts when he asserts that respondent and operant conditioning are distinct types. Watson had seen them as the same, and even many contemporary scholars fail to make a distinction. That Skinner found it important to discriminate between the two may signal a personal concern underlying the distinction between respondents and operants. Finally, Skinner's objection to punishment in particular is inconsistent with empirical evidence. Recall that Skinner complains that punishment does not really work: It is effective in reducing behavior only so long as the punishing contingencies are applied, with the behavior increasing again once these contingencies are removed. But reinforcement has been shown to have the same limitation on effectiveness: It is effective in increasing behavior as long as the reinforcing contingencies are applied, but the behavior decreases again once these contingencies are removed. Skinner's objection to punishment in particular may rest on personal sources. Let us turn now to Skinner's life history to examine its influence on his theoretical ideas.

LIFE

Our exploration of Skinner's life is greatly facilitated by the fact that he made many notes over his lifetime and drew on them to write an autobiographical chapter in his sixth decade and an autobiography of three volumes in his seventh. From these writings we can learn what Skinner found salient in his own personal history. It should not be surprising, then, that Skinner titles the first section of his autobiographical chapter "Early Environment," and that he begins the first volume of his autobiography with a description of the surrounding environment into which he was born.

Childhood

Burrhus Frederic Skinner was born on March 20, 1904, in Susquehanna, Pennsylvania, a small railroad town in the northeast corner of the state. Located between the river from which it took its name and the foothills of the Allegheny mountains, the town of Susquehanna had grown up around a depot of the Erie Railroad. The life of the town was ordered by the railroad shop whistle, with blasts signaling the beginning and end of the workday as well as of the noonday break. Not only were the town businesses paced by this whistle but also households were, as meals were prepared and served when the appropriate whistle blew. The effect of the whistle was pervasive, so much so that Skinner's mother had used this signal system as a metaphor for life in her high school graduation address as salutatorian. The pacing of Skinner's life by the town's whistle might be one potential source for his later theoretical emphasis on the influence of the environment on behavior, and on the importance of order and control.

Susquehanna at the beginning of the 1900s was representative of America as a whole in the midst of the "Progressive Era." A severe economic depression at the end of the 19th century gave way to a series of technological innovations that was to define the 20th century. Skinner remembers from his early childhood the introduction of electricity into the household and the first automobile his family owned. The ethos of the era was one of expansive optimism, a belief that the future would bring endless economic and social progress. Fed by a Protestant ethic of material success and social mobility, reformers adopted a focus on progress through action. American Protestantism claimed that it was through action that God was served and a state of grace assured; idleness was the worst of sins. This action orientation was applied in the use of technology and science to effect material and social improvement. By his own report, Skinner's family had fully adopted this prevailing belief that life was to be understood as progress through effective action. In this social context then might be found a source for Skinner's adoption of science as a means to progress, his focus on the behavior of progress in his first research experiments, and his theoretical emphasis on operants that act on the environment versus respondents that react to the environment.

The first person Skinner mentions in both his autobiographical chapter and the three-volume autobiography is his grandmother Skinner. The portrait he paints of her is not a flattering one. He depicts her as a foolish woman who put on airs and whose greatest intellectual achievement was to read a bit of the Bible every day, although he thought this was just a pretense. She moved hesitantly as if unsure whether she was properly dressed or doing the right thing, and she laughed nervously after every remark as if afraid she had made a mistake. Skinner expresses surprise, then, that this unadmirable character moved beyond her "poor white" family of origin, and indeed his account calls attention to his concern for the problem of how she managed this "escape." After introducing her family he writes: "A sister of my grandmother's moved out of that culture . . . Two or three brothers escaped, too, and so did my grandmother, though it is hard to say why."[22] He only apparently moves on from this theme in the next seven paragraphs, depicting his grandmother's appearance, sayings, cooking, humor, storytelling, frugality, and relationship with her pet canary. After all of this, the eighth paragraph begins: "Only one thing makes any sense of the fact that she escaped from her family background,"[23] and it is then clear that the problem of escape he had raised two pages before had remained incomplete in his thinking.

Skinner attributes his grandmother's ability to escape her family background to her having "aspirations." We may be surprised to find Skinner attributing causality to an inner quality such as aspiration, and indeed although his narrative contains a number of references to internal states he is usually careful not to give them a causal status. In this case it becomes clear as his narrative continues that Skinner takes a decidedly negative view of the effect of his grandmother's aspirations on his father and himself. As an only child Skinner's father received the full force of his mother's ambitions. She had once told Skinner that when his father was a baby she pinched his nose to make it look sharp and distinguished looking. But Skinner was sure that there were many other ways she had pinched his father as well and that these pinchings had had a painful effect. He attributes to his grandmother's ambitions for his father both his father's apparent conceit, which made him unpopular with other people, and his chronic drive for self-improvement and progress. The latter characteristic allowed him to escape beyond his meager beginnings as his mother had, but it also caused him to suffer profound feelings of failure and shame. Skinner describes his father at the time of his birth in the following way:

> Fifteen years had passed since my father had escaped from the Mechanical Engineering Department of the Erie Railroad and had gone to New York for that one-year course in law, and he had come a long way. The newspapers were correct in referring to him repeatedly as a rising young lawyer, but he was not to rise

much further. He was then about as effective, personally and professionally, as he was ever to be . . . Life was to abrade him, to wear him down. He struggled to satisfy that craving for a sense of worth with which his mother had damned him, but forty years later he would throw himself on his bed, weeping, and cry, "I am no good, I am no good."[24]

By Skinner's account his grandmother Skinner's demanding treatment had a negative effect on him as well. It was she who gave him his first religious teaching at the age of 5 or 6 in an effort to keep him from the temptation of lying. Opening the heating stove to expose the coal fire burning within, she told him that children who told lies were thrown in a place just like that after they died as punishment. Skinner's young mind was so impressed by the image that he suffered overwhelming torment when, soon after being shown the burning coals, he said that someone was his uncle and later learned that the man was actually a great-half-uncle. He had mistakenly told a lie, and the promise of punishment in Hell struck him with terror. Not long afterwards he knowingly told a lie to avoid punishment, only to be tortured for years with anguish over his future punishment in Hell. In a note he wrote a year after college he recalled: "I remember lying awake at night sobbing, refusing to tell my mother the trouble, refusing to kiss her goodnight. I can still feel the remorse, the terror, the despair of my young heart at that time."[25]

This is hardly the language we would expect from the behaviorist who denied the importance of emotions. Does he see emotions as a foolish curse that he suffered in childhood but outgrew with maturity? Alternatively, could it be that Skinner continued to be pained by such emotions into adulthood and so took efforts to deny them their power in his theory? He ended his account of his grandmother's training methods with the observation that he had never recovered from the spiritual torture of that threat of punishment. Thus, his theoretical belittling of emotions, as well as of punishment, may in part represent an attempt to defend against such painful experiences. And his long-term reaction to the threat argues against his apparent reason for deprecating punishment in his theory: that it is not effective in the long run.

Skinner's father picked for a wife a woman who was in some ways quite different from his mother. Grace Burrhus was intelligent and beautiful, and she had enough talent to be employed as a secretary before her marriage and as a pianist and singer at weddings and funerals after her marriage. But she shared with grandmother Skinner those qualities that Skinner thought had left a bad mark on his father and on him: an aspiration toward self-improvement and progress, a concern with looking and doing "right," even a tendency to laugh at mistakes, although this was specific to the mistakes of people she was not close to; shortcomings in herself or in her husband and son were judged violently as if they were a sin.

Grace pushed her husband to succeed and her son to grow tall, protesting when her father put a spoonful of coffee in the young Skinner's milk that it would stunt his growth. Along with her husband and mother-in-law, she held firmly to the prevalent ethos of progress and would play a part in passing this value to her son. She had rigid standards of what was right and was deeply concerned with what other people thought. Skinner recalls that when his report card in second grade recorded under "Deportment" that he tended to annoy others she showed great consternation. She was quick to take alarm when she saw any hint of deviation from the right path in Skinner's behavior, and her common phrases were "Tut tut" and "What will people think?" Skinner's mother liked to laugh at people who showed such errors as wearing a shirt and tie that failed to go together or mispronouncing a word, and she even collected examples of such mispronunciations to share with friends. When Skinner mispronounced a word or used incorrect grammar, however, she harshly corrected him with no hint of amusement in her stern response. That Skinner took her judgments on these occasions to heart is shown in his memory of mispeaking once as a child when his father brought their Congressman home to supper. When asked if he had ever been to Washington, Skinner replied, "No, I never were," and he reports that he suffered for a long while afterward from the thought of his error. Once when his mother heard him use a bad word she took him to the bathroom, put soap on a wet washcloth, and washed his mouth out. It was the only time he recalls being physically punished by either parent.

Skinner's father, Will, played his own part in perpetuating a strict atmosphere. When Skinner was discovered to have lifted a quarter from his grandmother's purse at the age of 4 or 5, he was lectured about the dangers of a criminal way of life. Some years later his father took him to a county jail to see the prisoners sitting in the bare room behind bars, and once while the family was on vacation he was taken to an illustrated lecture on life at Sing Sing Prison. After recounting these events in his autobiography, Skinner writes that he doesn't think they were done to frighten him, making the threat of fear salient by negation. Although his father never physically punished Skinner, he was not against using emotional manipulation, not only inducing fear by the implicit threats in the aforementioned examples but also inducing shame by social evaluation. Skinner was round-shouldered and had a tendency to droop in his posture, an inclination that led both parents to worry. His father dealt with this by slouching across the room with his hands dangling like an ape's to show Skinner how bad he looked. Skinner was powerfully influenced by these kinds of controlling maneuvers from both of his parents, and this may have led him later to seek control himself through the science of behaviorism. In his first experiments he would try a direct identification with his parents in exposing his rats to threats, but later he would reject punishment as a means of control.

One striking aspect of Skinner's autobiographical account is the inconsistency with which he describes the punishment he received as a child. After recounting the only time he had been physically punished (itself a rather unusual label for having his mouth washed out with soap), he says "I must have been punished in other ways because my parents' disapproval was something I carefully avoided."[26] Only a page later he claims he was not punished by his parents: "Unwilling to punish me, my parents showed some skill in finding alternative measures."[27] Two pages later he returns to the conclusion that he was punished with the remarkable statement: "I must have been punished in some way for very early sex play, perhaps even as a baby."[28] This series of contradictory statements indicates a confusion on Skinner's part in how to characterize his parents' aversive control of him. It is also noteworthy that the two times he says that he was punished he writes it as "I must have been," as if he does not remember actual examples yet decides he should reach this conclusion from other evidence. Skinner might characterize this failure of memory as a repression, that is, an avoidance of something unpleasant by failing to approach it even in thought. This personal aversion to punishment was later expressed in a theoretical rejection of it.

If Skinner's home environment was laced with aversive control, he found avenues of escape in building things and in studying animals. He was always building things, and in his list of the things he built, the first and the most frequent type of item he records is that which enables movement or travel. He built roller-skate scooters, steerable wagons, sleds, rafts, slides, kites, model airplanes, and tin propellers that could be sent high into the air with a spool-and-string spinner. He tried repeatedly to make a glider in which he himself could fly. It is tempting to see these devices as symbolic means of achieving both the progress that his parents valued and the escape from his constraining environment that he himself wanted. That he sometimes used invention explicitly to escape his parents' aversive control is shown in the following example.

At one point Skinner's mother began a campaign to get him to hang up his pajamas. Every morning as he was eating breakfast she would go upstairs to his room to check whether he had left his pajamas lying on the bed, and when she found that he had she would call to him to come immediately and hang them up, and he would have to stop eating to go upstairs and put them on a hook. She continued this for weeks over which time her morning call to him became increasingly unbearable. He writes: "It did not make me any more inclined to hang them up before coming down to breakfast, but it was nonetheless aversive, and I escaped in the following way."[29] The closet was near to the door of his room, and he rigged a pulley system from a hook in the closet to a sign hanging above the door. When his pajamas were in place on the hook the sign remained above the door out of the way. But as soon as he took his pajamas off the hook at night the sign fell down to the middle of the doorway so that he ran into it when starting to leave his room the following morning. The sign read: "Hang up your pajamas!"

His contact with animals also seems to have served as a means of dealing with his parents' constraining maneuvers. The town of Susquehanna was set in a river valley with fields, hills, and forest. Skinner explored this natural world extensively and caught many animals to bring home and study: chipmunks, frogs, turtles, snakes, butterflies, bees, and fireflies. It is striking how his descriptions of his play with these animals reveals a recurrent theme of him trapping them and their forcefully trying to break free, as if Skinner is acting out in his relationship with animals the role his parents took toward him. He writes, for example, "I had a cage-like mousetrap that caught mice alive, and I used it to catch chipmunks. I could never tame them, and I let them go when red marks developed on the sides of their snouts as they tried to force their way between the wires of the trap."[30] Just a few sentences later the same pattern recurs with a different captive: "I could catch a bee in a hollyhock blossom, folding the petals together to make a small bottle, the bee buzzing furiously until I tired of the game and released it."[31] Skinner is a different captor than his parents, however, in being moved to release his captives.

A similar pattern occurs in his narrative 30 pages later, but this time it is his father who has done the catching and he declines to let the captive free. Writing about fishing with his father, Skinner says, "For bait my father caught minnows with a net in the shallow water near our cottage. He would put a hook through the back of a live minnow (I never watched him) and throw the struggling creature overboard. The minnow sometimes took revenge by weaving in and out among the eel grass so that the line could not be pulled in without breaking it."[32] Skinner's distaste for his father's capture of the minnow is made salient by his isolated comment that he could not watch his father hook it, and this distaste stands in contrast to his comfort with baiting hooks himself, recounted only one paragraph before this one. It may be that in this case he identifies more strongly with the captive rather than with the captor. Support for the idea that the young Skinner identified with the minnow who suffered under his father's constraint is found in his personification of the minnow, depicting it as a "struggling creature" who "took revenge."

Although Skinner may have identified with the minnow who struggled against his father's control, by Skinner's report, he himself never revolted. He writes: "I was never aware of the control exercised by my family or my associates in Susquehanna, but it was nonetheless irksome . . . I accepted all this as I had been taught to do; I had never learned to protest or complain or even to try to find out what was wrong."[33] In his first experimental designs in graduate school Skinner would combine his childhood patterns of building things and capturing animals as a way to express his concern with escaping a constraining environment, and his theoretical distinction between respondent and operant behavior can be seen to reflect his concern with passive acceptance versus active revolt in relation to this environment.

Beyond the mitigation provided by building things and capturing animals, another source of relief from the oppressiveness of Skinner's home life came in the form of a younger brother, Ebbe. Born 2½ years after Skinner, Ebbe was an easygoing and good-humored boy of whom the young Skinner was very fond. Skinner used to call his brother "Honey," a term he picked up from his mother. He and Ebbe were constant playmates, and Ebbe's role as an early reinforcer is shown in a memory Skinner had of a day when Ebbe was in bed sick with a cold. Working with the boards of orange crates to fashion a stool, Skinner brought his creation in to show his brother. Ebbe responded with such delight that Skinner went right back to make a second stool, and this pleased Ebbe so much that Skinner promptly went back and made a third. Their mother finally had to intervene to stop him from making still more. Joy came easily to Ebbe and he took delight in things that his parents would have scorned. Skinner gives an example of this when he recounts a time when the family was sitting in the library and Ebbe got up and went to the kitchen. He came back a minute later laughing hilariously as he reported that he had intended to go to the toilet, and only discovered that he was in the kitchen after he had started to urinate into the coal pail. Only one paragraph earlier Skinner had recounted his parents' reaction of troubled concern when he himself had had a similar moment of absent-mindedness and made a faulty salute in a Boy Scout rally. This contrast between Ebbe's style and that of his parents probably had an impact on the young Skinner, and it may have fed his later sensitivity to the distinction between reinforcement and punishment, and his preference for the former.

Tension emerged between the two boys as Ebbe grew older, however. In part, this was because Ebbe found it as easy to laugh at his older brother as at himself, and Skinner did not like to be laughed at. The examples Skinner recalls in his autobiography indicate that he was especially sensitive when Ebbe teased him for "putting on airs," such as when Skinner referred to his father's secretary as "Miss Jessie Sykes" or reported information on the anatomy of a peanut that he had gleaned from an advertisement. In part, the tension resulted from the fact that Ebbe grew to be a much better athlete and more popular than his older brother. That the tension reflected Skinner's concern with maintaining a dominant position is suggested not only by the previous examples but also in his account of an interaction between them when Skinner was making discoveries about his sexuality. Experiencing an erection, he showed it to his brother who displayed great interest and started to play with it. Skinner reports that at that age he felt that to ejaculate was to be demeaned or defeated, and thus that he saw his brother as trying to put himself in a superior position. Skinner announced to the disappointed Ebbe that he could take that kind of stimulation forever without having an orgasm.

There is also some evidence that Skinner was jealous of Ebbe's greater closeness to their parents. When reporting this greater closeness in his autobiography, Skinner writes that Ebbe "enjoyed" more expressions of affection from both parents as if he wished for more himself. Skinner quickly follows this, however, with the assertion that there was plenty of affection to go around. He also takes pains to assert in three different places that there was no rivalry between them, and wonders whether "the lack of sibling rivalry is disappointing"[34] to his readers. That he needed to negate rivalry so many times would be enough to raise suspicion about its authenticity, but to have it come on the heels of the aforementioned examples of competition between them makes it very tempting to doubt his assertion to the reader of a lack of rivalry, as we would doubt his assertion to Ebbe that he could resist ejaculation forever. We will soon find an event in his college years that gives further evidence of Skinner's competitive feelings, and of their impact on his theoretical model.

By high school Skinner was exploring sexual relations with girls, and one theme appears over and over in his descriptions of these relations: progress. In particular, his main concern was to see how far he could advance up a girl's leg. With Marion Knise he had a well-established limit of 3 inches above the knee; with Margaret Persons they had an argument on his first approach up her leg and he "never made any further advances";[35] with Leslie Gilbert he wondered whether he might have married her if instead of being so concerned with how far he could go up her leg he had shown her some affection; with a fourth girl he "had never been able to make any progress with her."[36] We have seen that this theme of progress was part of the general ethos of the Progressive Era;

here it may have been amplified by a biological source. In any case, this theme of progress would recur in Skinner's later work, being used to justify his choice of science over art and being applied in his first experiments on the behavior of the laboratory rat.

When Skinner's senior year arrived, his class had to choose a motto for the graduation exercises. Skinner suggested "Contact!," the title of a story by Frances Noyes Hart that was based on the word aviators use at takeoff. Skinner reproduces a part of the story in his autobiography:

> It's waiting—waiting for a word—and so am I and I lean far forward, watching the figure toiling out beyond till the call comes back to me, clear and confident, "Contact, sir?" and I shout back, as restless and exultant as the first time that I answered it—"Contact!" And I am off—and I'm alive—And I'm free! [37]

Skinner welcomed his departure for college as a chance for escape from his oppressive home environment.

Young Adulthood

Although Skinner hoped that Hamilton College would be an opportunity for freedom, in his first year he found it to be a mixed opportunity. Classes were run on a schedule as strict as the daily activities had been in Susquehanna, with a bell in the chapel tower replacing the railroad shop whistle. The bell tolled 12 times at the beginning of each period, and students who were not in their seats by the 12th stroke were marked absent or late; only a few such absences were excused. Here was another environment that controlled his behavior by an orderly schedule, serving as a basis for the attention paid in his theory to the influence of the environment on behavior and to the issues of order and control. Freshmen were subjected to hazing by upperclassmen, and Skinner recounts a time when he was "captured" by two sophomores and tied to a chair in a classroom. He reports: "I did not resist; I simply let my captors tie me up without protest."[38] As in his years at home, he was submitting to the control of others, and this passivity rather than active attempt to change the situation perhaps found expression later in his theoretical distinction between respondent and operant behavior. Yet Hamilton did provide new

opportunities for freedom, such as in the use of an honor system during examinations. Skinner also found himself writing poems as he had never done at home and being reinforced when some were published in the *Hamilton Literary Magazine.*

On balance, however, in his first year Skinner was most impressed by the constraints and requirements imposed by the college, and he was disappointed to find college more of a burden than an incentive. He showed some signs of homesickness, and on a lonely excursion to the nearest city one day, he wandered into a bookstore and bought a book called *Homes in America* that he sent to his parents. But he was soon ashamed of the sentimental inscription he had written inside the book, in an echo of the earlier ambivalence we saw over the relative affection he and Ebbe received from their parents. In his visit home during the spring vacation of his freshman year, a traumatic event was to bring this ambivalence to the fore.

On a Sunday morning, he and Ebbe drove their parents to church and then met a friend of Ebbe's in town for a sundae at the drugstore. By the time they had driven back to their house Ebbe was complaining of a headache, and within a short while he was obviously in great pain and frightened, and he cried for them to call a doctor. Skinner stood by helplessly as Ebbe's friend called a doctor he knew lived nearby. In the 15 minutes it took for the doctor to arrive Ebbe had fallen unconscious; food was flowing out of his mouth. Skinner asked the doctor if he should go get his parents from church and was told that he should. He drove so fast that his mother, not aware of the seriousness of Ebbe's condition, complained about being bounced about. When they arrived at the house they found the maid standing on the front porch crying that Ebbe was dead. A poorly done autopsy at the time gave the cause of death as acute indigestion, but Skinner showed the report to a medical friend years later who guessed it was more probably a massive cerebral hemorrhage.

Skinner's description of his stunned and disoriented parents is a compelling one. His mother threw her arms around the still warm body of her son while his father walked from room to room in a kind of trance repeatedly saying "For heaven's sake, for heaven's sake." Skinner's account of his own reaction is much harder to decipher. In the autobiographical chapter he wrote in his sixth decade he reports, "I was not much moved. I probably felt guilty because I was not."[39] But in the autobiographical volume he wrote a decade later he says specifically "I was far from unmoved."[40] In this account he reports that Ebbe's death had a devastating effect on all of them, and he emphasizes his own ineffectiveness in being unable to do anything for his brother. Here it is implied that it is through a feeling of shock that he was stunned into a helpless immobility. He writes, in a rather odd analogy, "Just as I allowed myself to be tied to that classroom seat by two hazing sophomores, so I submitted to that tragic loss with little or no struggle."[41]

What is going on here? Should we draw from his earlier account the conclusion that Skinner was actually lacking in feeling at his brother's death, and that his later claim to being moved is a false claim of feeling, resulting from his guilt in having none? After all his actual statement in the second account, that he was "far from unmoved," is a noteworthy way to put it, using a double negative to say that he was not not moved. Or should we draw from his later account that Skinner did in fact feel deeply at his brother's death, but that his inability to control the situation to prevent the tragedy and its devastating effects led him to a feeling of stunned numbness that he had earlier misidentified as a lack of feeling? Now perhaps the double negative should be seen as an effort to avoid the powerful negative feeling that did exist. An answer to these questions might take us a long way in understanding the role of personal experience in Skinner's theoretical discounting of the importance of emotion.

There is one more part of the story yet to be told that should aid our understanding, although this piece too is told in a way that makes it not immediately easy to decipher. Surprisingly, however, although Skinner's two autobiographical accounts differ in their report of whether he was moved, they are virtually identical in their report of this aspect of his reaction. In both accounts, right after reporting that he was/was not moved and in the same paragraph, he continues with this observation:

> I once made an arrowhead by bending the top of a tin can into
> a flattened cone. I fastened it to the end of an arrow, and when I
> shot it straight up into the air, it fell back and struck my brother
> in the shoulder, drawing blood. Many years later I remembered

the event with a shock when I heard Laurence Olivier speaking Hamlet's lines:

> . . . *Let me disclaiming from a purpos'd evil*
> *Free me so far in your most generous thoughts,*
> *That I have shot mine arrow o'er the house,*
> *And hurt my brother.*[42]

What can he be thinking here to put this observation after his report of Ebbe's death? Is he telling us that he felt guilty and in some way responsible for his brother's death?

No further hint is given in the autobiographical chapter, where he immediately moves thereafter to a new paragraph on a new topic. This incompletion may represent Skinner's avoidance of something unpleasant. In the volume written a decade later, however, there is one more paragraph before he shifts to a new subject. This paragraph begins "My brother and I had never competed for the same things."[43] That he negates competition with Ebbe on the heels of the Hamlet quote suggests that he may indeed have felt guilt and thus a need to deny any competition with his brother. The guilt that he recounts in his first report would now be understood not as guilt for feeling no emotion but rather as guilt for his competitive feelings. And the lack of felt emotion would have resulted from a repression of those feelings, that is, an avoidance of the inner experience of inclinations toward hostile behavior against Ebbe. Now, too, we would understand why in the second report Skinner calls attention to the fact that it was Ebbe's friend rather than he himself who had called the doctor, for this failure to help Ebbe would also be likely to invoke guilt over inclinations to harm him. If Skinner had competitive feelings toward Ebbe that he had repressed, this would be consistent with the fact that in his autobiography he gave a number of examples of competition between them but explicitly and repeatedly denied any competition.

Some particular examples Skinner chose to use in his analysis of human behavior in *Science and Human Behavior* (1953) now become noteworthy when we adopt this perspective. When he analyzes emotion, Skinner's first and most frequent example is of the emotion of anger, and when he illustrates how angry behaviors can be both innate and learned, the example he gives is that of one child attacking another. Then, when he turns to explicating the Freudian defense mechanisms, the example he uses to illustrate repression is that of sibling rivalry. In this analysis he asserts that rivalry between two brothers for affection and other reinforcers from parents can lead one to aggress against the other, and that the negative consequences of this can lead the aggressive brother to feel guilt and to repress his aggressive tendencies. Thus, for Skinner, sibling rivalry was a ready example for illustrating anger, guilt, and repression.

These observations suggest that Skinner had competitive feelings toward Ebbe, that these feelings caused guilt and a need for repression, and that his need to repress these feelings at the time of Ebbe's death may have contributed to his numbness and immobility. If this is the case, it would illuminate other aspects of Skinner's life. For one, we see at the time of Ebbe's death a sequence for Skinner that has implications elsewhere: Angry feelings lead to guilt about negative consequences of this anger, which leads to repression and immobility. His analogy to the hazing incident makes more sense in light of this sequence: He submits without a "struggle" because he feels guilty of the negative consequences of expressing his anger. This same sequence also finds an echo in his pattern of submission to his parents' control without protest, while at the same time showing sympathy for the "struggling" minnow who took revenge on his father.

A second implication of this discovery of guilt over competition with Ebbe is that it might explain in part his ambivalence toward his wish for a more affectionate relationship with his parents. Skinner had reported that Ebbe enjoyed more affection with their parents, yet in his description of defense mechanisms he had written that rivalry with a sibling over parental affection can lead to negative consequences. Ebbe's death may have brought Skinner guilt in particular about his wish for greater closeness with his parents, serving as one reason why he was led to regret the sentimental inscription he had written in the gift he had sent them only a few months before. Ebbe's death then appears to have made powerful demands on Skinner to deny angry feelings as well as affectionate wishes. This event may well have played a role in Skinner's later denial of the importance of emotions and wishes in his theory.

When Skinner returned to Hamilton he returned to writing, although after his freshman year he focused more on short stories than on poetry. He became aware that many of his stories were references to his relationship with his parents. From one story in particular we learn that another reason for Skinner's resistance against his wish for more affection with his parents may have been that his parents had not provided good satisfaction for this wish. The story, written toward the end of his college career, is about his behavior freshman year of sending a book home to his parents. It provides a remarkable window into his emotional life.

> Father and mother had laughed at Henry's first letters. Prosaic descriptions of college, the food, and his health, but with them an occasional unguarded note of homesickness. This pleased father and mother. They felt proud and happy that being away from home was hurting their son. It proved to them something they had sometimes doubted: that he really loved them.
>
> His overtones of homesickness increased as the months passed until a book came, carefully planned to reach home on mother and father's wedding anniversary. It was a large book, a gift edition in blue and gold, called *Beautiful Homes of History*. On the first page was carefully written:
>
> "To father and mother, whose home surpasses the beauty and holiness of any of these. Henry."
>
> Mother read it with moist eyes, and hated to have father smile at it. She did feel a little uncertain about it; but then, it was so unexpected! It really *was* dear of Henry! They both felt peculiarly happy. But after it was put on top of the bookstand, father occasionally laughed at it; and sometimes mother smiled too, although it made her feel guilty.
>
> Two months afterward Henry came home for the holidays. But during the first hour when he told them his joyous history, no one spoke of the book. No one even spoke of homesickness. Mother looked at the boy before her, and wondered about *Beautiful Homes*. There was something incongruous there, between the inscription and Henry.
>
> That night before she went to bed she went to the bookstand and ran her fingers over the cool gold letters on the blue cover. She read the words in a whisper: "Beautiful Homes of History." Then with a little swell of feeling she lifted the cover.
>
> But the first page had been removed with a sharp knife.[44]

It is unclear what elements of this story are literally true, but by Skinner's own account the story is about his behavior freshman year and there is very likely an authenticity to the emotional patterns displayed. What is revealed is a son who is ambivalent about showing his love to his parents: His parents have come to doubt that he really loves them and his homesickness only seeps through when he is not guarding against it. When we see the parents' response to his expressions of love we find a reason for his guardedness: They ridicule his tender feelings with laughter and gain pride from the idea of hurting their son by their distance. In the end the son deals with his dilemma by disavowing his expression of feeling. If this story speaks to Skinner's own relationship with his parents, it provides another personal basis for his discounting of emotion in his theory: He had been demeaned for the expression of feeling and so had responded by repudiating it entirely.

By the end of his time at college there were many things pointing Skinner to a career in writing. He was one of four seniors who had attracted attention on campus as writers and were involved with a number of faculty members in weekly meetings modeled after the Round Table at the Algonquin. He had had the opportunity to visit socially with such writers as Aleck Woollcott, Edna Ferber, Carl Sandburg, and Robert Frost at Hamilton or at Bread Loaf Summer School. It is not surprising, then, when in his autobiography he reports his decision senior year to spend the following year writing a novel. What is surprising is his decision to do this at home. True, we can imagine reasons for doing so, such as the economic savings in living with his parents. But we can also imagine reasons against it, such as the fact that whereas college had provided a supportive environment for free expression, his home had not. In any case, the curious fact is that although his autobiography gives ample justification for his choice to pursue writing, the rationale for his choice to go home is omitted.

He wrote his parents telling them of his decision and received back a long and considered letter from his father representing their view. The letter, reproduced in full in Skinner's autobiography, made clear that his parents were very dubious about his plan. A few weeks after this letter from his father came a letter from Robert Frost that took a very different tone. Skinner had sent Frost some of his short stories to evaluate. Frost's letter, also reproduced in full in Skinner's autobiography, ended with the following paragraph:

> Those are real niceties of observation you've got here and you've done 'em to a shade. "The Laugh" has the largest value. That's the one you show most as caring in. You see I want you to care. I don't want you to be academic about it—a writer of exercises. Of course, not too expressly, overtly caring. You'll have to search yourself here. You know best whether you are haunted with any impatience about what other people see or don't see. That will be you if you are you. I am inclined to say you are. But you have the final say. I wish you'd tell me how you come out in thinking it over—if it isn't too much trouble—some time. I ought to say you have the touch of art. The work is clean run. You are worth twice anyone else I have seen in prose this year.[45]

Unlike his parents whom Skinner had experienced as ridiculing his feelings, Frost encouraged Skinner to care. The story that Frost liked best was the one that he saw most caring in, "The Laugh." In an echo of a theme we saw in Skinner's story about "Beautiful Homes," "The Laugh" was a story about a husband who demeans his wife by laughing at her. Frost was encouraging Skinner to pursue writing, and Skinner felt that this was all the evidence of his promise as a writer that his parents could ask for. He writes this conclusion in his autobiography as "I should be allowed to try my wings."[46] The particular phrasing he uses here is telling. Skinner sees the pursuit of writing as a kind of escape ("to try my wings"), yet rather than forcefully breaking away from his parents he wants them to sanction this freedom ("I should be allowed"). This may explain in part his choice to go home to write: He was hoping that his parents would actively release him as he had released the animals under his constraint.

But it was not long after he returned home before Skinner realized the tragedy of his choice. He found himself fully unable to write. Despite his wish to produce something, no thoughts or feelings forced their way out of him and onto the blank page. The impotence of any inner life in motivating his behavior was painfully obvious to him, and the power of the external environment was felt more forcefully. Skinner turned to blaming his parents, both for his going home to write in the first place and for his inability to write once there. The following is from a note he wrote to himself at the end of the summer after arriving home.

> My family ties prevent my living simply alone, "struggling to write." . . .
>
> My family ties prevent me, not because I have a great deal of devotion and respect for my father and mother, but because they have suffered very much in the last four years and because my leaving them would increase their present anxiety to an unbearable degree.
>
> Thus they are unwittingly forcing me into my present course.
>
> True, they have offered me a year to stay at home to write. But if the first three months of that year are exemplary, this will be the condition:
>
> My father and mother will be patently ashamed to explain to friends what I am "doing." I have already felt the sting of implied "You ought to go to work. If you were my boy—." My father will assume that I am doing nothing. He will come home at noon and scowl at me in my smoking jacket and slippers. He will tell me to do this around the house or that with the car with the implication: "You have nothing to do—."
>
> Mother will say at least once a day, "It's going to be pretty hard, son, for you to settle down to work when you can't play the piano for an hour after breakfast, or read all afternoon."
>
> If I go for a walk Mother will ask meaningfully: "All alone—?" To be alone in Scranton is a sin.
>
> Father will laugh with half-veiled disgust if I make a date to go walking with a girl at half-past eight in the morning to discuss Dostoevski.
>
> I will accept an invitation to a piano recital with tea afterwards and Mother will say, "Don't you think that's so effeminate?"
>
> I will ridicule a sermon, with the parental rebuke, "It isn't right for you to do that! Those are the men who get things done in the world."
>
> Without ever inquiring into my ideas father will flutter his hand in the air and talk of my "highfalutin theories." . . .
>
> I am too sensitive to my surroundings to stand it.
>
> I could do little or no creative work during a year here. It was a big and important mistake that I ever thought I could. At the end of that year according to my agreement I would admit (outwardly) failure and go to work.[47]

Although Skinner had hoped that his parents would sanction his freedom, instead they "prevent" him from "struggling" to write and thus "force" him into his present course. The first research designs he would pursue in graduate school would reflect the concern Skinner now had for how to progress and escape in the context of a restraining and threatening environment.

He was in a bad spot. Although Hamilton had been an environment that reinforced his writing, his parents created a punishing environment for it. Along with their disparagement of feeling that we saw in his short story, "Beautiful Homes," we now see also a disparagement of thinking, dismissing his ideas as "highfalutin" and belittling his discussion of Dostoevski. Value is given to men who get things done and writing is viewed as doing nothing. That Skinner could not progress in his writing only lent support to this view. Skinner had come home to write because he could not forcefully break free, and on finding that his parents were not going to sanction his freedom as he had hoped, he began a process of resignation to their world view. He would give up the pursuit of literature to pursue science instead, and in his scientific theory he would adopt control as the primary goal and would reject free will as an impossibility. He would even embrace his parents' valuing of action in his focus on behavior as the phenomenon of interest, and their devaluing of feelings and thoughts in his claim that inner states should be treated as irrelevant. His preference for the study of operant behaviors that affect their environment over respondent behaviors that react to their environment can also be seen to rest in his parents' respect for effective action.

But as well as finding a way to move forward, Skinner also needed a way to justify his lack of movement during the Dark Year. He had agreed to admit his failure outwardly, as he wrote in his note, but he did not want to admit it to himself. The efforts that he took over the course of the year to account for his failure show a pattern of externalizing blame, and here we may find a basis for his later claim that behavior is determined from without rather than from within. At first he blamed his parents as seen in the previous note, saying that they prevented him from pursuing writing independently and thus forced him on his present course. His claim that he was too sensitive to his surroundings shows that he was deeply aware of the difference in the effect of his Hamilton versus home environments. Blaming his parents could not be the final solution for Skinner, however, for he was unwilling to revolt against them to pursue writing. He thus turned toward the end of the year to blaming literature itself as a method. This allowed him to divert blame from within himself but also to avoid blaming his parents. When at the end of the year he discovered Watson's work on behaviorism he found a systematic rationale for blaming his failure outward, for Watson's theory claimed that behavior was solely a function of environmental factors. He also found a system by which he could adopt those values his parents had transmitted, using science to effectively control behavior. Vulnerable to shame and guilt and eager to relieve himself of the failure of the Dark Year, Skinner embraced behaviorism with a tenacity that was not to weaken over the next 60 years of his life.

Adulthood

When Skinner entered graduate school in psychology at Harvard in 1928 he was already a devout behaviorist. His letters home to his parents that year reported that he was looked on as the leader of the behaviorist camp of graduate students and that he was prepared to solve the riddle of the universe. He was so convinced of the behaviorist system that when it came to his dissertation defense a few years later he was embarrassed by only one question from his examiners. One of his committee members asked him what were some of the objections to behaviorism. Skinner could not think of a single one. In 5 years as a graduate student at Harvard, and then another 3 as a prestigious Junior Fellow, Skinner systematically explored the environmental control of operant behavior in the laboratory rat. It was many years, however, before he would explicitly apply behaviorism to the analysis of human beings. When he first did so it was not in the form of empirical research, nor even in a scholarly treatment of the implications of his laboratory findings for humans. In an unlikely return to the pursuit of literature that he had abandoned at the end of the Dark Year, and to his own surprise, Skinner suddenly wrote a novel.

The novel, *Walden Two* (1948/1962) is about a utopian community operating on the principles of behaviorism. The story follows one character, Burris, as he is shown the community by its founder, Frazier; Burris is initially dubious but in the end a convert. Written in 1945, the book marked the turning point in Skinner's writings from empirical research reports on lower organisms to advocacy-oriented treatises on the implications of behaviorism for human conduct. But by Skinner's own account he did not plan to write the book at all. He simply found himself one day embarked on writing it. It was produced in a very different manner than his previous works as well. He had usually written his manuscripts longhand and slowly, averaging 2 minutes per word on his dissertation and on *The Behavior of Organisms* (1938). (And how like Skinner to compute this rate of behavior!) *Walden Two* was dashed off on a typewriter at incredible speed and finished in 7 weeks. He wrote in his autobiography: "Except for a bout of dramaturgy during my junior year at Hamilton, when I wrote a three-act play in one morning, I had never experienced anything like it . . . I wrote some parts with an emotional intensity that I have never experienced at any other time."[48] In his autobiographical chapter he admits about the book: "It is pretty obviously a venture in self-therapy, in which I was struggling to reconcile two aspects of my own behavior represented by Burris and Frazier."[49] Let us look at what was going on in Skinner's life at this time to bring him to this struggle and to its resolution in writing *Walden Two.*

In his final summer at Harvard in 1936, just before he left for Minneapolis to start his first teaching appointment at the University of Minnesota, Skinner met Yvonne Blue. An English major from the University of Chicago, Yvonne could talk easily with Skinner about literature, and they found themselves challenging each other with name-dropping. By the end of the summer they were engaged to be married and Skinner moved to Minneapolis as a fiancé. In a visit to Minneapolis that fall, however, Yvonne was less than thrilled with the town and her impending role as a faculty wife, and they agreed to postpone their wedding. After receiving a card from Yvonne breaking the engagement entirely, Skinner went to Chicago to try to change her mind, and they decided to be married right away by a local minister, returning together to Minneapolis at the end of the weekend.

As they started their life together it was clear that Yvonne not only did not relish the responsibilities of being a faculty wife, but also did not take easily to the early stages of motherhood. When she became pregnant with their first child Julie in their second year of marriage, Skinner wrote to a friend about Yvonne: "Having a baby is certainly no fun no matter how you look at it. Every now and then she gets scared as hell. Is just now feeling terribly self-conscious about her figure. She went to a young Faculty Wife's club yesterday and some fool made the five pregnant women present sit in a row. Poor Yvonne burst into tears in telling me about it."[50] After their daughter was born, Yvonne was so anxious that she called the doctor the first time she was alone with the baby and the baby cried. It was 5 years before Skinner and Yvonne decided to have another child, and in discussing it Yvonne said that she did not mind the child-bearing but she dreaded the first year or two of child-raising.

In 1944, when their second child Debbie was on the way, Skinner applied his technical skills to help solve Yvonne's distress. He designed and built what he came to call the *baby-tender*. It was a crib-sized space fully enclosed with sound-absorbing walls that muffled loud noises. A picture window on one wall had a curtain that could be pulled down to block out light while the baby was sleeping. The temperature and humidity of the air in the crib could be completely controlled so that the baby needed no clothes or bedcovers. Soiling could be immediately cleaned by unrolling a new section of floor sheeting from a 10-yard roll at the base of the unit. Skinner had designed the baby-tender to simplify the care of a baby, and it relieved the stress of caretaking in many ways. With sound muted and light blocked out Debbie slept well; with temperature controlled there were few clothes and no bedding to launder; with the sheet of flooring Debbie was kept clean enough that she was only bathed twice a week, and the sheet itself needed cleaning only once a week.

But Skinner's design reflected not only his wish to help Yvonne deal with the stresses of child-rearing; he was also concerned to relieve the stresses of the child. In describing the baby-tender at the time he wrote: "I am quite sure that many beneficial effects will follow, not only in easing the lot of the young mother but in building happy and healthy babies . . . The problem is two-fold: to discover the optimal conditions for the child and to induce the mother to arrange those conditions. The latter is frequently the more difficult."[51] Having children and seeing Yvonne's discomfort with mothering may have revived Skinner's concerns about his own treatment as a child, and he was eager to provide a better experience for his children than he himself had had. Many of the benefits he saw of the baby-tender were in its ability to eliminate negative influences on the child, such as the clothing that he viewed as confining or the airborne germs that could bring infection. Skinner wanted to use his behavioral science to control his children through their environment, but he wanted this control to be to their benefit in eliminating harmful forces.

He soon learned that others would not react so favorably to his vision of control. Enthusiastic about the potential of the baby-tender to have a positive effect on many mothers and children, Skinner approached General Mills about developing it commercially. Two of their engineers came to see it and one wrote a memorandum about it to the management. He raised concern about

> the possible psychological reaction against the device by the average mother who may not care to raise her baby in this way or may not trust the gadget. The thing, as I saw it, was a surprise and somewhat of a shock at first sight. It didn't seem to comport with my idea of the warm-hearted mother whom I envision as wanting to tote her youngster everywhere; also listen to his howls at night, but maybe there are enough long-haired people and cold-hearted scientists such as the professor who invented this gadget, to make a market for it.[52]

We are now in a better position to understand the struggle that was going on in Skinner and that found expression when he wrote *Walden Two* in the summer of 1945. Part of him had identified with his parents, in choosing to control as a scientist and parent and in denying the possibility of freedom. But part of him remained identified with his rats and children, who felt the negative consequences of aversive control and wished for freedom. The accusation that he was cold-hearted toward his own child required Skinner to face again the problems of control and freedom and their emotional consequences, and he would play out his struggle through the characters of Burris and Frazier in *Walden Two*.

Burris is a college professor, visiting a utopian community that was founded by an old classmate of his from graduate school, Frazier. As a potential occupant of the community and a man who values freedom, Burris represents one side of Skinner, whereas as the man who built the community and whose *idée fixe* in life has been to have control, Frazier represents the other. Over the course of the book Frazier shows various aspects of the community to Burris in an effort to convert him. At the core of *Walden Two* is a method of child-raising that protects the child from a host of negative forces.

Infants are raised in baby-tenders in a common nursery manned by those members of the community who enjoy child-rearing. When the question is raised whether the parents see their babies the reply is that as long as they are in good health they do, coming by every day or so to play with their children for a few minutes. "That's the way we build up the baby's resistance,"[53] it is said, and it is not fully clear whether resistance is being built to infection or to the parents. The baby-tenders are touted for the protection they offer from infection, the freedom they give from the constriction of clothing and blankets, and the soundproofing that prevents the infants from being disturbed by others. Frazier claims that thus when a baby graduates from the nursery it knows nothing of frustration, anxiety, or sadness. At that point, when the child is 3, the community begins applying behavioral engineering to build the child's resistance against situations that evoke frustration and other negative emotions that are "wasteful and dangerous."[54] They are taught such strategies as "out of sight, out of mind" and "love your enemy." About the latter Frazier says it is

> a psychological invention for easing the lot of an oppressed people. The severest trial of oppression is the constant rage one suffers at the thought of the oppressor . . . If a man can succeed in "loving his enemies" and "taking no thought for the morrow," he will no longer be assailed by hatred of the oppressor or rage at the loss of his freedom or possessions. He may not get his freedom or possessions back, but he's less miserable.[55]

This may have been the best strategy Skinner could find for dealing with the oppression of his own upbringing. But when Frazier designs his own community in *Walden Two*, he goes further. He does not, however, adopt freedom. Frazier says "If man is free, then a technology of behavior is impossible . . . I deny that freedom exists at all. I must deny it—or my program would be absurd."[56] What he does is to adopt control, but a benevolent form of control. Punishment is never used, and the use of force or threat of force is seen as incompatible with happiness. Instead control is always applied in the form of reinforcement. By this method, Frazier says,

> we can achieve a sort of control under which the controlled, though they are following a code much more scrupulously than

was ever the case under the old system, nevertheless *feel free* . . .
That's the source of the tremendous power of positive reinforcement—there's no restraint and no revolt . . . Restraint is only one
sort of control, and absence of restraint isn't freedom. It's not
control that's lacking when one feels "free," but the objection-
able control of force.[57]

By adopting this method with his own children, then, Skinner
could achieve the control he wanted but at the same time give his
children the feeling of freedom they wanted, and thereby also escape any rage they might feel toward him as he had felt toward his
parents. Skinner began writing *Walden Two* in conflict over his Burris and Frazier sides, but by the end of the book his Frazier side had
fully won out. Skinner embraced the utopian vision Frazier had
applied and from that point on he produced policy-oriented writings on the application of behavior analysis to human concerns.
In these writings he would emphasize the necessity of control and
the impossibility of freedom, but he would argue that control must
be applied in the form of reinforcement and not as punishment.

Skinner made this full identification with Frazier, however, at the
cost of admitting those unappealing personal qualities to which
the engineer at General Mills had referred. In a section toward
the end of the book that Skinner reports he had written in "white
heat," Frazier accuses Burris of not liking him and Burris finds
himself unable to counter the accusation. Frazier says:

> "You think I'm conceited, aggressive, tactless, selfish. You're con-
> vinced that I'm completely insensitive to my effect upon others,
> except when the effect is calculated. You can't see in me any
> of the personal warmth or the straightforward natural strength
> which are responsible for the success of Walden Two . . . Well,
> you're perfectly right," he said quietly. Then he stood up, drew
> back his arm, and sent the tile shattering into the fireplace. "But
> God *damn* it, Burris!" he cried, timing the "damn" to coincide
> with the crash of the tile. "Can't you see? *I'm—not—a—product—
> of—Walden—Two!*" He sat down. He looked at his empty hand,
> and picked up a second tile quickly, as if to conceal the evidence
> of his display of feeling.[58]

If Skinner had to accept that he was cold-hearted he could do so
by believing that his early environment had made him so, and this

made him only more eager to be an advocate of better methods of environmental control in his future writings.

CONCLUSION

When at the age of 86 Skinner gave his keynote address to the American Psychological Association he was dying of leukemia, but he still used the podium to fight for the adoption of behaviorism as the science of psychology. He died 8 days later, on August 18, 1990. Behavior analysis was not then and likely never will be the exclusive approach of psychology. But its influence on the field has been profound, and Skinner himself was rated the most important psychologist of all time in a 1991 ranking, beating out Freud, who had held the number one spot a decade earlier.[59] In its elegant simplicity and firm rooting in scientific method, Skinner's behavioral model has generated voluminous research. And like Freud's model, Skinner's has shown the power to capture the imagination of many outside of the field of psychology, both scholars and practitioners. Behavior analysis has been applied to such problems as how best to raise our children, to educate our students, to cure our ill, and to reform our criminals. There have even been multiple attempts to build real utopian communities modeled after his fictional Walden Two.

The intensity of the proponents of Skinner's model has been well matched by the intensity of its critics, however. After an article about the baby-tender appeared in the *Ladies Home Journal,* Skinner received letters from people asking for instructions on how to build one for their own baby, but he also received letters suggesting that if he wanted to shut his children away in a box he shouldn't have had them in the first place. After *Walden Two* was published in 1948, there were people who were so inspired by the vision it offered that they tried to make it a reality, but there were also people who saw his vision as that of a mad scientist who was a potential menace to Western civilization. Skinner's extremism probably fostered these strong reactions. In his final address to his fellow psychologists shortly before his death, he made an analogy between the vigorous opposition to Darwin's theory by those who want to maintain belief in a Creator and the stubborn resistance to behavioral theory by those who want to maintain belief in a Mind. The analogy drew claps of appreciation from some and gasps of astonishment from others. But it is not simply that Skinner's theory trampled on cherished values of American society like free will and a volitional mind. Many objected to the theory not because they felt it unappealing but because they believed it invalid.

There are two primary objections to Skinner's theory on the basis of its validity in providing an account of human phenomena. One is that the theory is derived from research on lower organisms, and that Skinner's generalization to humans is largely speculative. In order to have full control over his experimental conditions, Skinner worked with lower organisms such as rats and pigeons that were readily subject to his manipulations. But it is presumptive of him to claim that the principles he discovered for behavior in these organisms will apply equally to humans. Others have tested Skinner's principles in research with humans, however. In the last chapter we will look at this work.

The second main objection to Skinner's model has to do with its treatment of subjective phenomena. Skinner sought to explain observable behavior and saw subjective experience as merely epiphenomenal: That is, it is a by-product of behavior rather than something to be studied on its own terms. Yet some argue that in discounting inner states in this way, Skinner's theory has failed to illuminate just those things that are most important to understand if we are to understand what it is to be a person.

In contrast to Skinner's systematic bypassing of inner states, there are other theorists working with behavioral principles who have chosen to incorporate inner states into their theories. Albert Bandura incorporated thought into his model, arguing that the effect of environmental consequences on behavior is not direct but rather mediated by thinking; indeed we can be conditioned without ever behaving at all but only by cognitive processes such as attention and representation. Julian Rotter called attention to not only the role of cognitive expectancies but also the role of wishes or values, pointing out that people have different preferences for different environmental consequences and so will behave differently based on these preferences. Still, in these models the goal is to predict behavior rather than to understand subjective experience itself. A wholly different approach is taken by phenomenological theorists, who focus on subjective experience as the essence of humanness. We turn to a pioneer of this approach, Carl Rogers, in the next chapter.

SUGGESTED READINGS

Primary Sources

Skinner, B. F. (1938). *The Behavior of Organisms.* New York: Appleton-Century-Crofts.

Skinner, B. F. (1962). *Walden Two.* New York: Macmillan. (Original work published 1948)

Skinner, B. F. (1953). *Science and Human Behavior.* New York: Free Press.

Skinner, B. F. (1967). B. F. Skinner. In Edwin Boring and Gardner Lindzey (Eds.), *A History of Psychology in Autobiography, Vol. V* (pp. 387–413). New York: Appleton-Century-Crofts.

Skinner, B. F. (1971). *Beyond Freedom and Dignity.* New York: Alfred A. Knopf.

Skinner, B. F. (1974). *About Behaviorism.* New York: Alfred A. Knopf.

Skinner, B. F. (1976). *Particulars of My Life.* New York: Alfred A. Knopf.

Skinner, B. F. (1979). *The Shaping of a Behaviorist.* New York: Alfred A. Knopf.

Skinner, B. F. (1983). *A Matter of Consequences.* New York: Alfred A. Knopf.

Biographical Sources

Bjork, D. W. (1997). *B. F. Skinner: A Life.* Washington, DC: American Psychological Association.

Weigel, J. A. (1977). *B. F. Skinner.* Boston: Hall.

Other Suggested Readings

Elms, A. C. (1994). Skinner's Dark Year and Walden Two. In *Uncovering Lives: The Uneasy Alliance of Biography and Psychology.* New York: Oxford University Press.

Evans, R. I. (1968). *B. F. Skinner: The Man and His Ideas.* New York: Dutton.

Lattal, K. A. (Ed.). (1992). Reflections on B. F. Skinner and psychology [Special Issue]. *American Psychologist, 47.*

Nye, R. D. (1992). *The Legacy of B. F. Skinner.* Pacific Grove, CA: Brooks/Cole.

Siegel, P. F. (1996). The meaning of behaviorism for B. F. Skinner. *Psychoanalytic Psychology, 13,* 343–365.

Smith, L., & Woodward, W. (Eds.). (1996). *B. F. Skinner and Behaviorism in American Culture*. Bethlehem: Lehigh University Press.

NOTES

1. B. F. Skinner (1976). *Particulars of My Life* (p. 204). New York: Alfred A. Knopf.
2. Skinner, ibid., 204–205.
3. B. F. Skinner (1967). B. F. Skinner. In Edwin Boring & Gardner Lindzey (Eds.), *A History of Psychology in Autobiography, Vol. V.* (p. 395). New York: Appleton-Century-Crofts.
4. Skinner (1976). *Particulars of My Life* (p. 291). New York: Alfred A. Knopf.
5. Skinner, ibid., 298.
6. John B. Watson (1924). *Behaviorism* (p. 82). New York: Norton.
7. B. F. Skinner (1953). *Science and Human Behavior* (p. 14). New York: Free Press.
8. Skinner, ibid., 27–30.
9. B. F. Skinner (1956). A case history in scientific method. *American Psychologist, 11,* 223.
10. Skinner, ibid., 223–224.
11. Skinner, ibid., 224.
12. B. F. Skinner (1938). *The Behavior of Organisms* (p. 54). New York: Appleton-Century-Crofts.
13. Skinner's utopia: Panacea, or path to hell? *Time*, 1971, 47.
14. Skinner (1953). *Science and Human Behavior* (p. 162). New York: Free Press.
15. Skinner, ibid., 164.
16. Skinner, ibid., 167.
17. Skinner, ibid., 260–261.
18. Skinner, ibid., 284–287.
19. Skinner, ibid., 376.
20. Skinner, ibid., 31.
21. Skinner, ibid., 35.
22. Skinner (1976). *Particulars of My Life* (p. 6). New York: Alfred A. Knopf.
23. Skinner, ibid., 7–8.
24. Skinner, ibid., 38.
25. Skinner, ibid., 60.
26. Skinner, ibid., 61.
27. Skinner, ibid., 62.

28. Skinner, ibid., 64.

29. Skinner, ibid., 121.

30. Skinner, ibid., 52.

31. Skinner, ibid., 52.

32. Skinner, ibid., 82.

33. Skinner, ibid., 184.

34. Skinner, ibid., 134.

35. Skinner, ibid., 169.

36. Skinner, ibid., 213.

37. Skinner, ibid., 185.

38. Skinner, ibid., 195.

39. Skinner (1967). B. F. Skinner. In Edwin Boring & Gardner Lindzey (Eds.), *A History of Psychology in Autobiography, Vol. V* (p. 388). New York: Appleton-Century-Crofts.

40. Skinner (1976). *Particulars of My Life* (p. 210). New York: Alfred A. Knopf.

41. Skinner, ibid., 209.

42. Skinner, ibid., 210.

43. Skinner, ibid., 210.

44. Skinner, ibid., 202–203.

45. Skinner, ibid., 249.

46. Skinner, ibid., 249.

47. Skinner, ibid., 264–265.

48. B. F. Skinner (1979). *The Shaping of a Behaviorist* (pp. 297–298). New York: Alfred A. Knopf.

49. Skinner (1967). B. F. Skinner. In Edwin Boring & Gardner Lindzey (Eds.), *A History of Psychology in Autobiography, Vol. V* (p. 403). New York: Appleton-Century-Crofts.

50. Skinner, *The Shaping of a Behaviorist* (p. 216). New York: Knopf.

51. Skinner, ibid., 290.

52. Skinner, ibid., 291.

53. B. F. Skinner (1962). *Walden Two* (p. 96). New York: Macmillan.

54. Skinner, ibid., 102.

55. Skinner, ibid., 105–106.

56. Skinner, ibid., 256–257.

57. Skinner, ibid., 262–263.

58. Skinner, ibid., 249.

59. James Korn, Roger Davis, & Stephen Davis (1991). Historians' and chairpersons' judgements of eminence among psychologists. *American Psychologist, 46,* 789–792.

4

THE PHENOMENOLOGICAL APPROACH: CARL ROGERS

Carl Rogers had been practicing psychotherapy for over a decade before it struck him that he had a novel approach to offer the field. The occasion was an invited address he gave to the counseling program at the University of Minnesota in 1940. Rogers had just been hired as a professor at Ohio State University after having worked for 13 years at child psychology clinics. When he was invited that year to speak to the counseling program at Minnesota about the process of psychotherapy, he decided to give his talk the title "Newer Concepts in Psychotherapy." In this talk, Rogers began by first criticizing traditional methods of psychotherapy as outmoded. But Minnesota was known as one of the leading centers in the country for training in these traditional methods, and his talk aroused a great furor. It was this furor that confirmed for Rogers what his graduate students at Ohio State had been telling him that year: that he had something truly unique to say. Shortly after he returned from Minnesota he began to write a book, *Counseling and Psychotherapy: Newer Concepts in Practice* (1942), to introduce his new approach to psychotherapy. Out of this new view of therapy later grew a new approach to understanding persons, with radically different assumptions than those we have seen in previous chapters in the psychodynamic and behavioral models. Before we look at the theory of persons that Rogers developed, let us first look briefly at how he came to pursue the unusual methods of psychotherapy out of which this theory grew.

Upon graduating from college in 1924, Rogers originally intended to pursue a career in religious work. After considering various seminaries he chose to begin his graduate studies at Union Theological Seminary in New York, because it was reputed to be the most liberal seminary in the country. Yet still by his second year there Rogers found himself frustrated with having ideas fed to him. Along with a number of other students, he petitioned the administration to be allowed to set up a seminar with no instructor and no curriculum but the students' own questions. Somewhat to their surprise, the students were granted their request. In this seminar, a group of open-minded students took up important religious and philosophical problems, following their questions and doubts freely to see where they led. In Rogers' case, they led him out of religious work. He felt that the seminar played a profound role in his developing a philosophy of life that was truly his own, rather than one that was fed to him by others, and he decided that he could not choose a profession in which he was required to believe in a specified doctrine. The next fall Rogers left Union and religious studies, moving across the street to begin graduate study in psychology at Columbia University.

In the following years studying psychology, Rogers was exposed to the two approaches we have examined in previous chapters. His course work at Columbia first taught him to understand people from the outside by means of objective testing, as faculty members there scorned such things as intrapsychic dynamics and considered "Freud" a dirty word. Then his clinical internship at the Institute for Child Guidance trained him in the psychodynamic approach of understanding people through interpretation of unconscious dynamics. Rogers began his professional life as a therapist by relying heavily on this psychodynamic approach. In his early years working at the Society for the Prevention of Cruelty to Children, however, he became disillusioned with what he was to call "directive" approaches to therapy, whether those were based on behavioral or psychodynamic assumptions. In an autobiographical chapter he wrote later in life, he pointed to three events from these years that promoted this disillusionment.

The first event occurred when he was working with one of his first clients, a boy with a compulsion to set fires. Rogers had read a Freudian analysis that argued that delinquency is symbolic of sexual conflict, and that if the sexual conflict is uncovered the delinquency will end. Using this model, Rogers worked with the boy to eventually trace his desire to set fires to his sexual impulse to masturbate. Rogers was delighted with this analytic success. He thus ended the therapy and the boy was released from the detention home on probation. When shortly thereafter the boy was found setting another fire, Rogers was jolted. He later recalled this as a moment when he was struck with the realization that authoritative teachings could actually be wrong.

This incident began a shift in attitude that was exposed a few years later in the second event that Rogers recalled in illustrating his growing disillusionment with directive approaches to therapy. In his first year at the Society for the Prevention of Cruelty to Children, Rogers had led a discussion group on interviewing and had used a published account of an interview to demonstrate effective technique. The account was an interview a caseworker had conducted with a parent that Rogers originally had thought shrewd, insightful, and on the mark. But several years later, when Rogers dug up the interview to use again, he was appalled at what he found. Looking at this same interview, he now saw it as a legalistic line of questioning that convicted the parent of unconscious motives and wrung from her an admission of guilt. He now felt sure that "insight" gained in this way could certainly be of no lasting help to the client.

The third event occurred a few years after this one. Rogers had learned from his previous experiences to be more subtle in interpreting a client's behavior, but he was still assuming that his role was to direct the client toward his own expert understanding of the material. He had worked for many weeks with a mother who had a troubled son, trying to patiently lead her to the view he held of her case: that her early rejection of her son had led him to be the hellion that he was. But despite the client's obvious intelligence, she was entirely unable to see the pattern Rogers persistently tried to direct her toward. He finally gave up, telling her that although they had tried they had failed, and they may as well stop their contacts. The woman agreed and began to leave his office. But at the doorway she stopped and turned to ask him if he ever took adults for counseling. When he replied that he did she came back in, declared that she would like some help for herself, and sat down to pour out her despair about her marriage. This new direction resulted in a successful therapy for the woman and also for her son, and this convinced Rogers that it is the client who knows what direction to go in therapy. Thus, through this series of experiences, Rogers came to reject traditional directive approaches to psychotherapy and to develop a newer nondirective approach.

When Rogers moved to Ohio State and began to teach a graduate training course on techniques of psychotherapy, he began to explicitly distinguish his nondirective method of therapy from directive methods such as advice and persuasion or explanation and intellectual interpretation. He argued that directive methods operate by two basic assumptions: that the therapist is the one most competent to decide the goal of therapy, and that the therapist knows best how to get the client to the therapist-chosen goal. The nondirective method holds a fundamentally different set of assumptions: that the client, not the therapist, knows best the goal for his or her therapy and also knows best the direction to take to reach this goal. Whereas directive approaches imply by their methods that the therapist is superior to the client, who is incapable of responsibly choosing his or her own goal, the nondirective approach implies by its methods a valuing of the client's right and capacity to be independent and to maintain his or her own psychological integrity.

It is this argument that Rogers made when he addressed his listeners in the talk he gave to the counseling program at Minnesota. Introducing directive techniques as "outworn and discarded," he illustrated the directive techniques of advice and persuasion in particular, using a therapist's written account of an interview with a young man with social problems. In this account the therapist advised the client that his shyness was a defect and persuaded him to undertake a number of prescribed steps to change it. Rogers characterized the therapist's approach in this case as "vicious" and found it destined for disaster. On the one hand, he argued, for a client who has a tendency to be dependent, such an approach would drive him deeper into dependency and his growth would be impeded. On the other hand, for a client who has a good deal of independence, such an approach would require him to reject the therapist's suggestions in order to retain his own integrity. What Rogers did not say was that the therapist who had given this account was from the University of Minnesota and acting as Rogers' host at that very moment.

It is no wonder that Rogers' talk evoked the strong response that it did. He had come to an established program for directive methods of psychotherapy and had spoken out against such methods, even speaking out explicitly against one of the program's own members. In thus speaking out against one of the main authorities of directiveness, Rogers revealed himself to be playing the part of the independent individual who rejects the directions of an authority so as to retain his own integrity. We have seen how Rogers pointed to three events in his professional work as a therapist that fed into this rejection. But the autobiographical record also reveals that Rogers had shown a pattern of rejecting dogma and authority long before he had these experiences as a therapist. In his earlier studies in religion he had first selected the most liberal seminary in the country, next petitioned for a student-led seminar so that ideas would not be fed to him, and finally completely rejected the field because it required acceptance of a religious creed. Rogers had rejected the authorities of religion before rejecting the authorities of psychology. We might thus suspect that we will find personal as well as professional sources for the aversion to direction by an external authority that was an important kernel of Rogers' theory of therapy and his later theory of persons.

WORK

Rogers' book *Counseling and Psychotherapy* (1942) was published 2 years after he arrived at Ohio State. It was based both on his work as a therapist before coming to Ohio State and on his work in articulating the process of therapy to his graduate students during his first 2 years there. To teach the process of therapy in an advanced seminar with graduate students, Rogers initiated a training method that had never been used before in an academic setting: the analysis of recorded interviews of actual therapy sessions. At that time the published literature on psychotherapy consisted entirely of summary accounts of cases by therapists. Rogers found these accounts unsatisfactory from a scientific point of view, because they were potentially biased by the perspective of the therapist who made the summary. Such accounts were also insufficient for the purpose of clinical supervision, because a supervisor could only evaluate what the trainee knew to report of his or her clinical work. Previously Rogers had written that verbatim records of full cases of therapy would be a valuable contribution to the field. But recording technology at that time had made it difficult to capture verbatim records.

At Ohio State, Rogers found a graduate student with skill in radio and electronics, and with a grant from the department they were able to set up the necessary equipment and conditions to record clear interviews. The process required using two recording machines, alternating in use every 3 minutes, one recording on a 78-rpm disk for its 3 minutes while the disk on the other machine was being flipped or replaced to be ready for the next 3-minute interval. The stylus cut an actual groove in the disk so that shavings had to be continually brushed away, and because of the flipping of the disks transcribing the interview required moving from face 1 on one disk to face 1 on another, then back to face 2 on the first disk and so on. It was a laborious process, but with the enthusiasm of graduate students and a new professor it was eagerly undertaken. Rogers and his students thus began recording the therapy sessions conducted in the training program at Ohio State. From this process came the verbatim record of a complete therapy over eight sessions with a young man given the pseudonym "Herbert Bryan." When Rogers published the complete record of this case in *Counseling and Psychotherapy* (1942) it was the first such case ever to be fully recorded, transcribed, and published. An examination of the case reveals that it was an important source for illustrating Rogers' theory of therapy and for developing Rogers' theory of persons.

Early Case Study

Herbert Bryan was a young man in his late 20s who had come to the counseling center at Ohio State for help with what he saw as deep-seated problems. It was not the first time he had sought help. In high school he had attended a behaviorally oriented institute for speech defects to work on a speech impediment, but he thought the treatment too superficial and found no benefit from it. In college he went to a psychodynamically oriented university counselor to try to get to the root of his trouble, but this too provided no help. Mr. Bryan, an intelligent man who had read widely in psychology, then tried various techniques of self-therapy, ranging from an analysis of his childhood memories to a technique of behaving as if happy. He came to the counseling center at Ohio State with the feeling that all past methods had failed him and with the hope of finding a new and this time fruitful approach.

The audiotaped recording of the eight sessions of his psychotherapy would put at Rogers' disposal the word-for-word record of a full case of therapy. A close analysis of the particular remarks made by the counselor and their influence on the course of the therapy would allow Rogers to assess the value of his nascent theory of therapy. More than this, a detailed study of the articulate and sophisticated expressions of this intelligent client would also intimate concepts for Rogers' yet to be conceived theory of persons. Let us look at the record of the therapy of Herbert Bryan to see how his case provided an illustration of Rogers' theory of therapy and the foundation for Rogers' later theory of persons.

The full account of the case covers almost 200 published pages. Rogers reports each statement by the therapist preceded with a "C" to indicate the counselor, and each statement by Mr. Bryan preceded with an "S" to indicate the subject. He numbers these from C1 and S1 in the first interview to C614 and S614 in the eighth and final interview. The therapy begins as follows:*

C1. Well, now, we were so concerned yesterday about these various aspects of whether or not we were to go ahead with it, that I don't know that I have as clear a picture as I'd like to have of what's on your mind, so go ahead and tell me.

  S1. Well, as accurately as I can convey the idea, I would term it a blocking which has manifestations in several fields.

C2. M-hm.

S2. The—in my earlier childhood the symptom of blocking which was emphasized on my consciousness was in speech. I developed a speech impediment along about the sixth grade.

---

*From Rogers, Carl R. *Counseling and Psychotherapy.* Copyright © 1942 by Houghton Mifflin Company. Reprinted with permission.

Then, as I matured, I noticed a blocking in sexual situations. However, not—not in the voyeuristic situation, only in an intercourse situation; oftentimes I had difficulty there. Also an unpleasant tight feeling in the lower abdomen, as if, to use an analogy, there were some sort of a cold, hard axe or some other such thing pressing against the libido in such a way as to block it.

C3. M-hm . . .

S6. And sometimes it gets very excruciating. I just seem to be held down, as it were, blocked in all realms of life.

C7. A feeling of real pain, is that what you mean?

S7. Oh yes.

C8. M-hm.

S8. And then sometimes for short periods it mysteriously goes. I mean, there's no particular ideology with its going. I get release, and then I'm very active and very happy during these short periods.[1]

We have two threads to follow in looking at the unfolding case material. On the one hand, we want to understand Mr. Bryan's situation, to know what gives him trouble and why. On the other hand, we want to understand the process of therapy, to discover what the counselor does to help Mr. Bryan with his troubles. Let us keep an eye toward each as we look at excerpts from this case, picking up first the thread of the counselor's method. From the very first remark of the therapy, the counselor is taking a nondirective approach. His initial query, asking simply what is on Mr. Bryan's mind, is very broad and allows Mr. Bryan to choose for himself how to talk about his troubles. A traditional interviewer would have had a list of specific questions to pursue in an initial diagnostic interview and might have begun the inquiry with one of these predetermined questions. Here, the counselor makes it clear from the outset that what he wants to know is only how Mr. Bryan himself experiences his own situation. Further, when Mr. Bryan in his opening remarks makes a brief pause, the counselor simply encourages his line of thinking with a "M-hm." This kind of response enables the client to continue to explore his experience without the therapist determining the direction of that exploration. When a few sentences later Mr. Bryan expresses an excruciating feeling, the counselor speaks to simply reflect that feeling of pain back to him. This gives Mr. Bryan the experience of having this feeling understood without being judged, and this allows him to then go on to report times when he is free of the blocking.

By using this nondirective approach, the counselor provides from the very start an atmosphere in which Mr. Bryan is able to explore his own experience of his troubles. Turning then to our second concern, what does Mr. Bryan reveal in the first interview about his troubles? As an intelligent individual who had previously tried various kinds of therapy, Mr. Bryan proves to have a sophisticated view both of the nature of his troubles and of their origin. In his opening account we find him describing a palpable and excruciating blocking, showing itself in childhood in his speech and later in his sexuality. As the interview progresses he identifies this blocking as well in his pursuit of his work as a photographer and in other activities that he characterizes as involving "manly" initiative. Further, he locates the origin of this feeling of blocking in the harsh prohibitions his parents made of his childhood explorations of sexuality and initiative. Talking about his early exploration of sexuality he says:

> My mother even whipped me one time for talking with a friend of mine. She thought it was terrible. We had noticed, well, different animals and so forth, and she was very horrified. I remember she worked up to quite a dramatic climax. She said, "Well, did you talk about locusts?" and "Did you mention animals?" and then "Did you mention human beings?" Worked up to a climax, and then she whipped me for, well, for even mentioning the facts. I suppose I assumed that if it were horrible to talk about, it would even be more horrible to do.[2]

Later he depicts his father too as harsh and judgmental in the face of his childish explorations:

> I remember some very old nightmares that might be of interest. When I was very young, I could read at a very early age. I did a lot of reading. I read a book about Pike, the Western explorer after whom the Peak was named, and after I had finished the book I dreamed that I was ascending Pike's Peak, and when I reached the summit, there was my father, looking very, very stern. His aspect was intensely forbidding.[3]

Thus, in childhood, Mr. Bryan experienced his parents as forbidding his explorations of sexuality and initiative. His current symptoms of blocking suggest that at some level he has come to adopt his parents' prohibitions as his own, experiencing a physical blocking when he pursues activities of sexuality and initiative that his parents had previously forbidden. Yet he reports that, intellectually, he values his sexuality and initiative and rejects his parents' attitudes. The problem is, this intellectual evaluation on his part does not influence his gut feeling. He experiences an incongruity within himself, and is unable to align his gut feeling with his intellect. At the close of the first interview he tells the counselor:

> Here's the way I can perhaps illustrate it diagrammatically. Here (*pointing to head*) and here (*pointing to chest*) I am pretty balanced. I know exactly what I want and how to get it. But down here (*pointing to lower abdomen*) there's blocking...what it amounts to is—that I'm a pagan intellectually and in my heart, but in my guts I'm a perfect puritan.[4]

If this, then, is the nature of Mr. Bryan's trouble, what should the counselor do about it? Should he weigh in to support one side of the struggle and tip the balance in its favor? Although this might be the approach of a directive therapist, it is certainly not the approach this nondirective therapist would take. What he does instead is to help Mr. Bryan to fully explore his own experience of the two sides of his struggle, stubbornly refusing to judge one side as better or worse during the course of this exploration, and to make clear that it is only Mr. Bryan who can make the choice of which path to pursue based on his own very personal values. In the beginning of the therapy Mr. Bryan appears to look for external direction from the therapist and to feel frustrated not to get it. But the counselor persists in his unwavering faith in Mr. Bryan's capacity to direct himself, so that by the end of the therapy Mr. Bryan has been able to develop this faith in himself as well. An important turning point occurs in the fourth interview, as Mr. Bryan muses on his wish to find some kind of external directive for his choice, if not from the therapist then from a sort of cosmic rule. He says:

> If there were some cosmic yardstick, some sort of a cosmic absolute, uh—comparable to the religious person's absolute trust in

God, you see, uh—then I could have a philosophic proof that one set of values was definitely better than the other, but this way I know that I cannot have such a philosophic proof, or at least I haven't run across it. We can never prove values—we always have to assume them. I think as a philosopher you'll have to agree with me.

C314. I don't know whether it's as a philosopher, but I certainly would agree with you that, in situations of this kind, I don't think there is any proof that could be advanced that would prove one set of values rather than the other.

S315. Nothing out in the universe. It all must lie within ourselves.

C315. It comes right back to the naked self pretty much, doesn't it? Here are two general roads; which do you prefer? It comes right down to a personal and probably quite unphilosophical choice.

S316. Yes. In other words, I can't—I can't look to the cosmos and say, "Now which of the two roads do you approve of?" I can't—

C316. You can, and some people do, but it's doubtful if that is what really settles it.

S317. Yes, I imagine that when a person does make a change they oftentimes think that they're doing it for God, but they're really doing it for themselves. Well (*thoughtfully*), perhaps I don't need anything out in the cosmos, then.

C317. Well, there's just the chance that you've got enough within yourself.[5]

By the seventh interview Mr. Bryan has made his choice to pursue the "manly" activities of sexuality and initiative even though the struggle may be great. To deal with this struggle his prescription for himself is to force himself into difficult situations and dwell on any improvement he notices in his feelings, valuing the satisfaction he finds. Initially he begins to ask the counselor whether this prescription is a good one, but then he stops to reflect on the counselor's technique throughout the therapy. He says:

I was wondering whether your technique might not be to have every neurotic sort of prescribe for himself—that is—then I asked myself, does my prescription mean—does that above prescription that I made—does that mean that the technique would be generally the same for all people, or is it that every neurotic who seeks to do something about it can get an inkling of what to do in his own individual case, since he has a budding healthy desire—does that budding desire give each individual inklings of what to do for his own particular case, or is it sort of a generalized technique?

C497. I think it's both, and it seems to me that's a beautiful statement of it. That is, that each person—I don't care whether they're neurotic or not—essentially *has* to write his own prescription. I mean, if anybody could write it for him, why fine—why have him write it himself? But when you get right down to it, who knows what steps you can take and what steps would really improve your situation? Well, you don't know off-hand, but no one else can tell you either.

S497. Well, I got a pretty definite conviction there that the budding healthy desire has implicit in it means to its achievement for each of the individuals, and that the fact that they do want to do something about it will give them inklings of means to employ.[6]

Having found this faith in his own budding healthy desire, Mr. Bryan terminates the therapy himself in the next interview.

The therapy of Herbert Bryan provides a compelling case for the nondirective method Rogers sought to introduce to his students and to the field. Using this method, the counselor apparently was able to free Mr. Bryan from the obstacles that blocked his healthy development. The counselor accomplished this not by trying to instruct Mr. Bryan, but rather by his solid refusal to instruct. It is by this solid refusal to direct Mr. Bryan that the counselor most powerfully conveyed his faith in Mr. Bryan's right and capacity to direct himself, and it is when Mr. Bryan came to believe in this right and capacity himself that he became able to overcome the obstacles that blocked him. This is the primary point that Rogers sought to drive home to his readers in his 1942 book, *Counseling and Psychotherapy*, in which the case of Herbert Bryan appeared.

There are many ways in which we find Rogers eager to disabuse his readers of what he sees as the directive ways of traditional therapies. The first we might identify is in his very naming of his method of therapy, calling it "nondirective" so as to define it by its negation of these methods. Another appears when he first sets out to define the counseling relationship in his form of therapy, which he also defines through a negation of various other relationships that are authoritative in character. He writes:

> Perhaps the best way to begin the discussion is by explaining what the counseling relationship is not. In speaking of therapy at its best, we may make a number of negative statements. The therapeutic relationship is not, for example, a parent-child relationship, with its deep affectionate ties, its characteristic dependence on the one hand and the acceptance of an authoritative and responsible role on the other... Neither is the counseling relationship a typical teacher-pupil relationship, with its implications of superior and inferior status... Nor is therapy based on a physician-patient relationship, with its characteristics of expert diagnosis and authoritative advice on the part of the physician, submissive acceptance and dependence on the part of the patient.[7]

In making this claim Rogers was making a radical point for his time, seeking to overturn the dominant paradigm for psychotherapy. For it was typical in that era to use the language of "doctor" and "patient" when referring to the psychotherapy relationship, and with it to employ the attendant presumption of a hierarchical relationship between authority and subordinate. Whether in a psychodynamic therapy where the therapist was expected to be viewed as a parent-substitute, a behavioral therapy where the therapist gave homework assignments akin to a teacher, or in a medical approach where the therapist prescribed drugs, no prevailing therapy was free of the assumption that it was the therapist who knew best. Rogers was seeking to dismantle the authority of the "doctor" and to empower the "patient," and he introduced the terms *counselor* and *client* to mark this departure from the prevailing convention. Indeed, Rogers would successfully revolutionize the field of psychotherapy by this transfer of power and of responsibility.

But what was the source for this insight that Rogers was able to contribute to the field? It appears as if it was called for by Herbert Bryan himself. Blocked by the authoritative posture of his parents and continuing to seek this authority from his counselor, it was only by finding faith in his own capacity for self-direction that he was able to overcome his impasse. But by now we should know that what a theorist extracts from his or her observations is not only a function of the events themselves but also of his or her way of looking at them. The case of Herbert Bryan seems to make salient the issue of rejecting external authority, but there are already signals that this issue was personally salient to Rogers himself. We have seen in the brief autobiographical record so far that Rogers found his way to the field of psychology because he could not abide the external directions of religion. And as we look now at his book on his new form of therapy, we find that he defines his approach by emphasizing the directiveness of other approaches and characterizing his own through a negation of this posture. Could it be that Rogers was introducing this issue to the case of Herbert Bryan more than was warranted?

One thing that would seem to make this unlikely is that the case of Herbert Bryan was recorded and presented verbatim; indeed Rogers himself was offering this method of verbatim accounting in order to avoid the biases that can be introduced by general summaries of a case. Because of this invaluable contribution we are able to reexamine the case more closely. In doing so, we discover that in fact the issue of external direction is not one that Mr. Bryan himself introduced to the therapy. Let us look closely at an exchange that occurs in the very first session.

Mr. Bryan is discussing his feeling of blocking and wondering how it can be overcome. He says:

> I feel that there's some sort of a hidden touchstone that provides the driving force for the oppression, and that there is—I feel it is a blind impulse, rather immune to logic, but of course not necessarily immune to change, that is, I mean, there are other ways besides logic, of course—
>
> C52. In other words, you haven't been able to reason yourself out of it—nor has anyone else, is that it?[8]

So far so good, until we look again with closer attention. The counselor's reflection that Mr. Bryan cannot reason himself out of his situation seems to be on the mark, but why has he added the extra clause: "nor has anyone else"? This issue does not appear at all in Mr. Bryan's remarks. The interchange continues:

> Yes. In other words, I even get the impression that I have a full cognitive appreciation of the difficulty, and that even if I

were—even if there were no more new ideas to come out, that would have nothing to do with the change . . . I don't believe that anybody is ever persuaded by logic or reasoning—it's emotional undercurrents which undergo the change, and logic, that's just a rationalization—sort of a rack to hang your coat on.

C53. In other words, you feel that nobody could persuade you out of this situation.[9]

Now it is clear something is amiss. Mr. Bryan is calling attention to the difference between logical reasoning and emotional conviction. The counselor, in distinction, is calling attention to the issue of being persuaded by another. In his first response the counselor had attended to Mr. Bryan's issue before adding his own, and he had ended his remarks with a query: "is that it?" Now he has dropped Mr. Bryan's issue and dropped his question whether his rephrasing is correct. And in his next remarks we find that Mr. Bryan begins to accept the shift in focus that the counselor is now pushing:

No. I feel that I already know the logic of it, but that doesn't effect a cure. Now, I feel that in the last analysis—I think that psychoanalysis is probably a matter of prestige—prestige persuasion. I feel that if I get a confidence in you, that you know more about it than I do—that regardless of the logic—that is, I feel I am your equal in logic, but that you are my superior in certain emotion-changing techniques.

C54. In other words, if you felt that gradually you had enough confidence, and so on, in me, I might be able to bring about some change in you, but you couldn't very well do that by yourself.[10]

The shift has now been made, from a focus on the issue of logic versus emotion (introduced by Mr. Bryan) to that on the issue of internal versus external direction (introduced by the counselor).

If we can see that the counselor has introduced this shift in focus, does Rogers? When he presents this case in the book, Rogers not only provides the line by line exchange between the counselor and Mr. Bryan but also offers his own commentary on the exchange as it unfolds. At times in the book Rogers is critical of the counselor's approach, but for this exchange he is not. When in C53 the counselor asserts his reinterpretation of Mr. Bryan's struggle as one of internal versus external direction, Rogers as the book author writes in a footnote about this remark that it "clarifies the attitude that is being expressed."[11] And in his footnote to the counselor's statement in C54, Rogers praises the counselor for recognizing Mr. Bryan's "dependent feeling" and says that "if he had failed to recognize it, undoubtedly it would have cropped out again."[12] We should be wary when an author uses a term such as "undoubtedly". In this case it reflects a certainty that Rogers felt about the importance of the issue of dependency on external direction to the client, but his certainty may have derived instead from its importance to Rogers himself. In fact, in the very remark that Mr. Bryan had made in S50 before the beginning of this exchange, he had said this: "Well, after all, the whole thing is occurring within me, and it's what might be termed a war within my own house."[13] There is no hint of relinquishing his responsibility to an external authority here.

Why does Rogers fail to see the bias introduced here by the counselor? The answer is that Rogers shares the counselor's bias, for he himself is the counselor of Herbert Bryan. This fact is indirectly conveyed to us at the end of the case, when in the concluding minutes of the last interview Mr. Bryan says to the counselor: "You're sort of a pioneer in this, aren't you? Is this largely your own technique?"[14] Although Rogers never explicitly identified himself as Mr. Bryan's therapist in his 1942 book, he later acknowledged that he was. Furthermore, Rogers later came to acknowledge that despite his belief in following the client's lead, he had displayed "subtle directiveness"[15] in the case of Herbert Bryan. Ironically, one way that he did so was by directing Mr. Bryan to the issue of being directed by another. When we find Rogers' vehement rejection of external direction coupled with his own unwitting act of directing another, we might be led to the hypothesis that Rogers' personal interest in this issue derives from his having experienced unwanted direction in his own life. We will look for evidence of this when we turn to his personal life. At this point, however, we are ready to look at the theory of personality that he elaborated from his therapeutic work.

The Theory

By 1959, Rogers had extracted from his therapy experiences an explicit theory of the nature of persons and the course of their development both in and out of therapy. He presented this theory in a paper titled "A Theory of Therapy, Personality, and Interpersonal Relationships, As Developed in the Client-Centered Framework." At the core of this theory is the proposition that individuals are born with one exclusive motive, which he calls *the actualizing tendency*. This is an innate tendency to develop all of our capacities so as to maintain or enhance ourselves. According to Rogers, this inborn motive toward actualization is an inherently positive and trustworthy impulse toward the growth and development of one's own *organism*. As infants we experience our world in terms of this goal of actualization, evaluating positively those experiences we perceive as maintaining or enhancing our organism and evaluating negatively those experiences we perceive as impeding this maintenance or enhancement. From birth, this organismic valuing is based on the individual's own experience, what Rogers calls *the phenomenal field*. Rogers emphasizes that it is our subjective experience that is crucial and that determines our valuation and consequent behavior, not some postulated objective environment apart from the organism. For example, a stranger might speak to two infants in exactly the same voice, but one infant might experience the sound as stimulating and so smile, whereas the other experiences the same sound as aversive and so cries.

With development, the individual becomes increasingly autonomous and differentiated in line with the actualizing tendency. An important consequence of this development is the differentiation of *the self*. A portion of our experience gets elaborated into a concept of what is "I" or "me" or "myself." This self-concept consists of those qualities we perceive ourselves to have, the relationships we perceive between ourselves and other people and objects, and the values we attach to these perceived characteristics. It is through our interactions with the environment, especially interactions with other people, that the conceptual pattern of a self is formed.

At this point in the child's development, the evaluations of others become important due to the individual's *need for positive regard*. The individual has a need to experience from others attitudes such as warmth, respect, sympathy, and acceptance. But here emerges the potential problem of development: Often the positive regard of another will be conditional on the individual being a particular way. And often, the positive regard of another will be at odds with the individual's own organismic valuing process. For example, in our own organismic experience we may find it enjoyable to break objects, but our parents may not likewise evaluate this behavior positively. Now we are confronted with a dilemma. If we admit to ourselves that we get satisfaction from experiences that others judge negatively, then this is inconsistent with our self-concept as someone who is good or loveable. Rogers suggests that the normal resolution to this dilemma is that the individual comes to pursue those behaviors that have been positively evaluated by others, rather than those that have been experienced as positive to the actualization of his or her own organism. We live not in terms of our own organismic valuing but rather in terms of values that have been introjected from others, or *conditions of worth.* We cannot regard ourselves positively unless we live in accord with those conditions.

But this resolution has tragic consequences. The values that we have introjected from parents or other intimate figures are experienced as if based on our own sensory and visceral equipment. As a result, our valuing has become divorced from our own organismic functioning and determined instead by the attitudes of others. This establishes a state of *incongruence* between self and experience that is the basis for psychological maladjustment. Experiences that are congruent with the conditions of worth are conceptualized accurately in awareness. But those experiences that run contrary to these conditions of worth are felt as threatening and must be distorted or denied to awareness. This leads to the common neurosis of humanity: We live not as whole persons open to all experiences but rather in estrangement from basic aspects of our experience.

According to Rogers, defensiveness against the threat of perceiving incongruent information applies to all individuals to some degree. Under certain conditions, however, when a significant experience suddenly or obviously demonstrates a substantial incongruence between an individual's self and his or her experience, this process of defense is unable to operate successfully. The result is that the individual will experience anxiety at the coming awareness of the incongruity, the organismic experience will be accurately symbolized in awareness, and the self-structure will be broken and a state of disorganization will result. This is the phenomenology of an acute psychotic breakdown.

What, then, are the conditions by which a common neurosis or acute psychosis can be reversed? According to Rogers the individual's own actualizing tendency can be trusted to move him or her forward toward growth, health, and adjustment, but the obstacles that have impeded this normal process in the first place must be removed. In place of the conditions of worth, the individual must experience from a counselor or other significant person that their positive regard is unconditional. Regardless of how the individual feels or acts, he or she is seen as worthy and lovable, prized and valued as a whole person. When a counselor feels and shows such *unconditional positive regard* toward experiences of which the client is frightened or ashamed, as well as those with which the client is pleased or satisfied, then the client can learn to accept all organismic experiences as part of the self.

Along with unconditional positive regard, however, the counselor must also show *empathic understanding*. If unconditional positive regard is conveyed when the counselor knows little of the client it is of no great value, because further knowledge could disclose aspects of the client that the counselor would not regard positively. If the counselor displays empathy, however, he or she perceives the internal frame of reference of the client with accuracy, sensing the other's hurts and pleasures. When the counselor thoroughly knows and empathically understands the wide variety of the client's feelings and behaviors and still experiences unconditional positive regard, then this is a very profound thing indeed.

Rogers had identified these qualities of unconditional positive regard and empathy as two of the therapeutic conditions in his 1942 book. But in that work he had also identified a third therapeutic quality, a refusal to influence or coerce the client, the quality of being nondirective. By his 1959 paper Rogers had changed the name of his therapy from nondirective to *client-centered*, and he had dropped this third therapeutic condition from his list of defining qualities. But a new third quality had now been introduced, that of *congruence*. By congruence Rogers refers to the counselor's genuineness in the therapeutic relationship, the accurate awareness of his or her own experience in the relationship. Thus, if the counselor is experiencing threat and discomfort in the relationship but is only aware of feeling acceptance and understanding, then this incongruence will have negative consequences for the therapy. The counselor cannot help the client overcome incongruence if he or she is not congruent in the relationship himself or herself.

In the ideal therapeutic relationship, then, the counselor is congruent, empathic, and experiences unconditional positive regard toward the client. Through the combination of these qualities the counselor establishes the conditions for the client's growth toward acceptance of the full range of experiences. This leads the client toward psychological adjustment, which is characterized by an openness to experience without defensiveness, congruence between self and experience, and living by an internal locus of evaluation rather than by externally determined conditions of worth.

Let us now return to the case of Herbert Bryan to see how we can find in it the basis for this elaborated theory of personality. The "budding healthy desire" that Mr. Bryan discovered at the end of the therapy is the actualizing tendency that he was endowed with at birth. It is this tendency that led him initially to be drawn to experiences of sexuality and initiative because they were subjectively felt to be organismically satisfying. But in early childhood his parents set up conditions of worth that were at odds with these organismic values, conveying that their positive regard for him was conditional on his avoiding such behaviors. When as a child he enjoyed exploring sexuality by watching and talking about animals, his mother responded with horror and whipped him; when as a child he pursued fantasies of exploring initiative in a dream about climbing Pike's Peak, he perceived his father as looking intensely stern and forbidding. In order to retain the love of his parents he introjected their values, coming to feel that his own sensory and visceral equipment negatively valued sexuality and initiative through his experience of a blocking sensation. Although intellectually he believed that sexuality and initiative are good behaviors, his valuing was divorced from his own organismic functioning and determined instead by his parents' attitudes. This incongruence between his experience and his self-concept led to the feeling of internal division or incongruence that he identified as his reason for seeking therapy.

The therapy proceeded by the counselor's conveying to Mr. Bryan his empathic understanding, unconditional positive regard, and congruence. From the first statement by the counselor that asked in an open-ended way for Mr. Bryan to convey what is on his mind, the counselor made clear that his wish was to understand Mr. Bryan's internal frame of reference. The counselor attempted to come to know Mr. Bryan's own experience and to show empathy for his feelings, reflecting back to Mr. Bryan those feelings he expressed. In this way Mr. Bryan was encouraged to explore the range of feelings he himself had, including those he had previously denied. As Mr. Bryan undertook this exploration, the counselor made clear that he had unconditional positive regard for the full range of experiences Mr. Bryan had. He did not judge Mr. Bryan nor did he direct him toward certain choices; rather he conveyed that he valued Mr. Bryan's right and ability to choose what he prefers. When in the middle of the therapy Mr. Bryan wondered whether he could look to the cosmos to ask "which of the two roads do you approve of?," the counselor recognized that to seek external approval is a possibility, but he also expressed genuineness when he conveyed that he found it doubtful that such an approach settles the question. Instead he indicated that he trusts that Mr. Bryan may have the answer within himself. This combination of unconditional positive regard and congruence was also conveyed in the penultimate session, when the counselor indicated that he found Mr. Bryan's statement about his budding healthy desire to be beautiful and true. As a result of these therapeutic conditions Mr. Bryan came to regain an internal locus of evaluation, trusting in his own budding healthy desire to make the right choices for himself and no longer feeling the need for therapy.

It should be clear by now how Rogers' theory offers a vital alternative to the two theories we have studied previously. It is a theory that puts at its center the individual's own organismic experience as a valuable directive force. Unlike Skinner's theory in which the role of the external environment is decisive, Rogers' theory asserts that it is the individual's own subjective experience of the world that is paramount and that determines his or her course in life. And unlike Freud's theory in which the individual's basic impulses are seen as dangerous, Rogers' theory trusts the goodness and growth potential of the individual's internal tendencies. It is a theory pervaded with humanity and optimism. Rogers' work as a psychotherapist was one important source of this theory for understanding persons, and we have seen that the case of Herbert Bryan in particular provided evidence for his theoretical concepts. But as we have also seen, Rogers' own personal experiences may have made him more sensitive to some phenomena than to others among his therapeutic observations, and may have even in part led to the formation of the phenomena themselves, because he was the therapist for Mr. Bryan. Let us turn to Rogers' personal life to see if we can find sources for his theoretical concepts in it.

LIFE

When Rogers was in his 60s he was approached by the editors of a series called *A History of Psychology in Autobiography* and asked to contribute a chapter on his life. The chapter he wrote appears in the same volume of the series as one by Skinner. But whereas Skinner went on after this to write a complete autobiography of three volumes, Rogers had no interest in such a task, saying at one point that he preferred to look forward rather than backward. He did, however, provide interviews and written material, including diaries, for a full-length biography by Howard Kirschenbaum, and later provided another set of interviews for an oral history by David Russell. It is from these various sources that we can extract a picture of Rogers' life.

One thing we might be struck by at the outset is some similarities between Rogers' upbringing and Skinner's. Most importantly, both had parents whose religious beliefs led them to employ strict parenting styles. But although Skinner eventually identified with his parents, and his theory shows the effects of this identification, Rogers eventually rejected his parents' judgments, and his theory shows the effects of this rejection. In an interview conducted late in life, Rogers himself remarked: "Some of the most fundamental aspects of my point of view and my approach are sort of the reciprocal of what my parents believed."[16] Although he did not elaborate on this statement at the time, we find support for the idea in his life story.

Childhood

Carl Rogers was born on January 8, 1902, in the town of Oak Park, Illinois, just outside of Chicago. Like Skinner, he grew up in America in the 20th century and was influenced by its prevailing cultural values. The value of progress that we saw in Skinner's work appears in Rogers' work as well, but with the coloring of his own particular palette. For Rogers we find the idea of progress in his focus on the actualizing tendency, an innate and singular human motive that directs the individual to grow and develop toward self-enhancement. Rogers further postulated that the actualizing tendency leads the individual toward increasing autonomy and away from control by external forces. This stress on independence from external control may also be seen to echo another basic aspect of American culture: the founding of the nation through rejection of British control. Although this link may intuitively seem like too much to claim, we will find later that it appeared in Rogers' own imagery: He made an explicit analogy to the Declaration of Independence when talking about an individual's drive toward autonomy and freedom. Finally the concept of democracy, where power is held by the people in the absence of class distinctions, is also found expressed in his theory. The ideal therapeutic relationship, he asserted, is one in which the client is seen to have the knowledge and power to determine his or her own path rather than the therapist having authority over the client.

Rogers was the fourth of six children of Walter and Julia Rogers, preceded by two brothers and one sister and followed by two more brothers. His parents had both been raised on farms, and when he was 12 they bought a farm and moved the family farther away from Chicago. One reason for this move was that they were practical individuals who believed strongly in the virtue of hard work. But the main reason, according to Rogers, was that "they were concerned about the temptations and evils of suburban and city life and wished to get the family away from these threats."[17] Among these threats were such things as dancing, playing cards, watching movies, and drinking soda.

Rogers' parents were both deeply religious, and his mother in particular became increasingly fundamentalist over time. Every day after breakfast, whether there were guests in the house or not, the family would gather in a circle for Bible reading and prayers. One of his mother's favorite Biblical phrases that stuck in Rogers' mind was "All our righteousness is as filthy rags in thy sight, oh Lord." That is, people are at their core utterly sinful. Anxious to protect their children from the temptations to sin, the parents kept a close watch on Rogers and his siblings. As Rogers described it, they were "in many subtle and affectionate ways, very controlling of our behavior."[18] Although he felt sure that his parents loved him, he felt equally sure that they would judge negatively his private thoughts and feelings if they only knew them. Many of Rogers' later theoretical ideas can be seen as a rejection of this world view held by his parents. His parents had believed that people are sinful in their most basic nature, and so had taken the responsibility of judging and directing their children. In contrast, Rogers would assert the essential trustworthiness of an individual's inner being, and so argue that he or she needs to be left free of conditions of worth and external direction.

As a child, however, Rogers showed himself eager for the positive regard of others and sensitive to any lack of it. He was frail in stature and shy in personality, and easily prone to tears. He felt that his parents loved his next older brother Ross more than they loved him, and the feeling was strong enough that he developed the idea that he had been adopted. He was the butt of teasing from his siblings, although teasing was apparently a prominent way all the children related to each other. In the autobiographical chapter he wrote as an adult, Rogers recounted that the children in his family all teased each other unmercifully and that this teasing had a biting edge to it. But his siblings took issue with this account when they read it, insisting that the teasing was all in good fun and part of a playful comradery. They saw Rogers as especially sensitive to the teasing, however, and easily hurt.[19] Thus, he was as a child particularly vulnerable to feeling a lack of positive regard from others, and so in outlining his theory was aware of the problematic role this need for regard could play in the developing person.

In the face of this teasing from siblings and the negative judgments from parents, Rogers kept to his inner world a great deal, and kept this inner world to himself. Looking back from adulthood he reported:

> My life was a very, very private thing . . . I simply knew somehow that what most interested me would not be of interest to other people and might be sort of scorned or thought of as very strange by other people. So the thought of sharing it never occurred to me.[20]

He was a dreamy youngster, so often lost in fantasies of his own creation that this too became a source of teasing from siblings and concern from parents. His brothers and sister needled him about this by calling him "Professor Moony" after an absent-minded comic strip character of the time. Around his 12th birthday, his father took him along on a 2-week business trip to visit various construction sites on the east coast, and Rogers later surmised that "it was an attempt to help me become more interested in real life than fantasy."[21] In one of his writings, he went so far as to say that his childhood fantasies "probably would be classed as schizoid,"[22] by which he meant perhaps to emphasize their lack of contact with reality. At another time he mused that he could easily have become schizophrenic.[23] It is in this childhood immersion in subjectivity that we might find the origin for his later theoretical emphasis on the subjectivity of organismic experience and the phenomenal field.

In moving their family to a farm when Rogers was 12, his parents were probably hoping that this too would spur their son to take more notice of the real world. They assigned him various chores around the farm, including milking the cows and riding the cultivator. The experiences that seemed to have had the most powerful effect, however, were those in which he had primary responsibility for rearing from infancy lambs, pigs, and other animals. The project he pursued with most passion was the rearing of luna moths. One day while walking in the woods surrounding the farm, Rogers came upon two luna moths just emerging from their cocoons. He looked in wonder at the marvelous creatures, as large as a small bird with long swallowtail wings, pale green in color with spots of purple. From that moment on he was fascinated. He got books on moths to read about them. He found and raised their caterpillars, collecting the particular kinds of leaves they needed for food. He attentively nursed them for days and weeks through their 12-month cycle, until at last their cocoons opened to reveal the glorious creatures. It was a process of emergence that he remembered "very vividly" into adulthood, and it may have played an important role in leading to his theoretical emphasis on growth and development via an innate actualizing tendency.

Indeed the whole farm life probably made this salient to Rogers. In one of his papers, in which he was seeking to emphasize that the actualizing tendency operates even in the most maladjusted individuals for whom it is not so apparent, he wrote:

> I remember that in my boyhood, the bin in which we stored our winter's supply of potatoes was in the basement, several feet below a small window. The conditions were unfavorable, but the potatoes would begin to sprout—pale white sprouts, so unlike the healthy green shoots they sent up when planted in the soil

in the spring. But these sad, spindly sprouts would grow 2 or 3 feet in length as they reached toward the distant light of the window. The sprouts were, in their bizarre, futile growth, a sort of desperate expression of the directional tendency... In dealing with clients whose lives have been terribly warped, in working with men and women on the back wards of state hospitals, I often think of those potato sprouts. So unfavorable have been the conditions in which these people have developed that their lives often seem abnormal, twisted, scarcely human. Yet, the directional tendency in them can be trusted.[24]

As a child at home, Rogers dutifully followed the directions laid down by his parents. But one incident gave a foreshadowing of his future rebellion against authority. A small, 1-acre plot of land had been fenced off by the previous owners of the farm, and after reading some books on feeding and growing techniques, Rogers persuaded his father to let him and his younger brothers use this field as an experimental plot. For a year they worked the field, conducting experiments comparing different kinds of grains and having great fun doing it. After that year, however, Rogers' father said that he wanted to take the fence down and include the plot with the main field. Rogers suspected that the farm foreman had a hand in this decision, embarrassed by what onlookers would think of the odd things going on in this plot next to a respectable field. Rogers recalled his response later:

> That really got me. I felt it was unfair and unjust. I fought and fought for that, and lost, and was really angry and upset. I remember crying about it. They'd taken away something that was very precious to me and my brothers for no sound reason. I felt very unjustly treated.[25]

Here we see him ready to stand up for what is personally meaningful, finding it precious, despite the fact that others see it as odd and embarrassing.

Young Adulthood

When Rogers left home for college in 1919, he initially continued to follow the directions laid down by his family. He went to the University of Wisconsin, not because of any evaluation of the school itself, but because both of his parents and all three of his older siblings had gone there and it was expected that he would do so as well. In his first year he roomed with his brother Ross, who was then a senior, in the YMCA dormitory. His religious upbringing made the YMCA a congenial home, and he joined a group that met every Sunday for worship, study, and social activities. His deep involvement in religion, as well as his willingness to be led by an external power, are revealed in a diary he kept at the time. In November of his freshman year, for example, he wrote about a Fellowship meeting:

> "Dad" Wolfe spoke on "Selecting a Life Work." Oh, it's wonderful to feel that God will really lead me to my life work, and I *know* He will, for never has he deserted me. Just the same, tho, it is an awesome thing to think that a wrong decision will wreck my life, but oh, how I'll try and keep my life in tune with God, so that He can guide me. I have plenty of ambition, in fact I sometimes think I'm too ambitious, but if I can only keep that terrible swelling force within me in the right path, I know all will be well.[26]

At this point in his life he was assuming an attitude of dependence on an external authority, and seeing the swelling force that came from within himself as "terrible" and needing to be reined into the right path.

Although Rogers had come to Wisconsin expecting to study agriculture in preparation for a career in farming, he soon abandoned this plan in favor of a career in the ministry. He became increasingly absorbed in religious activities, helping to organize religious conferences on his own campus and traveling to conferences in other states. This involvement brought him an opportunity in his junior year that was to profoundly alter his life course. A conference of the World Student Christian Federation was being planned in Peking, China. From across the United States, 10 youths were chosen to represent their country as delegates to the conference. Beyond going to the week-long conference in Peking, they would also take part in various meetings and speaking engagements throughout China, Hong Kong, Korea, Japan, the Philippines, and Hawaii over a period of months. When Rogers was selected as a student delegate to this conference, he wept with surprise and joy. He felt sure that his selection meant that God had a great plan for him.

In February of 1922, he and other students and professional workers boarded a ship for China. Although his previous exposure had been to religious belief of a conservative and evangelistic kind, on this trip Rogers found students, leaders, and scholars from all parts of the country and all types of experience with divergent religious beliefs. In them he found a group of open-minded individuals eager to explore their religious understandings in uninterrupted discussions on the 3-week voyage across the ocean. They asked themselves the most basic questions that for Rogers' parents had been unthinkable to ask, such as whether Christ was really the son of God or simply a man like other men. In the face of evidence that sincere and honest people could have such divergent religious beliefs, Rogers' thinking was stretched in ways it had never before been stretched. The result was that his views became liberalized, and he realized that he could no longer go along with his parents' beliefs. Only 5 days into the journey he wrote in his diary:

> We have had many discussions already on lots of the doubtful points, and I am thankful beyond words that we are with a group of leaders who are all forward-looking, young minded people, who are still building up their own faiths, not dogmatists who are sure that their own interpretation is the only one. The more we talk and think, the more I am finding it possible to define what I myself believe.[27]

This exposure probably impressed on Rogers the variability of subjective experiences, and the idea that there is not one external truth but rather that it is up to each individual to discover his or her own truths.

This view would only be enhanced when Rogers arrived in China and met the 600 delegates from China and 200 from other countries. After the conference in Peking, he travelled with an African American and a Native American from the United States, as well as with students from China, England, France, and Germany. Along with taking part in religious meetings and giving talks, he was able to see close up many aspects of life that were vivid experiences for him: the sight of Chinese prisoners kow-towing in a filthy hole that

was their cell; being pulled in a Japanese rickshaw by a man serving as a draft animal; hearing of the brutality of a Russian prison camp from a recent escapee; seeing children in the Philippines who suffered such poverty that the skin hung in flaps from their bones. These were experiences that deeply moved the sensitive young man and awakened in him a sense of social responsibility. In his diary, he no longer talked about God choosing him or leading him, and instead began to talk of his own responsibility for religious as well as political and social choices. More than any other event in his life, this journey helped Rogers to develop his own mind about things and to become an independent person. It is likely that this profound experience was important in leading Rogers to the theoretical idea of the self. According to Rogers' theory, as we develop autonomy we come to differentiate a self-concept, consisting of perceptions of our own characteristics, our relationships to aspects of the world, and the values attached to these perceptions. This trip accomplished just this type of autonomy and developing self-concept for Rogers.

It is important that this development occurred while Rogers was out of the reach of his parents. This allowed his developing self-concept to be a truer expression of his organism, not distorted by the conditions of worth inherent in his parents' dogmatism. Throughout the 6 months of his trip, Rogers recorded his life-transforming experiences and emerging thoughts in a diary, and he sent a copy home at intervals to his family. But the mail service was so slow that there was a delay of 2 months for any reply to arrive from his parents. So he continued to pour out his new ideas in heartfelt letters for 2 months before they could be brought up short by his parents' negative response. By the time his parents' replies caught up with him, his new world view was fully established.

It is surprising, however, that in his autobiographical chapter he indicates that he had

> no notion of the consternation that this was causing in my family...I had been able freely, and with no sense of defiance or guilt, to think my own thoughts, come to my own conclusions, and to take the stands I believed in. This process had achieved a real direction and assurance—which never after wavered—before I had any inkling that it constituted rebellion from home.[28]

Why was he able to share his thoughts with his parents so openly now, without any thought to their likely disapproval, when he had previously kept his inner world private for fear of their negative evaluation? One possibility is that he was under the pervasive influence of what he would later term unconditional positive regard and empathic understanding. The interpersonal culture among the delegates during the journey through the Orient was one of genuine acceptance, valuing one another regardless of individual differences in religious belief or culture. Further, they each made honest efforts to understand one another, to be open to the ideas and empathic to the feelings that each individual brought. This pervasive culture of unconditional positive regard and empathic understanding may have been a powerful antidote to the conditions of worth that Rogers had previously known from his parents, making him aware of the therapeutic power of these conditions when he later developed his theory of therapy.

Rogers returned from this trip in August to meet head-on the negative judgments that had been festering at home with each of his diary installments. But he now was determined not to be bullied by his parents' conditions of worth, and the family atmosphere became one of pervasive tension with periodic eruptions of verbal fireworks. Many of the arguments in this period centered on interpretations of religious scripture, but Rogers was also the first child to insist on the freedom to take up dancing or to join a fraternity. Despite his willingness to do battle, Rogers was very unhappy with finding himself at odds with his parents. His younger brother Walt reported, in looking back from adulthood, that he thought Rogers kept trying to fight things out despite his discomfort because he so wanted their mother's approval.[29] This is expressed by Rogers himself in a letter he wrote at the time, after having just tried to stick up for Walt to their parents:

> All I did was to beg that they should try and see things from Walt's point of view, because if they didn't he *would* be apt to drift away from them ... Oh well, what does it all matter? I'm an ass to think I can change things at home, or that I can ever do anything to make father and mother anything but unhappy.[30]

The conflict with his parents was to take its toll on him. Soon after his return from the Orient, Rogers began to experience abdominal pains of increasing severity. It was clear that these pains did not result from something he had picked up while abroad, because he had been troubled with similar pains intermittently from the age of 15. Now they became severe enough to require a thorough medical assessment, and it was discovered that he had an ulcer. It had become so serious that he had to be hospitalized for 5 weeks, and thereafter had to follow an intensive regime of medical treatment for 6 months while he lived at home. In reporting this event in his autobiographical chapter, Rogers pointed out that three of the six children in his family developed ulcers at some point in their lives, although he had the dubious distinction of developing his at the youngest age. He attributed his and his siblings' ulcers to the "gently suppressive family atmosphere,"[31] but it hardly seems likely that "gentle" suppression could cause such severe effects. In any case, he was probably right in identifying the family atmosphere as decisive in the outbreak of his ulcer at this point, because there is evidence of the role of stress in promoting ulcers. What is even more intriguing, given what we know of Rogers' theory of personality, is to discover the particular psychological factors associated with this illness.

A review of over 70 research studies examining the role of psychological factors in peptic ulcer disease found a number of factors to yield inconclusive results. But the authors of this review concluded that one psychological factor proved powerful across a range of studies: Ulcer patients show "a conflict linked to the dependence/independence balance."[32] For example, in a study seeking to predict which of over 2,000 army recruits would later develop a duodenal ulcer (the type Rogers had), a strong predictor was having shown greater conflicts over needs for dependence in psychological interviews and tests. This, of course, echoes an important theme that we have seen in Rogers' theoretical work. In the talk he gave at Minnesota to introduce his therapeutic approach, he spoke passionately against directive methods that would impede an individual's growth and threaten his or her integrity by fostering dependence. In his writings on therapy, he sought to destroy the prevailing view of the therapeutic relationship as a hierarchical one between an authoritative doctor and a dependent patient. And in his final theory of persons, he defined maladjustment in terms of the introjection of attitudes from others, and health in terms of the independent reliance on an internal locus of control. A psychological struggle over the issue of dependence versus independence thus played an important role both in his personal life and in his professional theory.

Rogers' theory suggests that there may have been something more going on as well in the formation of his ulcer. In his theory, he specifically identifies neurotic symptoms as the consequence of incongruence between the self that is accepted in awareness and one's actual organismic experience. Is there any evidence that Rogers was experiencing such an incongruence at this time? I would suggest that there is. When Rogers was on his trip through the Orient he sent home to his parents the diary that recorded his changing religious views. By his own account he had no idea that this would constitute any rebellion from home. Yet his mother's beliefs were conservative and fundamentalist, and when faced with his changed religious views she "essentially disowned [him] psychologically."[33] Was there no part of him that saw that his new ideas would be in conflict with her strongly held beliefs? Earlier I suggested that the supportive culture he found among the delegates during this trip overshadowed his parents' conditions of worth. But the fact that he felt complete ignorance of his rebelliousness suggests that there may have been more going on. Rogers may have been denying to conscious awareness his own organismic inclination to rebel against his parents, and the ulcer that flared up when he returned home may have resulted from his having to face this incongruent part of himself head-on.

Having noted this possibility, another instance comes to mind in which Rogers seemed to be unaware of his own organismic inclinations to rebel against authority. Earlier I recounted that when Rogers introduced his budding ideas in a talk he gave at the University of Minnesota they were received with great furor, no doubt because his remarks were aimed at overthrowing the traditional methods of therapy that Minnesota was famous for. In fact, the case study he critiqued in his talk had come from one of Minnesota's own therapists. But in reflecting on this talk later, Rogers reported:

> One thing that was astonishing and embarrassing to me was that I had found a very good advice-giving interview—an account of it—and I suppose it was in literature that came from Minnesota, but by the time I'd put it into my paper I wasn't aware of where

it had come from. After my talk I discovered that it was the chairman of the meeting.[34]

He appears to have been genuinely unaware of the source of this case while he was attacking it at Minnesota, but when he first found the case he presumably knew its origin. Is this mere forgetting, or an inability to accept in awareness his inclination to antagonize authority? The recurrence of this pattern of unwitting rebellion, and the association between the first expression of it and the onset of his ulcer, suggests that Rogers may have been denying to awareness an incongruent organismic inclination. We will see later that Rogers identified another time in his life when he was forced to face organismic experiences that he had been denying, with negative consequences for his psychological health.

For the 6 months of his recuperation from his ulcer, Rogers was unable to return to the University of Wisconsin. Coupled with the 6 months he had spent abroad he was put back a year, to graduate in 1924. One benefit of that 6 months of recovery at home, however, was that he was able to be close to Helen Elliott. When Rogers lived in Oak Park he and Helen had lived a block apart, going to the same school and riding their bicycles together, and when they both went to the University of Wisconsin they began dating. After 2 years Helen had transferred from Wisconsin to the Chicago Academy of Fine Arts to get professional training for a career as a fashion artist. But they had kept up their courtship by mail, and when they were together again in person during his recuperation Rogers found Helen's support to be a balm. It was she who taught him to dance, and to whom he wrote and spoke about his conflicts with his parents. By the following fall they were engaged, and upon his graduation they were married and moved together to New York City where Rogers would start graduate school.

Rogers' parents disapproved both of the marriage and of the graduate school. As to the marriage, they liked Helen but thought it absurd for their son to marry while he was still a student. As to the graduate school, in distinction, they were in favor of his going to seminary but were deeply disturbed by his particular choice. Rogers had chosen Union Theological Seminary because it was the most liberal in the country. For his fundamentalist parents, this meant that it was the devil in disguise. In a material expression of their conditions of worth, Rogers' father offered to pay all expenses for both him and Helen if he would go to Princeton instead, which was at that time a center of fundamentalist thinking. Rogers rejected the offer indignantly, now fully embarked on a path of his own choosing.

He would now, over and over again, make choices that reflected his need for freedom from external direction. When later he wrote about a student-run seminar he had helped to organize at Union, the issue of freedom recurred in his account: "I am truly astonished at the freedom which was granted to us... The whole seminar was very freewheeling... I wanted to find a field in which I could be sure my freedom of thought would not be limited."[35] When years later he was tempted away from his position at Ohio State by an offer from the University of Chicago to establish a counseling center, again the issue of freedom seemed paramount in his experience of the opportunity. In his autobiographical chapter he wrote about this experience: "I learned to set the staff free... It was a time of innovation in our educational methods and in our freewheeling administrative process... We were also experimenting with much freedom of expression of interpersonal feelings... There was enormous freedom for creativity."[36] This need for freedom had its source in the restrictive family environment he now left, and it would be expressed in his theoretical proposition that healthy development consists of increasing autonomy from the control of external forces.

Adulthood

We have now found personal origins for most of the important concepts Rogers was to offer in his theories of therapy and of persons. There is one aspect of his theory that emerged later in his thinking, however, and whose source therefore is probably found in experiences that occurred after his professional life was launched. In his 1942 book *Counseling and Psychotherapy*, Rogers identified the three essential characteristics of a therapeutic relationship to be unconditional positive regard, empathy, and nondirection. By his 1959 paper offering his elaborated theory, he had dropped the third characteristic of nondirection and had offered in its stead the characteristic of congruence. We have seen that Rogers came to recognize the subtle directiveness he had shown in the case of Herbert Bryan, and his realization of this may have led him to deemphasize the quality of nondirection. But what led him now to emphasize the importance of the counselor being genuine about his or her true feelings toward the client? In introducing this element in his 1959 paper, Rogers wrote:

> The "growing edge" of this portion of the theory has to do with point 3, the congruence or genuineness of the therapist in the relationship. This means that the therapist's symbolization of his own experience in the relationship must be accurate, if therapy is to be most effective. Thus if he is experiencing threat and discomfort in the relationship, and is aware only of an acceptance and understanding, then he is not congruent in the relationship and therapy will suffer.[37]

Although this was the growing edge of his theory of therapy, Rogers would claim later in this paper that it is this congruence of the counselor in the relationship that is primary, while unconditional positive regard and empathy are secondary to it. We might guess, then, that Rogers had been powerfully affected by an experience in which he himself had been defending against awareness of feelings of threat and discomfort in a therapeutic relationship, with negative consequences. And in fact he had.

In his autobiographical chapter, Rogers recounts such an experience occurring between 1949 and 1951 after he had moved from Ohio Sate to the University of Chicago:

> There were two years while I was at Chicago which were years of intense personal distress, which I can now look back upon coolly but which were very difficult to live through. There was a deeply disturbed client (she would be regarded as schizophrenic) with whom I had worked at Ohio State, who later moved to the Chicago area and renewed her therapeutic contacts with me. I see now that I handled her badly, vacillating between being warm and real with her, and then being more "professional" and aloof when the depth of her psychotic disturbance threatened me. This brought about the most intense hostility on her part (along with a dependence and love) which completely pierced my defenses.[38]

Rogers felt that he *should* be able to help this client and feel warm toward her, yet at times he genuinely felt threatened by her psychosis and his fear led to an aloofness that was not therapeutic. For a time he stubbornly persisted with the relationship although it was past the point of being helpful to the client. When she recognized his aloofness and responded with hostility, the relationship became destructive to him as well, and he suddenly felt that he himself was on the verge of a mental breakdown. Feeling an urgent need to escape, he contacted one of his colleagues and asked if the colleague could take over as her therapist that very day. When the client came in for her appointment that day, Rogers introduced the two of them and then bolted without further explanation. Within moments the client burst into a full blown psychosis with florid delusions and hallucinations.

Meanwhile Rogers, convinced that he himself was going insane, went home and told his wife that he had to get away at once. They were on the road within an hour and stayed away for 2 or 3 months on what they later referred to as their "runaway trip." The early moments were rough going—Rogers felt himself incapable even of walking into a store to buy some beer—but Helen's quiet assurance gradually relieved his terror. When they finally returned to Chicago he was past his crisis, but he was left with a feeling of utter worthlessness as a therapist and as a person. It was only after one of his colleagues offered to serve as his therapist that he was able to work through these feelings to a point where his fears diminished and his capacity to value himself increased. It is this traumatic experience, then, which made clear to him the importance of the therapist's congruence in a therapeutic relationship.

This experience also probably illustrated for Rogers the process of an acute psychotic breakdown that he would describe in his 1959 paper. According to this account, a breakdown occurs when a significant event suddenly or obviously demonstrates the substantial incongruence between an individual's self and organismic experience. Whereas previously the individual had defended against the threat of incongruent organismic experiences by keeping them out of awareness and thus denied to the self, this significant event forces the incongruity into awareness. The result is intense anxiety and a state of disorganization as the self-structure is broken. The individual now acts out those previously denied aspects of his experience, and as a consequence loses all confidence in himself or herself, feeling crazy and worthless. This is in fact the process that Rogers went through during this crisis. His self-image was that of a warm therapist, but this psychotic client evoked organismic responses of fear and a wish to withdraw that he could not accept into awareness. When her hostility broke his defenses and suddenly forced his fear and wish to withdraw into awareness, he urgently acted on those previously denied experiences and ran away. As a result of having thus acted out organismic experiences that he had previously felt the need to deny to his self, he lost all confidence in himself, feeling crazy and worthless. He was able to recover his self-worth only after undergoing a therapeutic relationship in which he received unconditional positive regard, empathy, and congruence.

Rogers and Skinner

We have now gone as far as we can to identify personal sources for Rogers' professional ideas. But before we leave Rogers' life story, let us see what we can learn from one more thing: the marvelous fate of the overlapping of his life and career with that of Skinner. The two men were born 2 years apart, Rogers in 1902 and Skinner in 1904, and they died 3 years apart, Rogers in 1987 and Skinner in 1990. Both fashioned a body of work that had a major impact on American psychology in the mid-1900s. And yet, although each was a passionate proponent of his own world view, their two views could hardly have been more different. They rarely had the opportunity to battle out their differences directly. Although both started their academic careers in the Midwest, Skinner shortly returned to the east coast to remain ensconced at Harvard for the rest of his career while Rogers traveled through a series of institutions in the Midwest and West as if not wanting to collect any moss. There were three occasions, however, when a special conference was organized so that the two men could meet eye to eye and spar. The most extensive of these meetings was the third, a 2-day event organized by the University of Minnesota in the summer of 1962. A transcript of the meeting shows that the two had no trouble identifying their differences.

In his opening remarks, Rogers outlined the important points to underlie their dialog with the following statement:

> Man has long felt himself to be a puppet in life, molded by world forces, by economic forces. He has been enslaved by persons, by institutions, and, more recently, by aspects of modern science. But he is firmly setting forth a new declaration of

independence. He is discarding the alibis of "unfreedom." He is choosing himself, endeavoring to become himself: not a puppet, not a slave, not a copy of some model, but his own unique individual self...To the extent that a behaviorist point of view in psychology is leading us toward a disregard of the person, toward treating persons primarily as manipulable objects, toward control of the person by shaping his behavior without his participant choice, or toward minimizing the significance of the subjective—to that extent I question it very deeply.[39]

When Rogers ended these opening remarks Skinner began his: "I always make the same mistake. In debating with Carl Rogers I assume that he will make no effort to influence the audience. Then I have to follow him and speak, as I do now, to a group of people who are very far from free to accept my views. In fact, I was just reminded of a story that I once heard about Carl Rogers and I will tell it now."[40] Skinner then told the following story: Rogers was sitting through a cold dawn trying to hunt ducks when none were about. Finally after hours of waiting, a lone duck flew by and Rogers took aim and shot, but at the same time another hunter from his own hiding place aimed and shot at the same duck. When the two men arrived simultaneously at the place where the duck had fallen, Rogers turned to the other hunter and said "You feel that this is your duck." But, as Skinner finished the story, in the end it was Rogers who brought the duck home. Skinner continued that he would do his best to prevent a similar outcome in the present instance. His remarks brought a laugh from all involved. But with this amusing introduction Skinner was also making a serious point, that even with his approach of empathic understanding Rogers is controlling others and leaving them far from free. Skinner then continued:

> The controllability of behavior is an old story, of course. Historians have always been delighted when they could prove the influence of some kind of biographical event on a hero. Biographers take the same line. The social sciences have certainly brought further evidence of a statistical nature, and an experimental analysis of the behavior of an individual organism has now essentially clinched the point...There are ways to control people that influence what they want to do. And there are ways

to control them that force them to do what they do not want to do. A shift from a legalistic coercive system to individual freedom, the whole theory of democracy, appears to take the good behavior of the citizen out of the hands of the police and turn it over to the individual himself. I suggest that the inner control which is then discovered is nothing but the product of another kind of external control which has been concerned with getting individuals to want to behave in certain ways, rather than coercing them to behave in those ways because of an external threat.[41]

The difference between them was stubbornly laid out by each. For Rogers, the value of psychology lay in its capacity to help the individual find freedom from external control, whereas for Skinner the value of psychology lay in its having experimentally proved that external control is unavoidable and freedom an illusion. The question before us now is, how did these two men form such opposing views? As we have already seen, their early lives had much in common. Both grew up in small-town America in the 1900s. Both had parents whose conservative religious beliefs led to a strict upbringing. Both were sensitive children who wanted approval. How is it that with these remarkable similarities they came down so differently on the issue of freedom versus control? Let us try to take on this question.

At the outset, we should first recognize that in one way Rogers and Skinner were alike in their view of freedom: For both, "freedom" was an all-important issue to deal with in their efforts to understand the phenomenon of being human. Recall that Skinner's first experimental studies in graduate school were focused on the issue of escape, and that he later devoted a whole book to the topic of freedom in *Beyond Freedom and Dignity*. True, he was denying freedom and free will, but still he was very much concerned with the problem. Rogers too showed great concern for the issue of freedom in his professional work, from his initial proposal of "nondirective" therapy to his later definition of the actualized person as one who is fully autonomous. But if we reflect back on Freud's theory, in distinction, we find that the issue of freedom does not appear as a salient concern. So whereas Rogers and Skinner came to different conclusions to the problem of freedom, they agreed that it was a crucial problem in a way that Freud did not.

One source for this shared concern with freedom may be found in the fact that Rogers and Skinner were both Americans. Indeed the importance of this influence is implied in the remarks each man made in their 1962 debate. When Rogers spoke about the human aim for freedom he used the imagery of a new "declaration of independence," explicitly drawing on an American icon. When Skinner offered his counter-argument he nonetheless drew on an equally pervasive aspect of American culture in referring to "the whole theory of democracy." It was not only this force of freedom in the larger culture that brought the issue to the fore for Rogers and Skinner, however, but also the countervailing force of control that existed in the subcultures of their families of origin. Both children were sensitive to the constraints imposed by their parents at home and were eager to tow the line for their parents' approval. Both also were surprised by their discovery of freedom upon going to college. But upon returning home their paths diverged. Skinner returned home to see if he could gain freedom with his parents' approval, but when he could not he gave up on freedom as a goal and instead identified with his parents' world view of control. Rogers, in distinction, upon returning home to find that his parents would not approve his freedom, opted for freedom at the cost of abandoning his identification with his parents. Why were these different choices made at this decisive point?

A few possible influences suggest themselves. For Skinner, identification with the parents was in many ways an easier path. Skinner was the first-born son, and by the time his choice of identification was firmly made, after the death of his brother Ebbe, he was the only surviving child. His autobiographical writings during this period explicitly address his inability to break from his family because of the loss his parents had already suffered. Rogers, on the other hand, was the fourth of six children who had felt that his parents preferred his older brother to him and had suspected at one point that he was adopted. Others before him had already taken on the role of identification with parents, and separation was for him an easier path. Further, Rogers found some important sources of support for this path in other people. He found this backing first in the intense group experience of his 6-month trip throughout the Orient, and he found it after he returned home in the love of his future wife Helen. Skinner, on the other hand, was fully cut off from similar types of support when he left Hamilton for home. He had no sympathetic woman to reinforce his push for independence, and he lost the opportunity for a supportive therapy relationship when his father failed to approve of the idea.

There may have been other reasons as well for their differing paths toward freedom versus submission to control. For Rogers, suffering a physical ulcer may have shown him in a palpable way, which could not be ignored, the cost of trying to live under his parents' world view. For Skinner, failing as a writer and seeing Ebbe die may have given him reasons that he needed to avoid the responsibility of free will. The determinants for each man were probably multiple.

CONCLUSION

Rogers continued to show a growth tendency throughout his life. When he was over 60, he resigned his most recent post at a midwest university to move to a private institute in California. There he began an intense involvement in the encounter group movement, teaching sensitivity training to such groups as medical school educators. In his 70s, he became deeply interested in the issue of world peace and expanded his activities further still. He organized the Vienna Peace Project to bring together leaders of 13 countries, and he led workshops on conflict resolution and citizen diplomacy in Northern Ireland, South Africa, and Russia. He was involved in these types of projects when he suffered a broken hip in early 1987, and he died from heart failure following hip surgery on February 4 at the age of 85.

By the time of his death, the influences of Rogers' theory and therapy were widespread and profound. They were felt in such diverse fields as medicine, religion, law enforcement, industry, and politics, and in such diverse countries as Ireland, South Africa, Russia, Japan, and Norway. Within his own field in his own country, in 1956 he was the first recipient of the American Psychological Association's Distinguished Scientific Contribution Award, in 1972 he was the first recipient of their Distinguished Professional Contribution Award, and in 1982 he was rated the most influential psychotherapist of all time.[42]

In the realm of psychological theory his most important contributions were twofold. First, he led the call for a phenomenological approach to understanding persons, which emerged as a third viewpoint in psychology to counterbalance the views offered by psychoanalysis and behaviorism. This viewpoint emphasizes the individual's ways of interpreting his or her experiences, and argues that it is these frames of meaning that determine the individual's course in life. Rogers' own version of phenomenology has now been overtaken by the version found in the cognitive approach to psychology. But in this cognitive approach his basic emphasis on the ways people construe their world is a vital and dominant force today. Other theorists working from this approach include Abraham Maslow, George Kelly, and Walter Mischel.

Second, Rogers initiated the empirical study of clinical phenomena in his research on the process of psychotherapy. Beyond providing the first published transcript of a full psychotherapy case, Rogers developed a systematic theory and submitted this theory to testing by the scientific method. In a field that had experienced a vast rift between clinical theory and scientific research, this was a radical and invaluable contribution. The dominant clinical theory of psychoanalysis had been belittled and ignored in scientific circles as the fantastic musings of biased individuals, in no small part because of the refusal of clinicians to submit their ideas to empirical testing. The dominant scientific program of behaviorism had likewise been belittled and ignored in clinical circles as being reductionistic and irrelevant, in no small part because it studied isolated acts of behavior displayed by lower organisms which seemed far removed from the kinds of phenomena revealed in a human psychotherapy session. But Rogers took on the task of bridging the rift between these two domains of psychology, while remaining fully aware of having to negotiate between the Scylla of personal bias and the Charybdis of reductionism.

Rogers himself worried about the legacy of his theory, however. At the beginning of his 1959 paper, "A Theory of Therapy, Personality, and Interpersonal Relationships, As Developed in the Client-Centered Framework," in which he provided the first comprehensive account of his theory, he wrote:

> I am distressed at the manner in which small-caliber minds immediately accept a theory—almost any theory—as a dogma of truth. If theory could be seen for what it is—a fallible, changing attempt to construct a network of gossamer threads which will

contain the solid facts—then a theory would serve as it should, as a stimulus to further creative thinking.

I am sure that the stress I place on this grows in part out of my regret at the history of Freudian theory. For Freud, it seems quite clear that his highly creative theories were never more than that. He kept changing, altering, revising, giving new meaning to old terms—always with more respect for the facts he observed than for the theories he had built. But at the hands of insecure disciples (so it seems to me), the gossamer threads became iron chains of dogma.[43]

Having built his life by resisting the shackles of authority and dogma, he did not want to be imprisoning others in turn. There are few criticisms that have been leveled at Rogers' theory that would be disturbing to him, then, except perhaps one. It can be argued that Rogers' theory merely restates in different language what has been said before by Freud and Skinner. If this is true, then perhaps Rogers has not broken free of the control of external authorities as he would wish to believe, and his own theory, as a reiteration of Freud's and Skinner's, serves only to strengthen the iron chains of dogma. Let us see in what ways this might be so.

For Freud, human psychology is understood in terms of the dynamic of conflict and defense. An individual's innate impulses conflict with parental censorship; after having internalized this parental censorship, the individual represses these impulses and allows them only distorted expression in neurotic or psychotic symptoms. But this same dynamic can be found in Rogers' theory, if we replace "innate impulses" with "organismic valuings," "parental censorship" with "conditions of worth," "internalization" with "introjection," and "repression and distortion" with "denial and distortion." And what of Skinner's theory? For Skinner, human psychology is understood to be a function of external contingencies. Behaviors that are reinforced will increase in frequency and those that are punished will decrease in frequency; private events, as correlates to behavior, follow the same functional relationships with external contingencies. But these functional relationships also find expression in Rogers' theory in the important influence of "conditions of worth" (Skinner's external contingencies) in determining the individual's behavior and "self-concept"

(Skinner's private events). There are, then, important parallels between Rogers' theory and those of Freud and Skinner.

It does not follow, however, that Rogers' theory is therefore nothing but a copy of Freud's and Skinner's in a new language. First, his theory turns a spotlight on a wholly different aspect of the human condition than in the theories of Freud and Skinner. Whereas Freud's theory calls our attention to the power of unconscious forces and Skinner's to the power of environmental forces, Rogers' calls attention to the role of subjective experience in determining a human life. He was a champion of the belief that "man's ultimate reliance is upon his own experience."[44] Second, to the extent that Rogers' theory has similar elements to the theories of Freud and Skinner, this may be a function not of his yielding to the dogma of these two authorities but rather of Rogers and the others independently capturing a valid aspect of the phenomenon of being human. In the next chapter we take on the question of the validity of the theoretical models offered by our three theorists.

SUGGESTED READINGS

Primary Sources

Kirschenbaum, H., & Henderson, V. L. (Eds.). (1989). *Carl Rogers: Dialogues.* Boston: Houghton Mifflin.

Rogers, C. (1942). *Counseling and Psychotherapy: Newer Concepts in Practice.* Boston: Houghton Mifflin.

Rogers, C. (1951). *Client-Centered Therapy: Its Current Practice, Implications, and Theory.* Boston: Houghton Mifflin.

Rogers, C. (1959). A theory of therapy, personality, and interpersonal relationships, as developed in the client-centered framework. In S. Koch (Ed.), *Psychology: A Study of a Science, Vol. 3.* New York: McGraw-Hill.

Rogers, C. (1961). *On Becoming a Person.* Boston: Houghton Mifflin.

Rogers, C. (1967). Carl R. Rogers. In E. Boring & G. Lindzey (Eds.), *A History of Psychology in Autobiography, Vol. V* (pp. 343–384). New York: Appleton-Century-Crofts.

Rogers, C. (1980). *A Way of Being.* Boston: Houghton Mifflin.

Rogers, C., & Russell, D. (2002). *Carl Rogers: The Quiet Revolutionary.* Roseville, CA: Penmarin.

Biographical Sources

Heppner, P., Rogers, M., & Lee, L. (1984). Carl Rogers: Reflections on his life. *Journal of Counseling and Development, 63,* 14–20.
Kirschenbaum, H. (1979). *On Becoming Carl Rogers.* New York: Delacorte Press.
Thorne, B. (1992). *Carl Rogers.* London: Sage.

Other Suggested Readings

Atwood, G. E., & Tomkins, S. S. (1979). On the subjectivity of personality theory. *Journal of the History of the Behavioral Sciences, 12,* 166–177.
Cain, D. J. (Ed.). (1990). Special issue: Fiftieth anniversary of the person-centered approach. *Person-Centered Review, 5*(4).
Evans, R. I. (1975). *Carl Rogers: The Man and His Ideas.* New York: Dutton.
Farber, B. A., Brink, D. C., & Raskin, P. M. (Eds.). (1996). *The Psychotherapy of Carl Rogers: Cases and Commentary.* New York: Guilford.
Greening, T. (Ed.). (1995). Special issue: Carl Rogers—The man and his ideas. *Journal of Humanistic Psychology, 35*(4).
Murray, E. J. (1956). A content-analysis method for studying psychotherapy. *Psychological Monographs: General and Applied, 70*(420).

NOTES

1. Carl Rogers (1942). *Counseling and Psychotherapy: Newer Concepts in Practice* (pp. 265–267). Boston: Houghton Mifflin.
2. Rogers, ibid., 271.
3. Rogers, ibid., 296–297.
4. Rogers, ibid., 286.
5. Rogers, ibid., 353–354.
6. Rogers, ibid., 406–407.
7. Rogers, ibid., 85–86.
8. Rogers, ibid., 277–278.
9. Rogers, ibid., 278.
10. Rogers, ibid., 278–279.
11. Rogers, ibid., 278.
12. Rogers, ibid., 279.
13. Rogers, ibid., 277.
14. Rogers, ibid., 431.
15. Carl Rogers (1946). Significant aspects of client-centered therapy. *American Psychologist, 1,* 420.

16. Paul P. Heppner, Mark E. Rogers, and Lucienne A. Lee (1984). Carl Rogers: Reflections on his life. *Journal of Counseling and Development, 63*, 18.

17. Carl Rogers (1967). Carl R. Rogers. In Edwin Boring and Gardner Lindzey (Eds.), *A History of Psychology in Autobiography*, (Vol. V, p. 346). New York: Appleton-Century-Crofts.

18. Carl Rogers (1961). *On Becoming a Person* (p. 5). Boston: Houghton Mifflin.

19. Howard Kirschenbaum (1979). *On Becoming Carl Rogers* (p. 5). New York: Delacorte Press.

20. Carl Rogers and David Russell (2002). *Carl Rogers: The Quiet Revolutionary* (p. 36). Roseville, CA: Penmarin.

21. Rogers (1967). Carl R. Rogers. In Edwin Boring and Gardner Lindzey (Eds.), *A History of Psychology in Autobiography*, (Vol. V, p. 346). New York: Appleton-Century-Crofts.

22. Carl Rogers (1973). My philosophy of interpersonal relationships and how it grew. *Journal of Humanistic Psychology, 13*, 4.

23. Rogers and Russell, op. cit., 96–97.

24. Carl Rogers (1980). *A Way of Being* (pp. 118–119). Boston: Houghton Mifflin.

25. Rogers and Russell, op. cit., 37.

26. Kirschenbaum, op. cit., 20.

27. Kirschenbaum, ibid., 24.

28. Carl Rogers (1967). Carl R. Rogers. In Edwin Boring and Gardner Lindzey (Eds.), *A History of Psychology in Autobiography*, (Vol. V, p. 351). New York: Appleton-Century-Crofts.

29. Kirschenbaum, op. cit., 32.

30. Kirschenbaum, op. cit., 38.

31. Rogers (1967). Carl R. Rogers. In Edwin Boring and Gardner Lindzey (Eds.), *A History of Psychology in Autobiography*, (Vol. V, p. 352). New York: Appleton-Century-Crofts.

32. Guido Magni, Francesco Di Mario, Luisa Aggio, and Diego DeLeo (1986). Psychological factors and peptic ulcer disease: A review. *Integrative Psychiatry, 4*, 44.

33. Rogers and David Russell, op. cit., 60.

34. Rogers and David Russell, ibid., 135.

35. Rogers (1967). Carl R. Rogers. In Edwin Boring and Gardner Lindzey (Eds.), *A History of Psychology in Autobiography*, (Vol. V, pp. 354–355). New York: Appleton-Century-Crofts.

36. Rogers, ibid., 364.

37. Carl Rogers (1959). A theory of therapy, personality, and interpersonal relationships, as developed in the client-centered framework. In Sigmund Koch (Ed.), *Psychology: A Study of a Science*, (Vol. 3, p. 214). New York: McGraw-Hill.

38. Rogers (1967). Carl R. Rogers. In Edwin Boring and Gardner Lindzey (Eds.), *A History of Psychology in Autobiography*, (Vol. V, pp. 366–367). New York: Appleton-Century-Crofts.

39. Howard Kirschenbaum and Valerie Land Henderson (Eds.) (1989). *Carl Rogers: Dialogues* (pp. 83–86). Boston: Houghton Mifflin.

40. Kirschenbaum and Henderson, ibid., 86–87.

41. Kirschenbaum and Henderson, ibid., 87–92.

42. Darrell Smith (1982). Trends in counseling and psychotherapy. *American Psychologist, 37,* 802–809.

43. Rogers, A theory of therapy, personality, and interpersonal relationships, as developed in the client-centered framework. In Sigmund Koch (Ed.), *Psychology: A Study of a Science,* (Vol. 3, p. 191). New York: McGraw-Hill.

44. Rogers (1967). Carl R. Rogers. In Edwin Boring and Gardner Lindzey (Eds.), *A History of Psychology in Autobiography*, (Vol. V, p. 351). New York: Appleton-Century-Crofts.

❦5❦

CONCLUSION

Now that we have come to the end of our study, let us reflect on the main thesis of this book and its implications. We have seen that each of the grand theorists of psychology developed a model for bringing order and meaning to the complexity of human life. Yet the model that each man introduced was quite different from those of the others. According to Sigmund Freud, the complexity of human life can best be given order and meaning by focusing on the role of unconscious sexual and aggressive wishes, which must be kept out of awareness but yet must find some symbolic expression. According to B. F. Skinner, searching out inner wishes or feelings or thoughts will only lead us astray; order and meaning will be found instead by focusing on observable behavior and the external environment that controls it. According to Carl Rogers, it is the individual's own actualizing tendency that brings order and meaning into a life, and thus understanding will only be found if we focus on the individual's subjective experience.

From within their respective paradigms in psychology, Freud, Skinner, and Rogers each believed that he had found the means for explaining the essential character of the human condition. Why, then, are their explanations so different? I have argued that the differences in these major models of psychology result in significant measure from differences in the personal lives of their originators.

In Freud's own life, sexual and aggressive wishes played an important role in his early childhood relationships, and his adult activities showed the effects of the repression and displacement of these unacceptable wishes. For example, we saw that when Freud undertook his own self-analysis, he uncovered a forgotten memory of a powerful sexual impulse he had felt toward his mother when he saw her naked at the age of 3. At the same time that he uncovered this sexual impulse, he also uncovered an aggressive impulse toward the younger brother who had taken his mother's attention away from him. When this brother died within a year of being born, the young Freud apparently felt that his own ill wishes were somehow to blame, for his self-analysis uncovered the residue of a self-reproach. Thus, Freud's early erotic attachment to his mother, his ill wishes toward the brother who appeared as a rival for her love, and this brother's subsequent death all impressed upon Freud the power of sexual and aggressive wishes and the need to deny them overt expression.

We saw ways in which these wishes found symbolic expression in Freud's adult life via displacement, however. For example, there was evidence that Freud experienced his psychoanalytic work as a displacement for his mother, and that he experienced Carl Jung as a displacement for his younger brother Julius. Although Jung was driven to pursue his own ideas, and voluntarily resigned his positions as journal editor and association president within the psychoanalytic movement, Freud saw Jung as a "usurper" out to steal psychoanalysis for his own. Freud even went so far as to display a neurotic symptom when the symbolic reenactment of his childhood rivalry with Julius overcame him, falling unconscious in Jung's presence when his repressed aggressive wishes were evoked. Freud's theory, then, reflects his own life.

For Skinner, too, his theory is a reflection of his own life experiences. For example, in Skinner's youth the power of external forces in controlling his behavior was palpable to him, as was the impotence of inner forces. Growing up at home he suffered under the control of his parents, but he never learned to protest against this control. In fact he did not even try to figure out what was irking him, because his parents had demeaned the exploration of feelings and thoughts. When he went to college he found an environment that valued this type of exploration, and he suddenly began expressing his feelings and thoughts through creative writing. He produced poetry and short stories that earned him a reputation on campus as a writer, and a letter from Robert Frost praising his talent pointed him toward a career as a writer.

But when Skinner returned home after graduation to pursue writing there, the control of the external environment over his writing was made powerfully apparent. Now that he was back in his home environment, where feelings and thoughts were disparaged, he suddenly found himself unable to produce anything. Despite his inner motivation to write, "nothing happened"; no inner feelings or thoughts forced their way out of him and onto the blank page. The impotence of any inner life in motivating his behavior was painfully obvious to him, and he felt that he had failed as a writer because he had nothing to say. But he could not accept responsibility for this failure, and sought to avoid the shame that it engendered. And so he turned to externalizing the blame, and saw his failed behavior as caused by his home environment or by literature itself. This attribution of cause to external conditions rather than to his own inner qualities lay the groundwork for the theory of behavior he would later develop.

Rogers' theory as well shows the influence of his personal life experiences. For example, as a child he was deeply immersed in his own subjective world, and as a young adult he displayed a unique directional tendency that was at odds with the direction laid down by his parents. We saw that he was a dreamy youth whose siblings teased him for being an absent-minded professor. For a long while he was so immersed in his private subjective experience, and so unconcerned with its relationship to the external world, that looking back from adulthood he surmised that he might have been at risk for schizophrenia. Rogers' parents moved the family to a working farm when he was in middle childhood, probably in part to spur their son to take more notice of the external world. Tending the animals and crops on the farm, as well as an independent project raising luna moths, impressed Rogers with the fact that all living things have an innate tendency to grow toward their own unique potential.

At first this tendency did not find expression in his own life, as Rogers followed the directions laid down by his parents. But he discovered this tendency within himself when in college he joined a delegation to a religious conference in China. In his childhood home he had been exposed to a dogmatic religious belief system that did not allow him to discover what he himself believed. On this trip he was exposed to open-minded individuals who sincerely held a range of beliefs, and in exploring religious questions with them he was able for the first time to discover his own views. This impressed on him the idea that there is not one external truth or reality to be known; rather, it is up to each individual to discover his or her own truths. Years later this personal discovery would find expression in his professional theory.

Thus, personal experiences shaped the professional ideas of these grand theorists of psychology. Let me reiterate an important point that I raised at the outset, however. It is not my claim that the personal experiences I identify in this book were the only sources of the theorists' ideas; far from it. It has been my goal to reveal the influence of personal life experiences on these theories, but other factors certainly played a role as well. For example, many scholars have elaborated the role of social–cultural forces in theory building in general, and on the theories of Freud, Skinner, and Rogers in particular. I paid some attention to the influence of such broader forces in my review. I addressed briefly the influence of anti-Semitism on Freud's thinking, the effect of the Progressive Era on Skinner's theory, and the influence of American democracy on Rogers' ideas. But my attention to these factors was only fleeting. Much more could have been said about these and other factors, and indeed has been said. Because it is important that the point not be lost, that the personal experiences this book focuses on are only part of the story, let me spend some time here giving a flavor of the scholarship on social–cultural influences on these theories.

There is a voluminous literature on the role of social–cultural factors on Freud's theory in particular. For example, William Johnston has reviewed some of the influences of late-19th-century Viennese politics and culture on Freud's thought in his book *The Austrian Mind* (1983). Johnston recounts that during Freud's time, Vienna was the major city of the Austro-Hungarian Empire under the rule of Emperor Franz-Josef. This empire was a collection of a variety of peoples, Austrians and Hungarians as well as Czechs, Slavs, Poles, and others. As such, it was threatened from within by the nationalistic claims of its subject states. Emperor Franz-Josef took control of the internal threats to his empire by means of a bureaucracy, whose actions were enshrouded in secrecy and who acted to maintain this secrecy via censorship of the press. This pervasive culture of secretiveness and censorship might have led Freud to attend to the distinction between what is manifest versus hidden, and to the censorship of unacceptable impulses.

Johnston portrays not only this political climate but also a lively social climate in Vienna. In particular he points out that Vienna was preoccupied with sexuality, as evidenced by the presence of several disparate movements, including campaigns for birth control and against venereal disease. Sexuality was also a popular topic in literature and scientific writings, such as in Sacher-Masoch's novels dramatizing sexual masochism and Krafft-Ebing's treatise detailing the varieties of sexual deviance. Rather than being the first to broach a taboo subject, then, Freud fit in with a prevailing cultural trend in emphasizing the importance of sexual impulses in psychic life.

A number of scholars have also considered the role of Freud's Jewishness on his theoretical ideas. One of the most provocative analyses was offered by David Bakan in his book *Sigmund Freud and the Jewish Mystical Tradition* (1965). In this work Bakan argues that Freud's theory shows the imprint of the Jewish oral mystical tradition, or "Kabbala." Initially transmitted by word of mouth, the Kabbalistic tradition has secrecy as part of its nature. According to this tradition the secret teachings are conveyed by allusion rather than by direct expression, so that the true meanings can only be understood by those who are able to decipher the allusions. Thus, this too could have influenced Freud to attend to the distinction between manifest and latent, conscious and unconscious.

The "Zohar" is the most important written document in the Kabbalistic tradition. The Zohar casts its religious messages in terms of family and sexual relationships. It suggests, for example, that sexuality is the source of all energy, and that the act of a man's sexual union with his wife is symbolic of his relationship with the spiritual Mother. These ideas find a parallel, of course, in Freud's claim that sexual impulses are the fuel for psychic activity, and that a man's sexual impulse toward his mother is symbolically expressed in his sexual relationship with his wife.

Beyond the role of general social–cultural factors such as these, many scholars have focused on the influence of specific intellectual precedents on Freud's thinking. Henri Ellenberger has provided a thorough review of these influences in his book *The Discovery of the Unconscious* (1970). He identifies first the influence of the broad movements of Enlightenment and Romanticism, the former proclaiming the value of reason and the latter the value of irrationality. In the tension between these two movements might be found a basis for Freud's theory of the conflict between the rational ego and the irrational id. It is even more striking how many of Freud's specific concepts can be found in writings predating his own by a range of other thinkers.

The most obvious example is found in the writings of the philosopher Friedrich Nietzsche. Before Freud had written his *Interpretation of Dreams*, Nietzsche had written that the most essential part of the individual is unconscious and unknowable whereas consciousness is a kind of ciphered formula of this unconscious reality; that the unconscious is ruled by aggressive and self-destructive instincts; that psychic energy is damned up (Nietzsche used the term "inhibition" for what Freud would call "repression") and discharged through "sublimation" (a term Freud also used); that dreams and pathological symptoms reenact fragments of an individual's past history. Ellenberger identifies numerous other writers who also had previously expressed Freudian concepts: for example, the idea of the unconscious (e.g., Fechner, Herbart, Janet, Schopenhauer, von Hartmann) and of conflict between instincts toward sex/love and aggression/death (e.g., Darwin, von Schubert). To what extent Freud drew explicitly from these other thinkers, and to what extent Freud and the others were independently influenced by a prevailing climate of implicit ways of thinking, it is hard to say. In any case it is clear that Freud's theory emerged from a particular intellectual milieu.

Social–cultural influences such as these have been identified for the work of Skinner and Rogers as well. For example, Bjork (1996) has pointed out that to the extent that Skinner's theory replaces individual freedom with social control, it is an expression of a traditionalist ideology in America with roots in 18th-century Republicanism and 17th-century Puritanism. Williams (1981) sees

Skinner's views as reflecting the determinism of theologist Jonathan Edwards, who argued that free will is an illusion, and that what the individual experiences as free will is actually a product of habit rather than a consequence of a conscious will. Roberts (1985) has identified parallels between Christianity and Rogers' theory, such as in finding an analogy between the Christian view of God's love for sinners and Rogers' concept of unconditional positive regard. Kramer (1995) has pointed out that Rogers's concepts of the actualizing tendency and empathic understanding have an intellectual precedent in the thought of the psychologist Otto Rank, who gave a seminar to Rogers' first clinic and who had trained a number of social workers on Rogers' staff. The ideas of Freud, Skinner, and Rogers, then, have a basis not only in the theorists' personal life experiences but also in the social, political, religious, and intellectual contexts in which they lived and worked.

Beyond the role of personal experiences and social–cultural contexts such as these, each theorist's views were influenced as well by his genetic inheritance. Certainly each man's ability to form concepts at all was a function of his inherited human capacities, but also differences among the theories were likely influenced by differences in endowments. Long ago Carl Jung, struck by the differences in the theories of Freud and Adler, wrote:

> Both are obviously working with the same material; but because of personal peculiarities they each see things from a different angle, and thus they evolve fundamentally different views and theories. Adler sees how a subject who feels suppressed and inferior tries to secure an illusory superiority... This view lays undue emphasis upon the subject, before which the idiosyncracy and significance of objects entirely vanish... Freud sees his patient in perpetual dependence on, and in relation to, significant objects. Father and mother play a large part here... With Freud objects are of the greatest significance and possess almost exclusively the determining power, while the subject remains remarkably insignificant... This difference can hardly be anything else but a difference of temperament.[1]

This observation led Jung to posit the existence of two distinct attitudes in human personality, *introversion* and *extraversion*. The introvert, like Adler, emphasizes the internal, subjective world;

whereas the extravert, like Freud, emphasizes the external, objective world. It would be easy to see the expression of the introverted attitude in Rogers' theory, and the expression of the extraverted attitude in Skinner's. Research has shown that there is a biological basis for these different attitude types (e.g., Eysenck, 1990) and that they have a significant genetic component (e.g., Loehlin, McCrae, & Costa, 1998). This is only one example of how genetically inherited characteristics may have led our three theorists to form the particular theories they formed.

SCIENTIFIC VALIDITY

Thus, the theories of Freud, Skinner, and Rogers were influenced in important ways by subjective factors, whether from biology, social–cultural context, or personal experience. Let me return then to a question that I raised in the opening chapter of this book. If it is true that these three models of psychology are significantly based in subjective sources, does this mean that their claims to identifying general truths must be false? As I have already foreshadowed in the first chapter, this is not the conclusion that I come to. First, it is important to remember that these theories were also based in substantial measure on the evidence provided by systematic professional observations. Freud studied the dreams, symptoms, and everyday slips of patients and colleagues as well as of himself; Skinner studied the patterns of behavior displayed by rats and pigeons under various experimental manipulations; Rogers studied the changes that clients showed under different therapeutic conditions. Their theories were necessarily responsive to what was demonstrated by these phenomena.

I have argued that the theorists' subjective inclinations led them to choose the particular phenomena they chose to study, and to attend to particular things when observing those phenomena. Only some evidence emerges when studying dreams, or animal behavior, or the therapeutic process. And of those things that emerge, only some were focused on by Freud and Skinner and Rogers. Subjectivity played a role in determining what part of the world these theorists looked at, then. But to the extent that what they saw there was indeed a reflection of what they were looking at, it was a truth with applicability beyond their own subjectivity. This is in the nature of any scientific inquiry. Scholars of the scientific method have pointed out that subjectivity is unavoidable in the context of discovery, during which hypotheses are made. An individual's implicit ways of thinking lead him or her to look in certain places, to extract certain patterns from what he or she sees, and to relate these patterns to certain forms of meaning. In the context of justification, however, the general validity of these hypotheses can be tested by rigorous experimentation.

In the first chapter I gave an example of the role of subjectivity from the field of chemistry, in Kekulé's discovery of the structure of organic molecules. Let me now add an example from the field of physics and another from biology. The physicist Gerald Holton argued that the physical scientist regularly projects human characteristics onto nonhuman phenomena in order to interpret them. He wrote:

> Even in the most up-to-date physical concepts the anthropomorphic burden is very large. Particles still attract or repel one another, rather as do people; they "experience" forces, are captured or escape. They live and decay... Some critics of science are so wrong in thinking of modern science as entirely depersonalized, cold and abstract, devoid of all personal concerns.[2]

Here Holton declares subjectivity to be an inherent aspect of the scientific enterprise, as the physical scientist draws on his or her own human experiences to understand nonhuman phenomena.

The biologist Joshua Lederberg, who won the Nobel Prize for discoveries that established the genetics of microorganisms, made a similar argument when he was asked what he thought was required to make such discoveries. He answered that what is needed is

> the ability to imagine oneself *inside* a biological situation. I literally had to be able to think, for example, "What would it be like if I were one of the chemical pieces in a bacterial chromosome?"—and to try to understand what my environment was, try to know *where* I was, try to know when I was supposed to function in a certain way, and so forth.[3]

This wholehearted embracing of the process of empathy speaks of subjective experience as a value rather than as a limitation in scientific discovery. Indeed, if subjectivity not only is unavoidable but also is in fact a value, then it could be argued that psychology is in a stronger position for making accurate discoveries than these other sciences, because its practitioners are in a better position to use empathy successfully. We are more like other people than like physical particles or microorganisms. In any case, these scientists do not find the validity of their theories undermined by having a basis in subjectivity in the context of discovery. And subjectivity is not simply a characteristic of psychological inquiry, but is also in play for all scientific enterprises.

The question of the validity of a hypothesis must be answered in a separate stage, in the context of justification, where objectivity is required as hypotheses are submitted to empirical testing. Now, it is important to say that by "objectivity" we do not mean a pure knowledge without a knower, for that would be impossible. It is humans who "know." What is meant by objectivity in science is that the knowledge does not depend on a particular individual but rather is consensual and "extra-subjective" (Ziman, 1978). That is, hypotheses have been tested by a number of independent experts for external observational consistency and have been found to generate reproducible findings in a range of experiments. The question is, then, whether the three theories reviewed in this book stand up under this kind of scrutiny.

It is well beyond the scope of this book to assess the validity of each of our theorists' ideas by reference to the full body of relevant research. Year after year whole journals have been devoted to studies from within the psychodynamic paradigm (e.g., *International Journal of Psychoanalysis; Psychoanalytic Review*), the behavioral (e.g., *Journal of Applied Behavior Analysis; Journal of the Experimental Analysis of Behavior*), and the phenomenological (e.g., *Journal of Humanistic Psychology; Person-Centered Review*). But there is evidence that many of these ideas have held up quite well under empirical testing. For example, Westen (1998) conducted a literature review of research on Freudian theory, and concluded that there is strong support for the role of unconscious thoughts, emotions, and motives in guiding behavior. Domjan (2002) reviewed empirical work on the application of Skinnerian theory to humans, and found substantial evidence for the effects of reinforcement and punishment on behavior. Markus and Wurf (1987) undertook a review of research on the concept of the self, and found convincing support for the Rogerian idea of a self that directs intrapersonal and interpersonal processes. Although it is not possible to cover the research literature here, let us look at one illustrative example from each theoretical approach, to get a feel for how these ideas can be tested empirically.

Some have argued that Freud's theory is not testable, either because the hypotheses are too vague to be translated into a specific empirical prediction (e.g., Nagel, 1959) or because the hypotheses logically cannot be falsified (e.g., Popper, 1963). But in rebuttals, it has been shown that it is possible to identify evidence that would confirm Freudian hypotheses (e.g., Hospers, 1959; Salmon, 1959) as well as evidence that would falsify them (e.g., Edelson, 1984; Grunbaum, 1984). Still, Freud's theory does present special challenges for empirical testing. The most basic hypothesis of this model, on which the full system rests, is that people are driven by unconscious processes of which they themselves can give no report. How, then, can such processes be identified? Over the years researchers have come up with various ways to study the unconscious, such that now its existence is so well established empirically as to be accepted by even nonpsychodynamic psychologists (for reviews see Holyoak & Spellman, 1993; Kihlstrom, 1987; Schachter, 1992). What is distinct about Freud's theory, however, is the proposition that there is a *dynamic* unconscious, that unacceptable wishes are actively seeking expression and actively being censored. We will look at a study that addresses this particular hypothesis.

Patricia Morokoff (1985) did not set out to test Freud's theory. Rather, she was interested in the effects of a variety of factors on female sexual arousal. One factor she chose to study was guilt about sexuality. Previous research had found that women high in guilt about sexuality show inhibited sexual behavior. Morokoff wondered whether these women would show lower sexual arousal as well. She examined this with 62 women, most of whom were undergraduates but some of whom were university staff up to 53 years in age. The study was advertised as being about "films and sexual fantasy."

In the first experimental session, participants were given a self-report questionnaire to assess their level of guilt about sexuality. The questionnaire, a subsection of "The Mosher Guilt Inventory," involved 39 forced-choice items such as: "If in the future I committed adultery... a) I hope I would be punished or b) I hope I enjoy it." The total score across the 39 items was used to assess levels of sex guilt; that half of the sample with the highest scores formed the high guilt group and that half with the lowest scores formed the low guilt group. At the end of this session, the next session was described so that the women could decide whether they wanted to continue to participate in the study; they were asked to think about it and called later to see if they were willing to set up a second appointment. The reason for this consideration on the part of the experimenter will soon become apparent.

In the second session, each participant was randomly assigned to watch one of two videos. Half of the women saw an erotic video depicting a young heterosexual couple engaged in kissing, breast stimulation, genital stimulation, and intercourse. The 12-minute video was in color with a soundtrack of the sounds made by the couple. The other half of the women saw a nonerotic video that served as a control. Two measures were taken of the participants' sexual arousal, one a self-report measure and one a physiological measure. In the self-report measure, the women simply reported their answer to the question "How sexually aroused do you feel now?" on a 7-point scale from "no sexual arousal at all" (1) to "very strong sexual arousal" (7). The physiological measure was taken by a recently developed device that had been shown to accurately measure sexual arousal in women, a "vaginal photo-plethysmograph." Each woman self-inserted a probe that allowed for recording of vaginal pulse amplitude while watching the video. Physiological arousal was measured by the change in average vaginal pulse amplitude from the 1-minute before the video started to the 12 minutes of video viewing.

Results from this study showed that the pattern of sexual arousal to the erotic video was different for women with high sex guilt versus women with low sex guilt. High-guilt women reported less arousal on the rating scale than low-guilt women. However, at the same time, high-guilt women showed more physiological arousal than low-guilt women. These findings support Freud's hypothesis that unacceptable sexual impulses are defensively denied conscious awareness: Although the high-guilt women were physiologically more aroused than the low-guilt women, they consciously reported less arousal.

No one study can prove the validity of a hypothesis. None is without limits or invulnerable to alternative interpretations of its results. The most obvious vulnerability to an alternative explanation for this study comes from the self-report measure of arousal. It is not possible to know whether the self-report measure assessed the participant's conscious awareness of her sexual impulse or assessed her willingness to admit such an impulse to others. The Freudian interpretation of the findings depends on the assumption of the former. But is it not possible that women high in sex guilt recognized their impulses, and yet were unwilling to tell the experimenter about them? Two things suggest that the self-report measure assessed conscious awareness rather than willingness to report, however. First, all participants knew that the experimenter was getting a direct physiological measure of their sexual arousal. Denying this arousal in self-report would not hide the arousal from the experimenter, then, but only make the participant look like she was lying (to herself or the experimenter). Second, the high-guilt women did not simply report less arousal, they also showed more arousal physiologically. What could explain this pattern of findings? This pattern would make sense if the self-report measure was a measure of consciousness, because Freud has argued that an impulse retains its force when denied conscious expression (the high-guilt women) but discharges its force when consciously expressed (the low-guilt women).

Nevertheless, because any study has limitations, what must be done is to build support for a hypothesis across a range of studies using various methodologies. For example, some research on unconscious processes has used a methodology that does not depend on self-report, but rather rests on exposing stimuli to participants subliminally. Studies have shown that visual displays can be projected for durations too brief for someone to recognize consciously, and yet physiological activity in their brain is different when different stimuli are projected (Shevrin, Bond, Brakel, Hertel, & Williams, 1996) as is their subsequent behavior (Dixon, 1971). Silverman, Ross, Adler, and Lustig (1978) used this methodology to find evidence for the operation of unconscious aggressive impulses in males. Together with the study by Morokoff (1985), this gives evidence of the validity of Freud's hypothesis for aggressive as well as sexual impulses in males as well as females. As noted previously, Westen (1998) reviewed a range of such studies and concluded that there is ample support for Freud's idea that unacceptable impulses are kept out of awareness while yet affecting our physiology and behavior.

Turning to Skinner's theory, let us look at a study of the effects of reinforcement on human behavior. Stephen Higgins and his colleagues (Higgins, Wong, Badger, Ogden, & Dantona, 2000) wanted to know whether they could promote abstinence among cocaine addicts through the use of reinforcement. They pursued this question with 70 men and women who sought treatment for cocaine dependence at a university-based outpatient clinic. All participants were given counseling over a period of 24 weeks with attention to issues such as avoiding situations where cocaine is used, developing new recreational activities, and finding satisfying employment. Beyond this, participants were assigned into one of two conditions for supplemental treatment: "contingent reinforcement" or "noncontingent reinforcement."

Under the contingent reinforcement condition, rewards were given for abstinence from cocaine. Urine specimens were collected 3 days a week for 12 weeks and screened for a cocaine metabolite. For each screening that came up negative for cocaine the individual was given a voucher worth at least $2.50; the value of the voucher went up by $1.25 with each negative test, but with a positive test no voucher was given and the value of the next voucher was reset to $2.50. Thus, cocaine abstinence was reinforced, consecutive days of abstinence were reinforced more than isolated days, and cocaine use was not reinforced. In the noncontingent reinforcement condition, the same vouchers were given, but they were not contingent on cocaine abstinence. Rather, each individual in the noncontingent group was "yoked" to an individual in the contingent group, and he or she was given vouchers based on the urine results of the yoked individual. Participants in the noncontingent condition were told that the schedule of voucher delivery would be independent of their behavior and that they could not control the value of the vouchers they received. In the second 12 weeks a similar system was followed, but lottery tickets were given instead of vouchers.

What were the effects of this system of reinforcement? First, participants in both conditions stayed with treatment an equal amount of time: About three-fourths stayed through the first 12 weeks and one-half stayed for the full 24 weeks. These similar amounts of retention could have resulted from the similarity between the two conditions in amounts of reinforcement given, because both groups were given rewards as long as they stayed in the program. Of course, the similar levels of retention could have resulted from other factors, such as the similar rewarding properties of the counseling given, or similarities having to do with the participants rather than with the program, such as their level of addiction or motivation for cure. More important are the findings for cocaine abstinence, because the two conditions varied in making reinforcement contingent on this behavior. As Skinner's theory would predict, cocaine abstinence was significantly greater in the contingent reinforcement condition than in the noncontingent reinforcement condition. Thus, this study provides evidence that Skinner's theory of reinforcement applies to humans as well as to rats. As noted previously, Domjan (2002) reviewed a range of studies on the application of Skinnerian theory to humans and found substantial evidence for the effects of reinforcement on behavior.

Timothy Strauman and his colleagues (Strauman, Vookles, Berenstein, Chaiken, & Higgins, 1991) conducted a study that gave evidence for Rogers' theory that one's self-concept directs behavior. In particular, they looked at the effects of a person experiencing a discrepancy between their view of who they really are and their view of who others believe they ought to be. In previous research, Strauman and his colleagues had found that people who experience this type of discrepancy are more vulnerable to feelings of fear and anxiety (e.g., Strauman 1989; Strauman & Higgins, 1988). This study examined whether experiencing this type of discrepancy would also make people more vulnerable to eating disorders such as anorexia, because individuals with anorexia have characteristically been described as anxious and as working to live up to the expectations of others.

To address this question, Strauman and his colleagues studied 91 male and female undergraduates from an introductory psychology class. At the beginning of the semester, the participants were given a questionnaire to assess their self-concepts. The questionnaire, called the "Selves Questionnaire," asked participants to "list the attributes of the type of person you think you actually are" (actual self) and to "list the attributes of the type of person [X] believes you should or ought to be" (ought self). Participants were asked to provide the second listing of attributes from the standpoint of their mother, father, and closest friend. After providing the relevant attributes for each list, participants then rated the extremity of each attribute on a 4-point scale from "slightly" (1) to "extremely" (4). To measure the amount of discrepancy between the actual self and the ought self, each pair of lists was compared for the number of items showing a match (the same attribute was listed and given a rating within 1 point) or a mismatch (the same attribute was listed but given a rating discrepant by 2 or 3 points, or antonyms were listed such as "shy" and "outgoing"). For each participant, a score was assigned representing the largest discrepancy found between the actual self and the ought self (whether from the perspective of mother, father, or closest friend).

Two to 3 months later in the semester, the participants were given a questionnaire to assess their eating-related attitudes and behavior. This questionnaire, called the "Eating Attitudes Test," asked participants to rate the extent to which they endorsed maladaptive eating attitudes and behavior such as excessive preoccupation with food or dieting. High scores on this measure indicate anorexic attitudes and behavior. For each participant, their total score on this test was then correlated with their largest actual self–ought self discrepancy score. Results revealed a substantial correlation between these two measures, showing that the experience of a discrepancy between one's actual self and one's ought self was related to maladaptive patterns of eating. This study provides support, then, for Rogers' claim that our self-concept influences our behavior, and more specifically for his idea that experiencing a discrepancy between who we really are and who important others think we should be is a source of trouble. As noted previously, Markus and Wurf (1987) reviewed a range of studies on the self and found convincing evidence for the role of the self-concept in directing intrapersonal and interpersonal processes.

THE STUDY OF LIVES

The studies reviewed here and others like them have demonstrated that, despite the influence of subjective factors on theoretical ideas, some of the most important concepts of Freud,

Skinner, and Rogers have been supported empirically. These include Freud's idea that unconscious motives affect behavior, Skinner's idea that behavior is influenced by environmental reinforcement, and Rogers' idea that a subjective self-concept guides behavior. We really should not be surprised to find that many of the proposals of our three theorists are valid. These men introduced their models long ago, and yet the ideas are still vital today to people's ways of understanding themselves and others. This is true for the psychotherapist trying to develop an understanding of his clients, the writer trying to develop an understanding of her characters, and the adolescent trying to develop an understanding of himself. Surely this is so because the ideas have captured something useful to these efforts at understanding. The theories of Freud, Skinner, and Rogers resonate with people's experiences of themselves and others.

And yet, as we have seen, Freud, Skinner, and Rogers provided very different accounts of the human experience. How is it that such different accounts can each have empirical validity, and each be felt to capture something personally true? One way this can be so is that each theory illuminates different but real aspects of the human condition. Freud's theory calls our attention to the role of unconscious processes in determining human behavior. Skinner's theory focuses on the influence of environmental consequences. Rogers' theory points to the important role of subjective experience. This is not to say that each theorist fully ignored the domain of the other. Nor is it to say that these foci are the only essential characteristics of the three theories. But they are the essential features of these approaches that define them as distinct paradigms. What each paradigm does, then, is to focus on certain aspects of experience that all humans share. And these foci result in part from each originating theorist attending to what was most salient in his experience of his own life. Each theory has a truth to tell, then. But we may expect the importance of that truth to vary based on what is salient in the experience of the particular individual we are trying to understand, just as it varied in the lives of our three theorists.

As was pointed out long ago by Kluckhohn and Murray (1949), each person is in ways like all other people, in ways like some other people, and in ways like no one else. Freud, Skinner, and Rogers sought to identify what is true of all people. They were each right in that all people live with the influence of unconscious forces, environmental consequences, and subjective experiences. But there are also differences among people in the importance of these different factors to their living. For example, a body of work on "repressive coping style" has indicated that some people are more inclined than others to engage in repression. They score low on self-report measures of anxiety but physiologically they respond to stress with high anxiety; they also score high on measures of defensiveness, avoid negative feedback, engage in self-deception, and show deficits in self-understanding (Weinberger, 1990). Other research has revealed individual differences in people's responses to reinforcement and punishment. Extraverts are more sensitive to rewarding stimuli and condition more with reinforcement, whereas introverts are more sensitive to punishing stimuli and condition more with punishment (Gupta & Shukla, 1989). A third body of research has discovered individual differences in the extent to which people are guided by subjective experience, with some people guided more by their own internal attitudes and values whereas others are guided more by external norms and the expectations of others (Snyder, 1987).

There are also ways in which each individual is unique. On an evening in late December of 1888, an artist cut off part of his ear and gave it to a prostitute for safe-keeping. It is unlikely that this describes any other individual but Vincent Van Gogh. To understand Vincent as a unique individual, it may well be useful to draw on the models of psychology provided by Freud, Skinner, and Rogers. But these models should not be imposed wholesale, and the individual life made to fit them. Rather, ideas from these models can be extracted and tried on for their fit in the individual life.

It could be helpful, in line with Rogers' theory, to consider Vincent's subjective experience of self and important others at the time of his self-mutilation. For example, some evidence suggests that Vincent felt emotionally dependent on his brother Theo and that he felt profoundly abandoned by Theo at this time, because Theo had become engaged to be married that very day. Three of Vincent's mental breakdowns coincided with signs that Theo's care was being directed elsewhere (Theo's engagement, his marriage, and the birth of his first child). It could also be helpful, in line with Skinner's approach, to consider how reinforcing consequences make some behaviors more likely. For example, there is evidence that Vincent had found that when he was hurt the consequence was that others provided care, and after Vincent's self-mutilation Theo immediately came to him rather than spending the Christmas holidays with his fiancée as he had planned. It could also be helpful, in line with Freud's model, to know that people can engage in apparently nonsensical behavior when they must find a compromise between expressing and denying unacceptable impulses. For example, although Vincent may have unconsciously felt a need to monopolize his brother's love, his conscious love for his brother would have prevented him from denying Theo the marriage he wanted.[4] The theories of Freud, Skinner, and Rogers provide useful ideas for understanding persons, then, which can be drawn on as resources for illuminating a particular life in all of its complexity.

To understand an individual most accurately, however, is to understand that individual's own unique experience of the world. This will be accomplished not by imposing any a priori theory wholesale, but rather by finding ways to identify that individual's experience on its own terms. This is of course a difficult task. There is a risk that we will impose our own personal beliefs in trying to understand another, which is simply to substitute our personal theory of psychology for that of Freud or Skinner or Rogers. But if we can manage to understand the other on his or her own terms, the difficulty of the task will have been worth it.

A number of writers have pointed to the obstacles inherent in the study of individual lives, but they have also pointed to ways to negotiate these obstacles (e.g., Anderson, 1981; Bromley, 1986; Elms, 1994; Runyan, 1982). For many years, researchers in America were so worried about the potential of subjective bias in the analysis of individual lives that they avoided the task. In 1968, Rae Carlson reviewed all articles appearing in the two major journals devoted to research on personality and found that not a single one involved the extensive study of one or more individuals (Carlson, 1971). However, as our methodology for studying individuals has improved, this state of affairs has changed. For example, in each of the past 2 decades one of the journals Carlson reviewed has devoted an entire issue to the study of individual lives (McAdams & Ochberg, 1988; Nasby & Read, 1997).

In this book I illustrate one method by which the study of individual lives can be fruitfully accomplished. Applying this method to the lives and works of the grand theorists of psychology provides a rich portrait of the subjective sources of professional ideas.

NOTES

1. C. G. Jung (1977). *Two Essays on Analytical Psychology* (pp. 41–43). Princeton, NJ: Princeton University Press. (Original work published 1917)

2. G. Holton (1973). *Thematic Origins of Scientific Thought* (pp. 106–107). Cambridge: Harvard University Press.

3. H. Judson (1980). *The Search for Solutions* (p. 6). New York: Holt, Rinehart & Winston.

4. For further information on the life of Vincent Van Gogh, see A. Lubin (1972). *Stranger on the Earth: A Psychological Biography of Vincent Van Gogh.* New York: Holt, Rinehart, & Winston; & M. Tralbaut (1969). *Vincent Van Gogh.* New York: Macmillan.

REFERENCES

Anderson, J. W. (1981). The methodology of psychological biography. *Journal of Interdisciplinary History, 11,* 455–475.

Bakan, D. (1965). *Sigmund Freud and the Jewish Mystical Tradition.* New York: Schocken Books.

Bjork, D. (1996). B. F. Skinner and the American tradition: The scientist as social inventor. In L. Smith & W. Woodward (Eds.), *B. F. Skinner and Behaviorism in American Culture.* Bethlehem: Lehigh University Press.

Bromley, D. (1986). *The Case-Study Method in Psychology and Related Disciplines.* New York: Wiley.

Carlson, R. (1971). Where is the person in personality research? *Psychological Bulletin, 75,* 203–219.

Dixon, N. (1971). *Subliminal Perception: The Nature of a Controversy.* London: McGraw-Hill.

Domjan, M. (2002). *The Principles of Learning and Behavior.* Belmont: Wadsworth.

Edelson, M. (1984). *Hypothesis and Evidence in Psychoanalysis.* Chicago: University of Chicago Press.

Ellenberger, H. (1970). *The Discovery of the Unconscious: The History and Evolution of Dynamic Psychiatry.* New York: Basic Books.

Elms, A. (1994). *Uncovering Lives: The Uneasy Alliance of Biography and Psychology*. New York: Oxford University Press.

Eysenck, H. J. (1990). Biological dimensions of personality. In L. A. Pervin (Ed.), *Handbook of Personality: Theory and Research* (pp. 244–276). New York: Guilford.

Grunbaum, A. (1984). *The Foundations of Psychoanalysis: A Philosophical Critique*. Berkeley: University of California Press.

Gupta, S., & Shukla, A. (1989). Verbal operant conditioning as a function of extraversion and reinforcement. *British Journal of Psychology, 80*, 39–44.

Higgins, S., Wong, C., Badger, G., Ogden, D., & Dantona, R. (2000). Contingent reinforcement increases cocaine abstinence during out-patient treatment and 1 year of follow-up. *Journal of Consulting and Clinical Psychology, 68*, 64–72.

Holyoak, K., & Spellman, B. (1993). Thinking. *Annual Review of Psychology, 44*, 265–315.

Hospers, J. (1959). Philosophy and psychoanalysis. In S. Hook (Ed.), *Psychoanalysis, Scientific Method and Philosophy* (pp. 336–357). New York: Grove Press.

Johnston, W. (1983). *The Austrian Mind: An Intellectual and Social History*. Berkeley: University of California Press.

Kihlstrom, J. (1987). The cognitive unconscious. *Science, 237*, 1445–1452.

Kluckhohn, C., & Murray, H. (1949). *Personality in Nature, Society, and Culture*. New York: Knopf.

Kramer, R. (1995). The birth of client-centered therapy: Carl Rogers, Otto Rank, and "The Beyond." *Journal of Humanistic Psychology, 35*, 54–110.

Loehlin, J., McCrae, R., & Costa, P. (1998). Heritabilities of common and measure-specific components of the big five personality factors. *Journal of Research in Personality, 32*, 431–453.

Markus, H., & Wurf, E. (1987). The dynamic self-concept: A social psychological perspective. *Annual Review of Psychology, 38*, 299–337.

McAdams, D., & Ochberg, R. (1988). Special issue: Psychobiography and life narratives. *Journal of Personality, 56*(1).

Morokoff, P. (1985). Effects of sex guilt, repression, sexual "arousability," and sexual experience on female sexual arousal during erotica and fantasy. *Journal of Personality and Social Psychology, 49*, 177–187.

Nagel, E. (1959). Methodological issues in psychoanalytic theory. In S. Hook (Ed.), *Psychoanalysis, Scientific Method and Philosophy* (pp. 38–56). New York: Grove Press.

Nasby, W., & Read, N. (1997). Special issue: The inner and outer voyages of a solo circumnavigator: An integrative case study. *Journal of Personality, 65*(4).

Popper, K. (1963). *Conjectures and Refutations*. London: Routledge & Kegan Paul.

Roberts, R. (1985). Carl Rogers and the Christian virtues. *Journal of Psychology and Theology, 13*, 263–273.

Runyan, W. M. (1982). *Life Histories and Psychobiography*. New York: Oxford University Press.

Salmon, W. (1959). Psychoanalytical theory and evidence. In S. Hook (Ed.), *Psychoanalysis, Scientific Method and Philosophy* (pp. 252–267). New York: Grove Press.

Schachter, D. (1992). Understanding implicit memory: A cognitive neuroscience approach. *American Psychologist, 47*, 559–569.

Shevrin, H., Bond, J., Brakel, L., Hertel, R., & Williams, W. (1996). *Conscious and Unconscious Processes: Psychodynamic, Cognitive, and Neurophysiological Convergences*. New York: Guilford Press.

Silverman, L., Ross, D., Adler, J., & Lustig, D. (1978). Simple research paradigm for demonstrating subliminal psychodynamic activation: Effects of oedipal stimuli on dart-throwing accuracy in college males. *Journal of Abnormal Psychology, 87*, 341–357.

Snyder, M. (1987). *Public Appearances, Private Realities*. New York: Freeman.

Strauman, T. (1989). Self-discrepancies in clinical depression and social phobia: Cognitive structures that underlie emotional disorders? *Journal of Abnormal Psychology, 98*, 14–22.

Strauman, T., & Higgins, E. (1988). Self-discrepancies as predictors of vulnerability to distinct syndromes of chronic emotional distress. *Journal of Personality, 56*, 685–707.

Strauman, T., Vookles, J., Berenstein, V., Chaiken, S., & Higgins, E. (1991). Self-discrepancies and vulnerability to body dissatisfaction and disordered eating. *Journal of Personality and Social Psychology, 61*, 946–956.

Weinberger, D. (1990). The construct validity of the repressive coping style. In J. Singer (Ed.), *Repression and Dissociation* (pp. 337–386). Chicago: University of Chicago Press.

Westen, D. (1998). The scientific legacy of Sigmund Freud: Toward a psychodynamically informed psychological science. *Psychological Bulletin, 124*, 333–371.

Williams, D. R. (1981). Horses, pigeons, and the therapy of conversion: A psychological reading of Jonathan Edwards's theology. *Harvard Theological Review, 74*, 337–352.

Ziman, J. (1978). *Reliable Knowledge*. Cambridge: Cambridge University Press.

Author Index

Numbers in *italics* indicate pages with complete bibliographic information; n indicates note.

Subject Index